February-March, '73

To [illegible]

Leader
of the
Proletariat
– John

RACE, CLASS, and POLITICAL CONSCIOUSNESS

RACE, CLASS, and POLITICAL CONSCIOUSNESS

By JOHN C. LEGGETT
Preface by Richard Flacks

SCHENKMAN PUBLISHING COMPANY, INC.
Cambridge, Massachusetts

Schenkman Books are distributed by

General Learning Press
250 James Street
Morristown, New Jersey 07960

Cambridge, Massachusetts
Library of Congress Catalogue Card Number: 77-135340
Printed in the United States of America

To Malcolm X and
Martin Luther King

* * *

It takes two wings
for a bird to fly

John C. Leggett

in collaboration with:
Lynn Crescione
Norrine Gallisdorfer
Mike Halpern
Gunilla Napier
Jeffrey Starrfield

ACKNOWLEDGMENTS

We wish to express our indebtedness to Professor Herbert Blumer. Without his support, and that of the Social Science Institute formerly headed by Professor Blumer, the research materials that have gone into this book would never have been collected. Professor Blumer supported our study of fair housing at a time when major foundations refused to even consider our applications because of the alleged controversiality of sociological studies focusing on integrated housing.

We also wish to thank the Social Science Research Council as well as the President's Research Grant Committee of Simon Fraser University. Both subsidized our research efforts.

Irving Louis Horowitz, Anne Freedman, Deborah DeJames, Susan Olup, Lena Dominelli, and Janet Williams have helped immensely by making manuscript criticisms. In addition, we are particularly indebted to Werner Landecker for his helpful guidance on the work of Karl Mannheim, especially Mannheim's references to the distinction between conservatism and traditionalism.

To Sheila Gibson, Betty Howell, Orley Lindgren, Rebecca Marquis, Wendy Starrfield, Sharon Stern, and Sheila Trimble—all formerly undergraduate students at the University of California, Berkeley—we are thankful for hundreds of hours of work put into our civil rights research project. To the dozens of other students at Berkeley who worked on the interviewing and coding of the data, we owe our thanks.

Pat Ferguson read and criticized the text. Her suggestions helped to clarify ambiguities in the manuscript.

Above all we are indebted to Iris Leggett, for her critical comments and clerical work. To Jean Jordan and Mary Balfry we express our gratitude, for critical references and typing.

Also we wish to thank the persons who submitted to the interview questioning. Without them there would have been no study.

Finally, we thank the militant blacks and whites who made the action and created the interest in the topic about which we write and publish.

Contents

Preface

On the surface, the study described in this book concerns the distribution of public support for, and opposition to, a proposal to ban discrimination in the sale and rental of housing in Berkeley, California in the early Sixties. On the surface, its findings are just what one would expect—the issue divided the community along liberal-conservative lines.

But in analyzing his data, John Leggett has tried to probe beneath the obvious. In particular, in reporting his findings nearly a decade after they were collected, he suggests ways in which the opinion patterns concerning the now somewhat quaint issue of "fair housing" throw light on the more profound sociopolitical conflicts of the Seventies.

Everyone knows that Berkeley, California is hardly a typical American community. Berkeley is surely fascinating as a focus of study for its own sake, but one has a right to doubt that such a study would yield very much of relevance for understanding the shape of public opinion in the society as a whole. And yet, in the years since the present survey was conducted (1963) events in Berkeley have had an enormous impact throughout the nation. Leggett's study, I think, helps us understand some of the fundamental reasons for that impact.

One of Leggett's principal findings is that university affiliation had a powerful influence on support for "fair housing." The great majority of university employees and students supported the proposed ordinance (although a large number of students failed to vote). The impact of the university was, as Leggett points out, uneven—a substantial fraction of those affiliated with it voted "conservatively," and Leggett's study is helpful in identifying some of the determinants of such deviation from the prevailing academic consensus. But the data are quite clearcut—there *was* a consensus. By the early Sixties, a substantial voting-bloc consciousness had developed within the Berkeley academic community—certainly on the issue of race, but undoubtedly on other issues as well.

This finding may not seem surprising; most of us conceive of universities as centers of liberal politics, and, to a considerable extent, many major ones have been such centers for several decades. But it is well to remember that until the Sixties, the great majority of students in college and of college graduates came as Republicans and remained so throughout college and beyond. If the majority of liberal arts faculties have tended to vote Democrat since the New Deal, their numbers have often been offset by the Republican-leaning engineering, law school, medical school, "bus-ed" and "hard science" faculties.

By the early Sixties, however, it was clear that something was happening, especially at Berkeley, that was eroding the established pattern of university participation in politics. The university itself was expanding at an extraordinary rate: a much larger, more heterogeneous and more politically open student body had arrived; a vast network of research institutes was creating new sources of permanent employment for university graduates within the ambit of the university; the corporate growth of the university required great increases in numbers of personnel at many levels of skill and status. The university was moving from the periphery to the center as a source of economic growth, of jobs–it was coming to play a decisive role in shaping the economic, cultural and political life of its neighboring community. At the same time, major social issues provided a focus for political consensus among members of the university community–especially, at first, the issue of race, and somewhat later, the question of nuclear war.

By 1964, masses of Berkeley students were mobilized for political action, including protest against the university administration itself. The Free Speech Movement led some observers to talk about the students as a new "class"–playing some of the historical roles as an agency of change which radicals had previously assigned to the working class. In my view, such a metaphor contains considerable insight, especially if one defines the "new class" as consisting not only of students but of all those whose work required college-level training, who connect to the "knowledge industry," and/or whose perspectives have been significantly affected by connection to the multiversity.

For a number of interrelated reasons, the ranks of such people are rapidly growing–indeed "educated labor" has been the most rapidly growing sector of the entire labor force during the past decade. Leggett's data show that the political cohesion of this stratum was well-advanced by the early Sixties; by now, a similar process has occurred across the country–most obviously, in the university cities, the urban neighborhoods and suburbs where the mass intelligentsia are highly concentrated.

This rising quasi-class is of course deeply divided on many fundamental issues, and it would be absurd to contend that its prevailing sentiments are "revolutionary." Yet it is an opinion bloc, and it is likely to become even more so. Furthermore, despite its tendencies toward elitism, its prevailing sentiments point toward political alliance with other emerging self-conscious opinion blocs—the blacks, Chicanos, and other "third world" ethnic minorities.

This emergent coalition—reflected in Leggett's data—is already a potent force in American politics, both within the conventional political system and in the streets. It constitutes the most important force for basic change in the society. But it does not represent a majority of the populace. To constitute a majority, the new coalition would need to win the participation of significant proportions of the traditional popular base for social reform in this country—the white industrial working class. Leggett's data provide valuable materials for understanding the possible relationships between the new coalition and white workers. Leggett's data show the majority of the traditional working class, like the majority of the traditional middle class, opposes concrete reforms which would improve the position of blacks in the society. Nevertheless, his data suggest that the participation of white workers in a liberal Democratic Party, and in liberal unions, serves to maintain such workers as *political* supporters of civil rights, even if they are personally hostile to many egalitarian reforms. Insofar as workers continue to give political priority to economic security and continue to perceive the Democratic Party as their best assurance of favorable economic policy, then their hostility to civil rights reform is substantially neutralized by their political support for the Democratic Party. Further, some workers who are attentive to liberal arguments in favor of racial equality are undoubtedly influenced, as Leggett's data imply.

It is now being said that the traditional working class political support for the Democratic Party is rapidly declining. Leggett's data indicate that if that were to happen, white workers might then become a numerically substantial support for what would amount to a racist political coalition.

Leggett's data provide no concrete solutions to this critical dilemma facing the emergent coalition of the left. But they do suggest that that coalition must find some common ideological and organizational ground with substantial numbers of white workers to forestall the possibility of a majority coalition of the right. Beyond such a defensive perspective, however, lies the possibility that the building of such links could well result in a majority coalition of the left that could lend the society toward full equality and authentic democracy.

In any case, careful study of Professor Leggett's findings would repay anyone interested in understanding the transformation of the American political system which is now taking place.

Richard Flacks

ONE

Prologue:

Lessons Learned in Berkeley

Stokeley Carmichael said it: "White militants must organize the white community." That was five years ago. It hasn't happened, but the first steps have been taken. In April of 1971, Berkeley's left progressives and radicals were able to organize a sizeable section of the white community in the city's mayorality and city council election. Relying heavily upon the student population, but also working closely with the black community, the white radicals took the lead in electing both a progressive black mayor and three radicals to the Berkeley city council. During the electoral campaign, the white radical community was instrumental in both registering thousands of young people and publicizing the issues of police brutality, inadequate public medical facilities, landlord practices, city council shenanigans, and similar urban problems. The radicals defined these problems in ways quite different from traditional liberalism, for they emphasized the need to involve the people directly in local government. It should move to abolish such positions as the city planner and such organizations as a centralized police force. The New Left emphasis on citizen participation in all activities ran (runs) directly counter to the planning practices and bureaucratic styles of American liberals. They have traditionally favored decision-making by a political elite dependent on hired specialists.

Perhaps the April, 1971 election will serve as a model to be followed in towns such as Madison, Ithaca, and Ann Arbor. We don't know, but it would appear that the New Left can rally the necessary popular votes in local elections under certain conditions. If so, the New Left will have turned a corner. In any event, its members must move ahead and build a mass base for the movement. If not they will continue to rely upon a narrow range of strata to protest against American imperialism and domestic colonialism. Admittedly, the difficulties in building a mass base are many, but they are less threatening than continuing endless rounds of direct action that alienate working-class people and other potential allies from its cause. These bouts have failed to change significantly the structure of capitalism, let alone achieve socialism. We have not terminated the war in Vietnam. We have not stopped racism. Parallel to these failures is the shrinking base of support among students. Many have tired of sit-ins and similar tactics. Episodic politics have not been enough, and it is clear that most militant students now realize this to be the case. The cycle of student demands, collective protests, administrative repressions, minimal concessions, and student disengagement—until another event arises—has been found to be essentially nonproductive. The only alternative is to bring a sizeable portion of the working (and middle) class into the movement. Without divisions of troops there can't be anything more than skirmishes, devastating to the New Left leadership, rank-and-file, and cause. In this sense, the Berkeley elections prove promising, for the student and black radicals did well not only in their districts but in white working and middle class areas located quite some distance from student and New Left bailiwicks.

Given the Berkeley success, it might be useful to ask ourselves which sections of the working class seem most predisposed to listen. By no means are all workers hostile to New Left demands. Take the immediate withdrawal of troops from Vietnam, for example. The Berkeley radicals called for the immediate withdrawal of troops from Vietnam and pledged their support to the National Liberation Front. Despite this lop-sided commitment, the black and white radical candidates ran up large votes in all white districts, including those largely middle class and with sizeable blue collar minorities.

Nor is Berkeley unique. In Dearborn, Michigan, the anti-war mayor sponsored two successive referenda on the immediate withdrawal of troops from Vietnam, one vote in 1966, the other in 1968. The results proved encouraging. First, the percentage favoring immediate withdrawal increased sharply between 1966 and 1968, so that a majority of the 1968 voters in this medium-sized Detroit suburb favored the mayor's hard proposal. Second, a majority of working-class precincts in the eastern section of the city voted for immediate withdrawal. Dearborn is not the entire United States, but these kinds of votes, cast by Ford Rouge workers and others like them, are encouraging.

Further, in the area of race relations, a number of Cleveland white workers *did* vote for the successful black mayorality candidate, Carl Stokes, in both the 1967 and 1969 elections.

Similarly, in the study of the 1963 Berkeley Fair Housing referendum discussed in this book, we found that a sizeable minority of workers voted for the tough fair housing proposal when they had located in certain kinds of group associations and shared specific progressive attitudes on economy and culture. So let's not condemn what we have not yet analyzed. Let's not dismiss the working class from our political perspectives until we have studied its subclusters.

Yet few are analyzing the progressive political potential of the working class. It would appear that many New Left intellectuals–not just students but professionals as well–condemn the entire working class as if it were all of one coin. Some rely upon stereotypes such as "Joe," the ham-handed and cabbage-headed worker depicted in the movie by the same name, to understand a class whose heterogeneity defies the easy simplification. By contrast, some people romantically accept all of the working class as if it, the entire class, were the progressive force on all questions. The stance can only elicit disbelief from most of us. There is even another pattern, this one bizarre, among some who simultaneously reject and accept the working class as a font of wisdom. For them, when the political formula defies the day-to-day experience, these observers attempt to retain both.

Too frequently discussion of the working class proceeds as if John Stuart Mill's canons of logic had never existed, as if there were no rules of evidence. Admittedly sociologists do not have the final say on either logic or data; far from it. But their standards of empirical findings are superior to the "understanding" derived from disparate and inconsistent "insights" based upon newspaper readings, coffee-house gossip, small-group discussions, and naive citing of references to radical writings shrouded with biblical-like authority. Not Red books but hard data are needed to assess where working people are at.

Despite the 1971 Berkeley election, many of the New Left continue to condemn the *middle* class as if it too were all of the same cloth. *It* is described as out of touch, out of sight, perhaps out of luck or mind. Yet when New Leftists run candidates for office, whose support do they seek? When New Leftists go to jail, whom do they seek to bail them out and to accompany them to and through the courts? Who pays the bills? Not the New Left–they are generally "broke." The progressive professionals are sought out for ballot votes, free legal services, donations–the works. Yet the New Left is explainable. They seek support from their class of origin and destiny. Almost the entire work force of the New Left–the little band itself–derives from the middle class. Far from being classless, New Left members derive largely from the white collar strata, work in white-collar jobs, and act like middle-class people after they leave school for careers. There they join a class as mottled as the working class. So let's stop putting people in a "middle class" bag and then dropping it. Needless to say, the 1971 Berkeley election was a giant step in political reformulation.

In general, however, those on the left still suffer from stereotypy. What's happened? In our rush to put labels on people, our very categories have become caricatures of the sociological stereotypes we justifiably but ironically condemn. Nor are New Leftists the only ones to err in this regard. Older people, in many cases professors who should know better, speak of "working-class" this and "middle-class" that. These analysts avoid the painful task of creating a more complex and more useful set of categories. Their creation would allow us to compare working and middle-class subclusters to discover intra- as well as inter-class differences. Let's approach both classes with sophistication. Let's dispense with the tears. If, for example, large numbers of workers are authoritarian—and we have ample reason to believe that they are—let's find out who they are, why they are that way, and what can be done to get them out of that mess.

Again, if not all of the *middle* class is to be written off as hidebound and reactionary, then who are the potential allies of the New Left, what has made them that way, and what are we going to do about them? Ignore them? Not with J. Edgar Hoover breathing through our phones! "Who are our middle-class allies?" is the crucial question, and if radicals have come up with a technique superior to the social survey approach in ferreting out these people, we wish they would make it known. Certainly their objections to the use of surveys would be inconsistent with Marxism, for Marx himself in his later years used a newspaper mail questionnaire in an attempt to gauge the attitudes and activities of the Parisian working class. He, too, was concerned with its heterogeneity. All of us should take a cue from Marx, especially in gathering empirical materials in areas where Marxism has proved weakest. The complex relationship between class and race would be a good start.

More than the desire for intellectual neatness commands us to take these steps. We face certain political problems. The Black Panthers are right—hard, state-sponsored repression is with us, and we have to obtain as many allies as possible. If militant tactics or anarchistic acrobatics do not help build a united front, then we must stop these actions, criticize ourselves, and if need be, call for social reform as a way of widening the movement's base. The Black Panthers are also right when they say we must unite with those who are anti-fascist, even if this means putting away the Red books, the berets, and the fantasies about the elimination of imperialism now. It would appear that many have already learned that further desperate forays can only mean our political dissolution through state repression. During the present period, we must emphasize the creation of coalitions which will help us to establish organizations that will rework people's ideas on war, race, private property, the military, and their interconnections. An issue basis for such re-education might well be spectacles of governmental lying revealed in the Pentagon Papers. But before we can take advantage of such gifts, we have to become disciplined, and hard-working. We have to work on a continuous basis to build new groups and to invigorate old ones within neighborhoods, factories, and offices, wherever we encounter potential supporters. Working through these groups, we must reorder mentalities. Perhaps as important a task as any in this regard is the elimination of traditional, racist thought.

This book talks about whites accepting and rejecting blacks on the level of housing, an area filled with stereotypes. We discuss whites in terms of their backgrounds, their politics, and their attitudes. The book makes clear the combination of social characteristics and personal attitudes that predispose whites to go against racism and accept blacks as neighbors. Quite obviously, acceptance does not make these whites superior to blacks. White attitudes (and actions), however, *do* make them potential political allies with black people. Nor do these white attitudes make them allies of blacks on all questions. On the issue of jobs, for example, if and when black workers demand white jobs as the price of job integration, white workers will—and do—fight blacks irrespective of white workers' positions on housing. What should be made clear to both black and white is the need to demand an expansion of the number of available jobs as the basis for job integration. White workers are no more charitable than white intellectuals about giving up jobs. Imagine the white faculty at any college giving up one-quarter to one-half of their jobs to blacks in order to achieve job integration! You can't imagine it, nor can we. Blacks and whites must demand the kind of economic system that can provide the jobs necessary. And perhaps capitalism cannot do the job. In that case, some form of socialism must create the jobs. And perhaps that socialism will evolve slowly with local governments taking the lead in introducing non-capitalist forms of economic organization which can provide the jobs necessary—for both black and white. How local governments can obtain the necessary economic tax base to carry on this task, however, remains difficult to imagine.

This book has another relevant message, and it recurs time after time. If we are going to change the ways in which whites act toward blacks, we will have to change the everyday group associations of white people. Either we act to remove white people from racist churches or we strive to transform the altars. In any event, we cannot afford to ignore the reactionary socialization practices carried on by many religious groups, for they create traditional persons with racist dispositions. Again, either we work to create alternatives to unions or we move to revitalize them. We need to make unions more than bread-and-butter defense organizations generally hostile to, or indifferent towards, the demands of black people. On the neighborhood level, either we create local associations to help white people deal with problems of crime, taxes, inflation, schools, and *racial integration,* or we will by default abdicate this leadership to the hard-working right wing—the John Birch Society and its numerous cousins. In short, we either take the lead in attempting to resocialize the people or we allow this country to slide down the road to fascism.

But we must examine our intellectual folkways as well—the most perfidious formulation at the moment being the newly created tradition of viewing working-class people as uniformly authoritarian. Working-class authoritarianism—as it has come to be called, sometimes in hushed and embarrassed tones by those who wish to skip the problem and move on to radical action—finds its way into *TV and movie programming* where white workers frequently come through as ethnic morons; into *classroom discussions* where the professor espouses in his arrogant deliveries what he cannot demonstrate to be empirically the case; into *campus cafes,* where sloppy gossip passes for convincing analyses; into *youth meetings,* where gusto substitutes for careful specification of reason and marshalling of evidence. Working-class authoritarianism as rubric and barb has dribbled down to us in a multiplicity of forms. And it is accepted by many of us even though we should know better than to accept statements unless and until we have examined the evidence for the ideas expressed.

Who are the people who have coined this rubric? Many of us don't know, since we are the indirect and passive recipients of these ideas. But the label, working-class authoritarianism, does have a source. It is our job to examine and to expose it.

For the New Left and its faculty supporters there is another painful task—to examine evidence that runs contrary to pet prejudices, a key one being that Democrats and Republicans really are and always were near-identical on significant matters. In the 1970's, we shall discover that having been either a Democrat or a Republican during the early 1960's *did* make a whopping difference in the civil rights struggle—a fight now lost. But the losing of the fight does not demonstrate the absence of differences among people who were at the time of the contest located in quite different ideological and action positions.

Today the Democratic party is a wreck. Yet it is to progressive Democrats that we must go to help build a political coalition if we are to withstand the oppression now decapitating the leadership of militant black and white groups. Our doing so may well help to steer them towards a type of socialism in keeping with the decentralized preferences of a growing body of Americans. In moving in that direction, we cannot help but benefit from the kind of evidence presented in this book. The data strongly indicate that black and white militant decisions to seek out nonradical allies is essentially a good one. The actions and attitudes of many nonradical but progressive whites in the Berkeley Fair Housing of 1963 portended the Berkeley coalitions of the early

1970's, but there is a difference. Both center and left have taken a giant step to the left, with the young radicals taking the lead in what is in effect a united front. The move to build a united front in Berkeley and elsewhere does not mean, of course, that a scurry to build a left-center coalition has to be of the muddle-headed variety. For example, we must sort out the government mandarins from those intellectuals who serve the people. We must then exclude the mandarins from our coalition in order to prevent them from disrupting our organizational activity and consuming our time.

To some degree, this book will help us to make these kinds of distinctions, for it specifies those class and political affiliations that in one specific instance (the 1963 Berkeley Fair Housing election) predisposed whites to take the first step towards an interracial coalition. It also points up the significance of the university—its heterogeneity as well as its over-all impact. In a few years a good ten percent of this country's entire population may well consist of university and college students, faculty, and their immediate families. When one adds this ten percent to the approximately twenty percent of black and brown minorities, one can begin to appreciate the political potential involved. And there is another hopeful sign. Many of the protest leaders in American politics derive from both the academic and racial ghettos, the very ones on the increase in terms of absolute as well as relative size. May these spawning grounds continue to flourish.

Yet not all students and faculty are liberated by their educational experiences. Far from it. Who are the traditionalists—those made more bold and more facile by their "higher" educational experiences? This book examines the uneven impact of the university as well.

This introductory chapter is justifiably involved, yet there is something also to be said for cold, analytical commitment, especially when viewing those forces working for and against us. In the next eight chapters the analysis of the Berkeley fair housing vote falls into the tradition of committed but sober social science. But in the final chapter, when moving from what recently was to what currently should be, we shift gears. There we put our data on wheels and link our observations to what must be done.

TWO

Class and Race Relations

In urban America during the early 1960's there were two major classes and one significant race issue: blue- and white-collar groups tried to come to grips with the question of how blacks could attain first-class citizenship. Whites had to take a stand on the race issue if only because black demands forced them to. During this period of polarization within many communities, whites announced value positions and acted for or against the integration of blacks in such areas as work, recreation, education, housing, and so on. Why white people split on the race issue during the early 1960's is difficult to ascertain today, but perhaps their reactions stemmed partially from their class positions. If so, we would be wise to ask how working-class and middle-class whites differed on the question of integration of blacks and if group ties made a difference among both working- and middle-class whites, was the white working class responsible for the integration failures of the 1960s and, irrespective of blame, what are the consequences of integration failure?

Before trying to answer these questions, let's distinguish between the *intimate* and the *impersonal* areas of integration since we will be considering only one of them. The intimate areas include those settings where people get to know each other, either as knowledgeable acquaintances or as close friends. In both contexts, not only is there friendship but also concern for each other's well-being. Such ties can be found within the family, the school, the neighborhood, and the church. When we integrate minorities into these primary spheres, we are doing something quite different from helping them find niches within the impersonal realms of human relations.[1] The less intimate areas on the other hand would include certain occupational and distributive relationships—boss-employee ties at work and customer-clerk relations in stores. Such affective attachments among people can be quite limited, although even here highly cordial friendships may develop. However, these relationships are generally organized among impersonal lines, minimizing intimate involvements for those who wish to avoid them. In this sense the antiseptic settings differ considerably from the intimate spheres, for when groups stress affective ties, they make demands that have a wide range of consequences,[2] as we shall see.

Let us consider the relationship between class position and racial acceptance in one intimate setting—the realm of housing—for where someone lives helps determine where he will attend church and school as well as whom he will choose as a playmate or pal.[3] People who live together play together. If spatial propinquity thereby promotes the integration of church, school, and neighborhood life, there is a good chance that many friendships may lead to attraction, romance, and perhaps marriage. Under these conditions, racial differences and taboos may limit but not prevent fraternization leading to miscegenation and, in some cases, interracial marriage as well.

IMPACT OF CLASS ON ORGANIZATIONAL TIES AND GROUP BELIEFS

In the long haul, class relations largely determine racial ties, including the acceptance of blacks as neighbors, which is the subject of this book. In a foreseeable racially integrated community, work relations would be the principal determinant of where one lives, for class largely determines the ability to pay for housing, and the ability to pay is crucial to selecting a neighborhood in which to live. But class impact is by no means exclusively ecological, for class positions foster organizational ties, and these connections subsequently help determine how class-racial groups might combat or help one another.

The relationship between class and race can be partially understood if we focus on human ties such as those that occur at the periphery of as well as within political parties, and on people processes such as aging, buying, and moving. We would have to acknowledge that a person's class position helps determine type and incidence of his group affiliations. Where people stand on matters of property, work, and pay have a lot to do with how they affiliate with political parties, how long they live, how they age, whether they buy or rent a home, and how (if at all) they migrate. Class is the overriding determinant of human behavior, although it never appears as the only obvious factor.

Nonetheless, having made this necessary observation on the power of class in determining how people act—a view based upon centuries of historical and sociological observation—we must make another assumption. Once class has helped build group ties—such as those established in labor unions—and even while class continues to foster these relations, once group ties are set, once people processes are in motion, they acquire as "secondary determinants" a momentum to some degree independent of everyday work, property, and pay considerations, the primary determinants of human behavior. For example, once class conditions have contributed to belief construction on political party loyalties within a family, once these beliefs have acquired a solidity, the ongoing presence of these beliefs will operate somewhat independently of class connections, and these commitments will continue to deliver votes on election day. When class, status, and other considerations set a Democratic party preference within a large section of the urban, industrial, working-class community in one of our major cities, the very presence of this collective specification subsequently moves these workmen to go along with party choice on matters of candidates and issues (although, as is always the case, there will be a sizeable number of exceptions). Parallel belief construction within Republican, working-class families will also acquire a modicum of independence of material conditions, be they largely static or changing. Ideas, then, do acquire an autonomy whatever their structural sources and supports.

Perhaps by acknowledging this kind of limitation on class analysis we can begin to understand why black and white workmen remain so sorely divided at a time when their coalition might have challenged the power of those who have continued to benefit from working-class division and its corollary, the absence of a popular front among races within the blue-collar world.

In America, an upper class exists, coheres, and guides. As Domhoff has demonstrated,[4] a relatively small number of families garner the top prestige positions in the country and direct the leading corporations, insurance companies, and banks. This class also sets policies for research foundations, university corporations, foreign policy associations, economic advisory committees, and departments of labor. It also enjoys an exclusive social life, thereby contributing to its overall solidarity. Within limits, the upper class is thereby able to shape basic policies on such matters as level and incidence of blue-collar unemployment. In short, economic insecurity for blue-collar people remains to a high degree upper-class determined. This economic insecurity also has class consequences, especially in a multiracial working class.

From past observation[5] we have learned that economic insecurity contributes to working-class consciousness, especially among racial groups, marginal both with respect to division of labor and social acceptance; black insecurity can also intensify job competition among blue-collar people in various racial groups. In the United States this competition has contributed to interracial prejudices and antagonisms within black and white working-class communities. Over the years hostile beliefs have become customary.

These white subgroups—many of them ethnic as well as working class—have become the repositories of many traditions, including the authoritarian variety associated with avoidance of subordinate racial groups in potentially intimate settings such as neighborhoods. Working-class traditionalism thereby stands in the way of racial equality, for racial traditionalism provides mainstream working-class people (white blue-collar workers) with anti-egalitarian standards.

If what we assume is true—and considerable evidence would certainly suggest its plausibility—we should ask ourselves another question: Which group affiliations and people processes push working- (and middle-) class people to act contrary to the racist themes so obviously prevalent not only in working- but in middle-class worlds as well?

Clearly, progressive political party affiliation is a crucial factor in moving people to act contrary to traditional attitudes. In turn, this political tie has its origins largely in the intergenerational class and status group experiences of people—the underdog (person or group) generally ties up with reform or radical political parties and tries to use them to end economic injustices and to promote a measure of equality; the interests and experiences of upper-class individuals generally move them into conservative politics.

We are not saying that where one works or how much prestige one enjoys *directly* influence his actions in helping to liberate proletarian minorities such as blacks; in fact, we wish to prove the inadequacy of this formulation. From our point of view, class has an impact on race relations, but its force can be absorbed and redirected by a person's (or group's) connections.

A political party generally recruits on the basis of class interests, although in many instances it appeals to more than one class. Regardless of whom they seek, parties sometimes strive to (1) *reinforce* the perspectives of those in agreement with the party program; (2) *reshape* the attitudes of party adherents to make them consonant with the party program; and (3) *mobilize* party supporters in favor of issues sometimes unpopular among a sizeable minority of party rank and file. If these assumptions are correct, we should not be too surprised to find a relatively large number of mainstream working-class people acting contrary to their personal racist commitments and on behalf of subordinate racial minorities when they are formally affiliated with a progressive political party, one highly active and believable.

But before developing this thesis, we must make one point clear, namely, our position on racism and the mainstream working class.

LIBERATION FROM TRADITIONALISM: FROM COLLECTIVE ACTION TO COLLECTIVE THOUGHT

We assume that a racist ethic permeates the white working class, although it may be more deeply embedded within white proletarian ethnic groups than inside other layers of the blue-collar world.[6] Let us, in effect, grant to Lipset[7] and many others what would seem apparent in contemporary United States. However, in making this concession, let us not only make a distinction between conservatism and traditionalism, but also speculate about those forces that might liberate people (working and middle class alike) from traditionalism and link them to progressive sentiment. Karl Mannheim pointed to the difference between conservatism and traditionalism,[8] a very important one leading us to a discussion of those forces that operate to liberate workmen from discrimination in the short run and from prejudice in the long run.

Conservatism refers to the economic dimension, the propensity to favor the retention of property forms and ancillary class and legal structures. Of course, minor compromises on these and related matters may be acceptable, but conservatism favors keeping the basic forms intact. A new varnish, perhaps a brief sanding, may be acceptable, but under no circumstances should people tamper with the structure, under no conditions should people question the interests of the propertied so as to suggest some different way of allocating the strategic resources of the community. Conservatism, then, involves consciousness among the well-heeled, those who own a large chunk of society's fertile land, capital goods, or investment funds. In this sense large numbers of the middle class and their aristocratic ancestors would qualify as conservatives. In a general evolutionary sense, the working class would include relatively few adherents to conservatism.

On the other hand, workers will often stand behind certain traditionalist notions. *Traditionalism* may be either working or middle class in content, but in any event it refers to a particular range of prejudiced folkways or *mores* common to one class or the other.[9] These prejudiced views are nonscientific in quality and linger through time to help determine the behavior of consecutive generations, especially on matters of race.

Working-class traditionalism refers to subcultural values and norms expressed by intimate groups within which working-class people are embedded. These intimate groups would include working-class families, churches, schools, unions, bars, neighborhoods, and larger families (extended), all of which develop values, beliefs, and norms on an intergenerational basis and thereby create relatively sacred–hence unquestioned–subcultures. Territorially, workers create subcultures and subcommunities within certain areas, and later on they view these zones as their turf. (We are indebted to Stanley Lyman as well as Karl Mannheim for these insights.) Of course, when workers consider these districts their own, they may do so as a working class undifferentiated in terms of ethnicity or race. However, where ethnic stratification does occur inside the working class, one can expect that its nationalities will erect subcommunities, subcultures, and hence by definition, peculiar kinds of traditionalism. Consequently, there develop class-ethnic or class-racial groups with historical claims to bars, neighborhoods, and the like. Clearly, these subcommunities attempt to exclude many others, but especially those whom they perceive to be quite different in terms of sports and politics, religion and sex, alcohol and drugs, and other matters related to the intimate aspects of family life. So, for example, if Polish residents of a working-class neighborhood claimed certain areas as its own, they would certainly reject not only blacks but Anglos as well, although admittedly their resistance to Anglos would be less sharp; Poles would view blacks as extremely different from and quite destructive to the unquestioned preferences attached to the Polish subcommunity.

What is true of working-class traditonalism would also be the case, point by point, for middle-class traditionalism, including the potential of ethnic variation within the middle class, from Anglo through Jewish to Black—the full range of the ethnic hierarchy. All create their own intimate groups around activities such as religion, education, protection, and recreation. And these ethnic, middle-class enclaves also develop values, beliefs, and norms on an intergenerational basis. Each views these subcultural traits as beyond question; they too are resistant to ethnic or racial change.[10]

If we can discern traditionalism within both classes, and if we can locate ethnic variations within each of the two levels on matters of traditionalism, should one simply accept it or go on to ask the obvious question: What are the forces that liberate working- and middle-class people from tradition? In answering this question, we might benefit by making a distinction between liberating groups and liberating processes.

Liberating groups would be those collectivities that call for the realization of the beliefs associated with the French Revolution. Hence, these groups act fraternally[11] and, in the long run, press their members to rearrange their views. In the short run, fraternal ideology may or may not be a pertinent factor in pressing people attitudinally to accept others as racial equals, intimates or otherwise; but in the long haul, liberating groups hope to augment fraternal acts with egalitarian attitudes. This ideological supplementation would hold, among other things, that individuals and groups should be evaluated on the basis of their achievements and not on their ascribed statuses. In the long run, liberating groups also demand that racial pluralism be viewed as an alternative to racial assimilation. In the United States all minorities, including the proletarianized variety, should have the right to reject assimilation into a white Anglo-Saxon, middle-class subculture. Blacks, Mexicans, Indians, Puerto Ricans, Poles, and other subcommunity members should have the choice of rejuvenating and of extending their own subcultures to make themselves wholly distinctive from America's "charter group," the white Anglo-Saxons. Liberating groups hold that in diversity there is intellectual and other forms of stimulation, so why not view the creation of an America with multiple subcommunities as a healthy alternative to assimilation? Intergroup conflict might be inherent in a pluralistic arrangement, but perhaps this struggle could be both partially positive and generally less combative than the current effort to assimilate and integrate populations into a WASP frame. In any event, liberating groups today would appear to be warmer to the idea of ethnic pluralism than they were a short time ago when they stressed assimilation almost to the complete exclusion of the pluralistic possibility.

Perhaps liberating groups could find some structural support among the *liberating processes,* specific activities that often erase racist views and call for fraternal actions. These processes we associate, for example, with particular generational membership and migration from one milieu to another. At the same time, members of liberating collectivities would benefit from lack of participation within particular property forms, such as home ownership and the processes associated with them. Noninvolvement in property purchases weakens the racist ethic found at the heart of traditionalism and insulates nonbuyers from a key storage area of racism. When people avoid processes that are part of home buying and selling, they are less likely to associate with the traditional racist values embedded in the real estate community. Noninvolvement in home purchase, then, partially insulates one from the racist ethos of a key property group, and perhaps makes one more prone to support the ideas of emancipating collectivities. Of course this is not necessarily the case. However, renting should facilitate the impact of liberating processes and groups.

These liberating groups do not necessarily become strong forces acting for change unless social movements enter into and rework their policies and actions on matters of race. For example, formal political parties and university institutions do not become significant sources working for the elimination of racism unless and until social movements enter their environs and press hard for changes. An example during the early 1960's would have been the entrance of members of a civil rights group such as CORE or the "civil rights movement" into a local Democratic party organization. These movements need not be the sole source of liberating ideas, for nesting organizations (such as formal political parties) may already contain internal sources of themes favoring racial changes and eliminating traditionalism. Whatever the relative strength of external forces and internal commitments, when *movements* penetrate *liberating groups* and use *movement ideas* to translate *group beliefs* into integration practices, the two sets of ideas interact to become mutually supportable if not mutually exclusive. Under certain conditions, the total set of views can help create a strong collective ethic favoring either racial integration or egalitarian racial pluralism.

Ideas, whatever their tone, do not exist in limbo. They have group carriers. Key groups are those we associate with politics, education, and religion. Let us be more precise on matters of party affiliation, university connection, and religious tie.

Party Affiliation

When people make a decision to accept or to reject minority group members as neighbors, their choice should depend in part on the way in which these people affiliate with formal political parties. If voters are associated with a political group that continuously and honestly calls for integration and the use of the law to enforce integration, then this group will push many of its members towards the support of integration. Interestingly enough, norms, beliefs, and the influence of this political organization are often sufficiently compelling to make many prejudiced people vote for integration, even when they inhabit traditionalist neighborhoods most subject to the pressures of integration and hence most likely to experience racial intimacy and its expected consequences should minority group members move in.

Under these conditions a minority of white working-class people will frequently act for blacks, Mexicans, and other minorities when these white workers belong to a progressive or left-wing political group.[12] Proportionately fewer working-class people will act this way when they associate with an organization committed to fighting racial integration, for under these conditions group norms combine with personal attitudes to help produce globules of tradionalist *geist* and (hence) racist predisposition.

Of course, to state the difference so bluntly is to engage in oversimplification. Obviously, several qualifications are in order. We are discussing relative differences in the distribution of choices on questions of intimacy. For example, workmen may affiliate with the Democratic party in towns like Flint and Birmingham, Michigan or Berkeley, California, yet only a minority of them may vote in favor of fair housing legislation because of the lingering influence of traditionalism. Yet there should be a much larger proportion of Democratic than Republican workmen voting for fair housing legislation, because the Republican organization has lined up consistently and rigidly against fair housing and in favor of genteel white-collar racism. Obviously, also, when liberating group norms move people to vote in ways inconsistent with their traditionalist attitudes, and when these persons nonetheless retain strong ties with these traditional groups, then they will *in the long run* either (1) reject working-class subcommunities (and their class traditionalism) and accept liberated subcommunities and nonprejudiced attitudes or (2) disaffiliate from the liberating group.

Of course, there is a difference between liberation and affirmation. While liberation erases old traditional sentiments, the process of affirmation repeats progressive racial views—whether they lean toward assimilation or pluralism—and strives to link new predispositions to collective progressive racial views in an effort to cement new attitudes to already organized collective commitment. Political parties sometimes carry on both of these processes of liberation and affirmation. This dual tendency is especially noticeable when they contain new and past penetrations of civil rights exponents. Of course, a political party may lean towards one process or the other, either liberation or affirmation.

In Berkeley, for instance, during the early 1960's the Democratic party promoted both liberation and affirmation, since it was replete with the left-overs of the old Socialist party, the Communist party, the Progressive party, and ex-Adlai Stevenson supporters. These elements, and to a lesser degree the civil rights activists, did collect around the local California Democratic Council (CDC) chapters, themselves formally affiliated with the Democratic party of California. Consequently, we should not be too surprised to discover that a CDC-based Democratic party organization focused on race and carried on educational work in this area, although most of their efforts went into affirmation processes that took the usual forms—public discussions, platform planks, TV debates, legislative activities, and the like.

Admittedly, in Berkeley and elsewhere it was difficult to determine where liberation ended and affirmation began. Perhaps both were part of the same larger process of liberation-affirmation. Whatever the emphasis (or demarcation point), in 1963 a sizeable minority of the Berkeley middle class led in efforts to liberate and affirm, while the overwhelming majority of the working class proved conspicuous by its absence from such involvement. Still, the CDC-inspired activities may well have had an impact on many working-class people, some of whom undoubtedly derived racially egalitarian views from other sources as well, such as the International Longshoremen and Warehousemen's Union (a former CIO group with a relatively good record in promoting racial equality and exerting considerable political influence in the San Francisco Bay Area).

But what about the middle class? How significant is political affiliation for this group? Middle-class people—that is, the white-collar population—should vote overwhelmingly in favor of fair housing when they affiliate with a progressive or left-wing political organization with a fraternal ethos on race. This value commitment reinforces any egalitarian predispositions they might bring with them into a political party that they largely command.

But party affiliation is not the only consideration. Of those middle-class people who attach themselves to progressive and left-wing groups, a very large number derive originally from manual-worker populations. When these people move up the class order, they generally retain their sympathy for the underdog. There is a reason for this seeming inconsistency. New position is only partially significant in accounting for present action; loyalties are to a large degree related to early political experiences and, among people who have spent their youth on the bottom looking up through a progressive prism, many (but not all by any means) will maintain an empathic and hence sympathetic view when gazing down at the underdog population that no longer includes them.

On the other hand, when middle-class people belong to a traditionalist party, one by definition committed to maintaining the barriers of race, their views are often colored by the perspective of this organization. These views would be traditionalist despite the amount of formal education and total income common to the group in question. Previous education would simply provide these people with legalistic verbalisms useful for concocting sophisticated rationalizations constructed to keep blacks out of their neighborhoods and to buttress their traditionalist views on matters of race. In this setting, enlightened racism permeates many middle-class lives, with parents passing it on to their children. Hence, we should expect racist perspectives to be most pronounced among those raised within middle-class populations who give evidence of previous participation in a traditionalist political ethos and of continuation in this political milieu. In short, solid middle-class Republicanism may well be a sure breeding ground and a perpetuator of traditionalism with its built-in kernel of racism.

Solid middle-class Republicanism by no means represents the middle class. This heterogeneous stratum contains a multiplicity of subcultures, including the antithesis of racist Babbittry. What we have in mind is the university, for it is a repository of forces working both for liberation from traditionalism and affirmation of the Enlightenment. Of course, the university is not all of one cloth.[13] Like all progressive institutions, it too is divided between those who support racial equality and those who tie themselves to town traditionalism. In turn, the town ethos rests heavily upon the values of powerful business groups associated with commodity retailing and home resale.

Gown vs. Town

Our universities include a multiplicity of philosophies, and this book is no place to review them. However, one tendency demands our attention—the ideology of French revolutionary humanism with its call for the emancipation of mankind from theological *prejudice* and institutional *discrimination.* From the point of view of humanism, both prejudice and discrimination have had adverse effects upon large sections of mankind. For a number of reasons many university people have judged these racist ideas and practices as unfair. Of the critics, many have looked to the Enlightenment. Following Voltaire and akin French, English, and American philosophers, opposition has sprung up in many places: within the labor movement, inside cooperatives, and the like. But nowhere can one find greater enemies of institutionalized racism than in the left-progressive subcommunities inside the universities. Their speeches, writings, and money leave no doubt as to where they stand. Their presence in large numbers, however, should not lead us to equate left-progressive subculture[14] with a university ethos. On the contrary, the two phenomena are quite distinct and at times opposed to one another. Left-progressive subculture would appear to be an ethos more common to certain sectors of the university than to others. The values of liberty, equality, and fraternity are most evident in areas such as mathematics, foreign languages, library science, education, social science, and social welfare, among others, although this commitment penetrates throughout the remainder of the university.[15] With these differences in mind, we might view the university as a motley assembly of islands, some of which are more committed than others to the maintenance and revitalization of humanist traditions: equal educational opportunity; greater economic equity; unhindered political advocacy; and racial equality.

The progressive intelligentsia favors federal government involvement through limited regulation of the economy, while the more left-wing elements expect considerably more change, namely, the ending of imperialism. Whether liberal or left, however, these intellectuals are still pro-labor by tradition if not current inclination, especially when the blue-collar underdog suffers from racial discrimination as well.

Although previous ties to the working class are salient in accounting for these views,[16] more important would be the way in which academic work produces a scientific perspective consistent with the values of the Enlightenment. For example, science indicates that we cannot establish that races differ from one another in terms of intellectual endowment. Interestingly, this finding would be consistent with the Enlightenment, for it holds that we should not judge a man on the basis of racial status but, rather, on his personal achievement. This scientific finding would move university people to view man in evidential terms and hence to reject theological syllogisms that condemn blacks. Skeptical and empirical by academic training and professional association, university intellectuals generally reject Biblical tales and hold that racial pigmentation is demonstrably unrelated to the values and behavior of persons or groups, while the social and economic characteristics of racial collectivities are relevant and predictably related to behavior. Furthermore, as a correlate, these scientists would agree that as one alters the structural foundations of a racial collectivity, one thereby changes other aspects of how a group behaves. In this sense, man is no different from a rat, a fig, or a leaf. Given the scientific point of view held by many academicians, they would reject patterns of racial segregation rooted partially in stereotypic conceptions of man. Thus, the academician opposes both Babbittry and the Babbitt whenever one or both condemn minorities and foster segregation.[17]

However, we would be naive to overlook the way in which business groups have penetrated certain sections of the university and helped create a moral mood hardly in keeping with the acceptance of minority group members as intimates. Perhaps the business community has made the greatest number and most intensive contacts within schools of law, education, business administration, and most recently, hard sciences. In these three areas, if anywhere, one should find considerable faculty opposition to humanism, even though these fields—especially hard sciences such as biology, chemistry, and physics—depend considerably upon the scientific method. Much of the business community reinforces a traditionalist perspective on matters of race, especially within politically conservative circles. The wealthy often use their power to dictate discriminatory policies on race to the community, even when it is evident to academicians that there is a lack of scientific justification for the racism fostered by the Main Street businessmen. To much of the university community, racism rests not upon truth derived from scientific findings but coercion based upon property and power. Owners of strategic resources can use power to condemn and to confine a group through irrational myths derived from a form of racism rooted partially in Biblical inspiration.

Given the intellectual repulsiveness—nay, the scientific indefensibility—of the arguments arrayed by those who guard the outposts of segregation, university intellectuals have been more than willing to cast their lot for a fair housing ordinance, especially when they belong to a local party with a progressive tone.

Religion

Expectedly, hard opposition to racism should be found among university intellectuals well beyond the pale of organized religion. Religious groups are key carriers of traditional beliefs. Their moral commitments include racial views, more often than not positive in their treatment of dominant racial groups and negative, if not derogatory, in their definition of subordinate racial collectivities. Present-day Christianity would not be an exception. Being dominated by whites, it has traditionally defined non-whites as worthy of extraordinary treatment, more often than not exploitative or demeaning in quality. For whites in contemporary America, liberation from organized religion would mean nonparticipation. In passing we should mention that it is not unusual for large numbers of university intellectuals to place themselves well beyond the boundaries of organized worship of deities.

On the other hand, among university intellectuals in either the traditionalist party or organized religion, a disproportionately large number should be expected to vote against any form of interracial intimacy. When university intellectuals are found in *both* the traditionalist party and organized religion, then very few will act for proletarian minorities on matters of equality.

However, these hypotheses are not the key ones. Rather, they constitute combinations of more essential, more simple derivations.

In synthesizing our thoughts on party, university, and religion, we might formally specify the following hypotheses: (1) Everything else being equal, political progressives should surpass political traditionalists in voting for an ordinance forbidding discrimination in an area of intimacy (for example, a fair housing referendum). (2) University people should score more heavily for fair housing legislation than nonuniversity counterparts. (3) The nonreligious, as opposed to members of an organized church, should vote in disproportionately large numbers for fair housing.

SOURCES OF PREJUDICE AND DISCRIMINATION

Many writers would disagree with this formulation and reject the hypotheses just advanced. Of their arguments, two seem most important, and we would subsume them under two rubrics, one dealing with the significance of spatial propinquity, the other with race and job competition. The last category would contain those theories associated with working-class authoritarianism, including those of Seymour Martin Lipset.

In analyzing ideas on class position and racial intimacy, we might observe that there are at least two fascinating arguments supporting the proposition that workmen are more racist than others. The first argument is essentially ecological, for it points to the relevance of spatial propinquity as bringing together incompatible groups. The other point of view is economic, for it focuses on job insecurity and job competition as the ultimate basis for interracial strife among working-class people.

If one examines the central ideas associated with the ecological approach—one popularized decades ago by the Old Chicago School—and adds a dash of neo-Freudian theory, advanced by myself and countless others—then one might argue that spatial propinquity promotes sexual attraction, and that this proposition would seem especially true where community culture both rejects and romanticizes the sexual abilities of a subordinate racial group. When the culture forbids sexual relations between these persons, praises the sexuality of one and, at the same time, allows individuals from both to become pals, sexual attraction may well result.[18]

Within the white camp, accepting Negroes as neighbors has had more urgent meaning for the blue- than the white-collar population since integration in the areas of housing has been felt immediately by a higher proportion of manual workers. Housing integration generally means blacks moving into areas occupied by working-class whites. Under these conditions, integration has a predictable consequence. Blacks will go to school, church, and playgrounds with the sons and daughters of white working-class parents. Integration implies that black and white will often become intimate. White middle-class parents are generally spared such problems, since most live on the edge of the central city where blacks are either few in number or non-existent. Or, if blacks do move into these outer-edge neighborhoods, the white middle class can afford to move to a suburb where everything but castle moats, turreted walls, and boiling oil are used to keep the blacks at bay.[19]

Since working-class whites are the *white* ones who must live with the personal and social problems of interracial intimacy, one would expect that a relatively large number would do what they could to limit the presence of blacks in their neighborhoods. Indeed, this would seem to be the case, for racial disturbances have time and again erupted in these zones of racial transition.

At first glance, the ecological argument would seem to contain considerable merit. Unfortunately, it overlooks subcommunity clusters and subcultural rules which initially guide many—but by no means all—working-class evaluations and subsequently lead to restrictions on the entrance of blacks into white working-class neighborhoods. In other words, even if the ecological argument contains many valid assumptions, this line of reasoning fails to indicate the traditions around which many workmen react and, perhaps more seriously, neglects to account for those large numbers of workers who act in favor of integration, even in housing and hence the intimate spheres.

Perhaps, however, arguments that stress job insecurity and job competition advance more plausible theories. Let us consider several of them.

A few decades ago Louis Wirth argued that when white people belong to the upper classes, their job security makes them less prejudiced towards Negroes than would normally be the case among lower-class whites who, facing economic adversity in the form of economic competition, are moved to engage in racial conflict with Negroes. Wirth's analysis was consistent with the one advanced by Gunnar Myrdal who also focused on the way in which economic competition allegedly preempted political coalitions between poor whites and Negroes.

In recent years a number of scholars have followed in the footsteps of Wirth and Myrdal[20] and, of these, Seymour Lipset has presented a point of view most worthy of consideration. In his effort to advance an explanation for working-class authoritarianism, Lipset has argued:

> The poorer strata everywhere are more liberal or leftist on economic issues; they favor more welfare state measures, higher wages, graduated income taxes, support of trade unions, and so forth. But when liberalism is defined in non-economic terms—as support of civil liberties, internationalism, etc.—the correlation is reversed. The more well-to-do are more liberal, the poorer are more intolerant.[21]

This idea has become almost commonplace in sociology, and few doubt its veracity. Nonetheless, we might benefit from a close look at both evidence and argument presented to substantiate this point of view.

Lipset attempted to prove his general position by presenting information gathered by social scientists from many countries. For example, he used materials systematically gathered in 1958 from Austria, Japan, Brazil, Canada, Mexico, West Germany, The Netherlands, Belgium, Italy, and France to argue that a disproportionately large number of the lower classes were *not* in favor of the multi-party system.[22] (Unfortunately, he failed to tell us whether undemocratic views lead to actions that undermine a parliamentary political system.)

His analysis of class and prejudice follows the same pattern, for Lipset argues that American social studies demonstrate how the lower classes are the least tolerant of Negroes and Jews.[23] The reader is left with the obvious implication: working-class people would be the *least* likely to register a voting acceptance of blacks as neighbors. How can one account for this intolerance? Understandably enough, Lipset points to social environment in explaining working-class perspectives, and his presentation does make a good deal of sense, for he adopts what would seem to be a truism in social science: if a population is authoritarian and hence racist, it has become so because its circumstances have shaped it so.

According to this approach, working-class authoritarianism derives from lack of exposure to formal education, less frequent participation in organizations, limited reading in any setting, occupational isolation from the middle class, economic insecurity, and authoritarian patterns within families. All of these considerations combine to create a reluctance to accept deviants, be they Negroes, atheists, or Communists. At first glance, the evidence would seem to support this position. Take education for example. Using Samuel Stouffer's material on attitudes toward civil liberties in middle-sized American communities,[24] Lipset observed the impact of education and class on political tolerance. Although he thereby based his secondary analysis upon a sample that did not fully represent the American population, he nonetheless presented evidence with implications for the totality. In Table 1[25] we can see the relevance of *education* within all four strata: low manual, or lower working class; high manual, or upper working class, low white collar, or lower middle class; high white collar, or upper middle class. As expected, there proved to be a direct relationship between amount of formal education and political tolerance *within* each stratum. However, when we peruse the data, we should not forget that we are concerned primarily with the pertinence of class, not education. Consider the strata distributions *within* educational layers, for example, high-school graduates. We find that 40 percent of the low manual workers, 48 percent of the high manual workers, 47 percent of the low white collar, and 56 percent of the high white collar proved tolerant. Obviously, on this level class accounts for but a fraction of the variance in attitudes, since these differences are both meager and uneven. A 16 percent difference separates the low manual from the high white collar, while the percentage of high manual is greater than the proportion of the low white

Table 1. Relationships Among Occupation, Education, and Political Tolerance in the United States, 1955*

	Working Class		*Middle Class*	
Education	*% Low Manual*	*% High Manual*	*% Low White Collar*	*% High White Collar*
Grade School	13 (228)	21 (178)	23 (47)	26 (100)
Some High School	32 (99)	33 (124)	29 (56)	46 (68)
High School Grad	40 (64)	48 (127)	47 (102)	56 (108)
Some College	– (14)	64 (36)	64 (80)	65 (37)
College Grad	– (3)	– (11)	74 (147)	83 (21)

*Source: Seymour M. Lipset, *Political Man* (Garden City: Doubleday, 1960), p. 109.

collar. But perhaps the lesser educated are unique; surely class should prove significant among the better educated. Looking at the information for this category, the distributions are even more instructive, for class appears to be totally irrelevant–64 percent of the upper blue collar, 65 percent of the lesser white collar, and 65 percent of the high white collar samples are tolerant. The differences are quite minimal. Education proves to be the great equalizer.

Lipset's analysis of Stouffer's materials thereby demonstrated the salience of education and suggested the irrevelance of class. This last outcome proves to be ironic, for in his essay he repeatedly referred to the *combined* pertinence of education and class as helping to shape the authoritarian character of blue-collar workers. Yet, clearly, education operated independently of class in determining the views of workers, while class was without impact. Let us be more precise. Lipset's information strongly suggests that he did not want to demonstrate the independent statistical significance of class when controlling for a status consideration, namely, amount of formal education. Perhaps what he wished to suggest was the high incidence of intolerance among those denied a decent education by institutions directed in the interests of the middle class. Thus, class would have been important, but not in a manner discussed by Lipset. He could have considered the ways in which school boards control formal education and often neglect lower-class claims on matters of quality of education. Indeed, in another paper on education for young people (in Berkeley primary and secondary schools) Lipset has done this very thing, and his analysis is cogent, thoughtful, and convincing.[26] However, when dealing with white workingmen in his essay on working-class authoritarianism, he chose to avoid this course, focusing rather on the alleged peculiarities of experience common to individuals within the working class. The manual workers were simply undemocratic rascals because of unfortunate circumstances, not because they were systematically denied education and other values by institutions dominated by middle-class groups committed to shortchanging working-class youth. On the contrary, Lipset prefers to portray the middle class as the fountain of democracy and to view working-class reluctance to associate with the middle class as a further indication of their authoritarianism.

Presumably, minimal participation in voluntary associations augments structural deprivation and helps heighten working-class authoritarianism. Workingmen shy away from involvements that would make them less authoritarian and more democratic. Blue-collar workers fail to participate in our predominantly middle-class culture. Interestingly, reluctance to take part in such settings and failure to join the cacophony of middle-class club life makes them more bigoted. Indeed, negative consequences flow from the workers' reluctance to take part in the P.T.A., the League of Women Voters, and the Boy Scouts; workmen become inflexible in the realm of ideas. They subsequently rely upon black-and-white thinking and other less than subtle forms of cognitive, valuative, and affective ordering of experience.

Class isolation apparently accentuates this rigidity. According to Lipset, workers become especially authoritarian when they are located in industries that limit contact with the middle class. When workers are so fortunate as to be found in ". . . isolated occupations which require their living in one-industry towns or areas–miners, maritime workers, forestry workers, fishermen, and sheep shearers . . . ," they generally exhibit high rates of Communist support. And as we all know, Communists are authoritarians and therefore so are workmen who support them.[27]

Lipset's argument is fascinating but nonetheless fails to be acceptable, for he assumes what he should have demonstrated–the sequential derivation of one from the other–the way in which authoritarian personality characteristics result from isolated industrial environment and also aid Communist vote and membership. Yet we might view this criticism as picayune, since Lipset's remarks are only meant to be interpretive, not the last word on evidence. As speculation, his views appear to be plausible; perhaps they do add to our understanding of authoritarianism within the blue-collar world.

According to Lipset, not only economic structure but family form seems relevant in accounting for authoritarian characteristics inside the working class. Within the family, a battleground environment produces deep scars. Indeed, there is an immense amount of aggression in the ordinary lives of the lower class parents, sometimes taking the form of frequent use of physical punishment against children. Presumably, this punitive behavior differs fundamentally from the techniques celebrated and practiced by the middle classes who (by implication) prefer to use approaches marked by love, both in giving and withdrawal. The results are evident: middle-class families produce a paucity of authoritarian and a plethora of democratic personalities. In this sense, working-class kids are victimized by their class background. Their early socialization preempts democratic personality development.

Authoritarian tendencies thereby emerge at a tender age and later combine with economic insecurity to produce scapegoating. Personality and economic insecurity combine to frustrate workers and thereby to move them to lampoon minorities. Lipset uses this popular explanation in the following manner:

> A second and no less important factor predisposing the lower classes toward authoritarianism is a relative lack of economic and psychological security. The lower one goes on the socio-economic ladder, the greater economic uncertainty one finds. White-collar workers, even those who are not paid more than skilled manual workers, are less likely to suffer the tensions created by fear of loss of income. Studies of marital instability indicate that this is related to lower income and income insecurity. Such insecurity will of course affect the individual's politics and attitudes. High states of tension require immediate alleviation, and this is frequently found in the venting of hostility against a scapegoat. . . .[28]

The analysis seems plausible if not convincing, for many of us are fond of the explanation that connects insecurity with the tendency to scapegoat.[29] However, affection and validity are not equivalents. We must demonstrate the utility of the theory we find attractive. If the scapegoat theory is correct, one should be able to distinguish between workers who are *structurally* insecure and those who are not. One could then predict accordingly to *psychological* insecurity and correlated authoritarian personality characteristics. But nowhere does Lipset trace this causal connection. For example, he could have differentiated between (1) workmen found in relatively isolated enclaves marked by economic insecurity and (2) working-class populations located in circumstances characterized by maximal contact with the middle classes and minimal economic insecurity.[30] Had he made this distinction between polar types of subcommunities *within* the working class, he could then have predicted to a lopsided and heavy distribution of hostile sentiment among psychologically insecure workers within structurally unstable contexts. Other predictions would have followed. Presumably, the psychologically insecure and hence hostile workers should be disproportionately authoritarian, and furthermore, they should scapegoat as expected. Such scapegoating in turn should be associated with extremist politics of left and right.

In short, the end of the sequence has its complex derivation; but maybe we expect too much when we demand of the social scientist that he specify links and trace connections serially. Perhaps such an effort would be more in keeping with the field experiment, a context where the social scientist could contrive conditions and controls as well as trace cause and effect relations. If so, this criticism might be thought of as hair-splitting, for obviously Lipset's remarks are only interpretive and not conclusive.

Whatever the merits or weaknesses of Lipset's presentation on working-class authoritarianism, we would be unwise to ignore a large body of knowledge that lends credence to his views on authoritarian attitudes within the working class. As already mentioned, two eminent scholars, Louis Wirth and Gunnar Myrdal, have observed different classes among whites and commented on the relatively *low* levels of prejudice among the *upper* classes and the opposite tendency within the lower strata.[31] Simpson and Yinger have aptly paraphrased Myrdal on this matter by noting one of the consequences of high prejudice levels among white workmen—black and white workers fail to cohere within a united labor movement:

> When the feedbox is empty, says a Swedish proverb, the horses will bite each other. Lower classes are not naturally radical, or even liberal; they do not readily take a favorable attitude toward disadvantaged groups.[32]

Black and white wage workers, then, will not get along when both face near-subsistence. In fact, they may struggle against one another, while only the beneficent middle class can aid those shortchanged by subculture and unsettled by economic insecurity. This would seem to be Myrdal's message,[33] and it would appear to be in accord with Lipset's analysis.

We would be *wrong* to consider the views of Wirth, Myrdal, and Lipset as speculative pronouncements without supportive evidence, for we can once again draw upon the material cited by Simpson and Yinger to partially substantiate Lipset's views in particular. Survey research evidence repeatedly indicates that the lesser skilled, poorly educated, low-income categories seldom support civil liberties, at least verbally, when quizzed by survey interviewers. Perhaps more important, working-class people who express qualms about supporting the civil liberties of political minorities also seem to reveal authoritarian personalities and intolerant opinions *more* often than the middle class. For example, MacKinnon and Centers demonstrated that the *higher*-income groups were *underrepresented* among political authoritarians, and that the two lower ones scored just the opposite.[34] Cohen and Hodges conducted interviews among 2600 male heads of households in three northern California counties and found intolerance to be highest in the lowest stratum.[35] These attitudinal materials, then, would be consistent with Stouffer's findings and Lipset's views.

If we set aside our criticisms and follow the leads suggested by Lipset's theory and supportive information on working-class authoritarianism, we can specify the implications of his theory for an analysis of white residents in an American community: (1) A disproportionately large number of blue-collar workers should reject legislation that would allow blacks to live wherever they wish; (2) the lesser educated and the lower incomed should share the same behavioral pattern. If asked to vote on an issue such as fair housing, the supporters of the racial *status-quo* should find overwhelming numerical support inside the blue-collar world, among the lesser educated, and within the low-income categories. From the point of view of sophisticated conservatism, racism should draw its voting support from the white slag heap of the modern community.

We have already mentioned several criticisms of Lipset's theory, and perhaps we could say considerably more, but this is no place to comment in detail on some of the contributions and difficulties associated with his analysis.[36] Nonetheless, we might limit ourselves to an examination of three matters: (1) the distinction between attitude and act; (2) discrimination among the nonprejudiced; (3) action for integration among the prejudiced.

First, it is clear that when we attempt to relate class to acceptance of minorities, we should distinguish between *prejudiced attitudes* and *discriminatory acts.* Unfortunately, few writers, Lipset among them, make this distinction in their analyses and criticisms of various groups. Many social scientists generalize as if attitude can be equated with act, assuming that if a person is prejudiced he will discriminate; if he is nonprejudiced, he will integrate. However (as we shall see in Chapter 8) this neat equation is open to question. Second, because Lipset and others fail to make this distinction, they overlook the fact that many middle-class people may themselves fail to express prejudice but guide institutions to discriminate. Third, while working-class individuals may hold prejudiced opinions, they often have the kinds of associations that move them to help minorities.

Let us retain the distinction between thought and action and examine the second point above. Simpson and Yinger have commented on prejudice and discrimination within both the middle and the working classes. They rejected the understandable but faulty assumption that nonracist attitudes correlate directly with nondiscriminatory behavior. They have observed how nonprejudiced captains may steer race-biased ships:

> It is one thing to note that lower class whites get a higher prejudice score on verbal tests. It is another to discover what class of whites is most discriminatory. Middle and upper class people may have more skillful rationalizations and verbal disguises. They may recite the American creed

more spontaneously. They may have a great need to seem reasonable and tolerant. Hence their prejudice score may be low. These tendencies, however, could be accompanied by vigorous discrimination against minority group members–low wages paid to them, high rents charged for slum dwellings, exclusion from business and professional organizations, refusal to rent or sell property to them, ambitious programs to prevent them from voting.[37]

Although Lipset overlooks this point, he does note those situations in which *working-class people* have followed an underdog tradition and have acted for the rights of political minorities. Lipset has indicated how workers may struggle for civil liberties and defeat the efforts of middle-class citizens who on occasion may try to throttle the democratic process. He has pointed out how Australian workers supported their labor party when it led a successful fight against a middle-class political organization on a very important civil liberties issue: the attempt to outlaw the Communist party. Here he would agree with Miller and Riessman that in Australia, as elsewhere, the working class has often translated certain traditions–their equalitarian, antielitist, and cooperative values[38]–into democratic behavior. These commitments to democratic ideas plus worker sympathy for the underdog contrast noticeably with conformist orientations and authoritarian behavior common to large sections of the middle class. Its snobbism, intellectualism, status concern, fear of authority, competitiveness, conventionalism, plus its votes to outlaw the left made the Australian middle class anything but entirely democratic. In fact, these widespread characteristics play into the hands of authoritarian and totalitarian political movements committed to the manipulation of middle-class groups having these traits. Lasswell, Frankel-Brunswick, *and* Lipset have observed how the German Nazi movement successfully took advantage of these vulnerabilities.[39]

The middle class may act in ways to suggest they are in fact sometimes more authoritarian than manual workers. Lipset has made this very point in his essay, "Fascism–Left, Right and Center," in which he discusses center fascism as a middle-class phenomenon, much as left fascism draws from the working class, and right fascism finds widespread support within the landed aristocracy. Many significant points emerge in this fascinating paper, but the key one would seem to be that every class lacks insulation against the virus of antidemocratic sentiments. Those who burn books, destroy liberties, and silence criticism can be found at all class levels. Political totalitarians can be found within the middle class, especially when the economy collapses. In fact, the disintegration of economy is often associated with fascist movements, such as the German economic and political debacles of the 1920's and 1930's. Not too surprisingly, as Lipset himself has demonstrated, large sections of the middle class deserted the political center and joined the Nazi movement.[40]

CONCLUSIONS

Lipset's essay on fascism suggests that the working (and middle) classes can vary dramatically on matters of people's rights. He, and the authors of this book, see the way working people think and act on racial and other civil liberty issues depending to a large degree on where they stand with respect to political party allegiances. This crucial contingency largely escaped Lipset in his treatise on working class authoritarianism, a controversial but provocative essay in some ways inconsistent with his analysis of Peronista, Nazi, and Horthyite fascisms, which recognizes that under certain conditions both the working, middle, and upper classes can support some form of fascism.

Although critical of Lipset, we must recognize the importance of his insistence that we test our ideas through the use of empirical materials. In an age of sociological pop-essays, Lipset's writings, especially his earlier ones,[41] remind us of the necessity to wed idea to reality through evidence. This we have attempted to do as can be seen in the subsequent chapters of this book.

NOTES

1. When we make a distinction between personal and impersonal relations, we are obviously dependent upon the writings of such sociologists as Toennies, Cooley, and Mead. For a glimpse at their ideas on the importance of affectional ties, see Ferdinand Toennies, *Community and Society* (New York: Harper Torchbook, 2964), pp. 1-11; Robert H. Cooley, *Social Organization and Human Nature and the Social Order* (Glencoe: The Free Press, 1956), pp. 3-57; George Herbert Mead, *Mind, Self and Society* (Chicago: The University of Chicago Press, 1934), pp. 152-64.
2. Perhaps Shils and Janowitz have done one of the best jobs of alerting social scientists to the consequences of affectional ties within small and large groups. See Edward A. Shils and Morris Janowitz, "Cohesion and Disintegration in the Wehrmacht in World War II," *The Public Opinion Quarterly* 12 (Summer, 1948), pp. 280-315. Also see Herbert Gans, *The Urban-Villagers* (New York: The Free Press, 1962).
3. The Old Chicago School led in research on this matter of spatial propinquity and mate selection. For a particularly pertinent reference, see Ernest W. Burgess and Harvey J. Locke, *The Family* (New York: American Book Company, 1950), pp. 415-22. Most relevant would be those observations (pp. 415-416) that suggest but by no means demonstrate, that propinquity promotes miscegenation.

   > . . . The theory of propinquity assumes that persons marry in proportions greater than chance those who live near them, those they play with, those with whom they go to school, and those with whom they work. Stated in this way the theory merely affirms what is obvious, that marriage takes place between those who have an opportunity to meet each other. Therefore propinquity is

only a circumscribing factor in the choice of mates; it is not, or only in rare exceptions, a specific factor determining the individual person with whom one will fall in love. Propinquity is a specific factor in mate selection only in the situation of isolation, as where a man and a woman are shipwrecked upon a desert island, or two Americans meet in an alien culture, or two timid souls are thrown together by circumstances. . . .

The chief findings of three research studies indicate that there is a positive association between residential propinquity and marriage selection. In a study of 5,000 consecutive licenses of Philadelphia residents, Bossard discovered that over one half of the couples (51.9 percent) lived within twenty blocks of each other and one eighth (12.6 percent) resided at the same address. In a study made in 1931 in New Haven, Connecticut, Davie and Reeves, using methods similar to those of Bossard, found only 6.4 percent living at the same address before marriage, but that practically the same proportion as Philadelphia (51.3 percent) resided within twenty blocks of each other. In a later study of residential propinquity in New Haven in 1940, Kennedy discovered a slight increase in marriages of persons living at the same address, and a considerable increase of those living within twenty blocks of each other (18.5 percent), considering only those cases where both parties lived in New Haven. She concludes "that in the vast majority of cases marriage is an in-group affair; that is, the two contracting parties tend to be of the same race, nationality, religion, and socio-economic status." The relation between residential propinquity and mate selection may be a function of spatial segregation of the population according to cultural characteristics.

4. G. William Domhoff, *Who Rules America?* (Englewood Cliffs: Prentice-Hall, 1967), pp. 138-56.
5. John C. Leggett, *Class, Race and Labor* (New York: Oxford University Press, 1968), especially pp. 8-42.
6. A proletarian ethnic group would be an ethnic collectivity largely working class in composition. As such it would have relatively little prestige but perhaps a great deal of power, depending upon its level of consciousness and organization.
7. Seymour M. Lipset, *Political Man* (Garden City: Doubleday, 1960), pp. 97-130.
8. Karl Mannheim, "Conservative Thought," *Essays on the Sociology of Knowledge* (London: Routledge and Paul, 1959), pp. 74-164.
9. *Prejudice* here refers to an attitude based on information limited in scope yet used in judgment.
10. However, when an outside ethnic person has similar ethnic prestige, the person may enter the subcommunity, provided the intruder is willing to assimilate partially its subcultural ethos. At least this would seem to be the case.
11. *Fraternal action* means acting to accept another as an equal.
12. The local political group is obviously not coterminous with the larger political organization. Not only are its boundaries different, but its programs and policies are generally dissimilar.
13. We do not want to imply that all university intellectuals are on the left.

Indeed, there are divisions, and they become most apparent during moments of university crisis. If anything, the left is a small minority, especially among faculty.

14. *Left-progressive subculture* refers to the values of liberty, equality, and fraternity that we associate with radical and center political parties plus related social movements and voluntary associations. This subculture spells out a consensus from the center to the far left on (1) the desirability of restricting state and corporate power over private lives; (2) the necessity of closing the wealth gap in every country; (3) the importance of treating people as equals irrespective of their class and racial backgrounds.
15. Seymour Martin Lipset, "American Intellectuals: Their Politics and Status," *Political Man, op. cit.*, pp. 313-36.
16. Seymour Martin Lipset and Hans L. Zetterberg have compiled an immense amount of information on the relationship between a person's previous class background and his present political choice. Their evidence clearly indicates that when middle-class people come from the working class, a disproportionately large number of them will vote for liberal or left-wing parties that have led in the struggle for racial and other forms of equality. See their "Social Mobility in Industrial Societies," in Seymour Martin Lipset and Reinhard Bendix, *Social Mobility in Industrial Society* (Berkeley: University of California Press, 1959), especially pp. 64-72.
17. For a discussion of this matter, see Lipset's "American Intellectuals: Their Politics and Status," in *Political Man*, pp. 319-22.
18. One should not forget the ecological distribution of classes and ethnic groups when discussing racial integration. Too often we view residential integration as an interindividual affair when, in fact, what occurs is a struggle among (1) white groups largely of ethnic origin and generally committed to the preservation of residential turf, and (2) blacks generally from upper working- and middle-class backgrounds and understandably concerned with using their legal and moral rights to break out of the black ghetto.
19. Here, as elsewhere, the law proves to be largely irrelevant. Clever lawyers can evade court bans on restrictive covenants, and when the lawyers fail, a middle-class mob often takes over to harass and in some cases to victimize the black interloper.
20. W.E.B. Dubois would have dissented from Myrdal's views. Dubois indicated how white and black manual workers united—if only for a short time after the Civil War—within the incipient populist movement in order to solve the Southern land question and ancillary problems. See his *Black Reconstruction in America* (New York: Russell and Russell, 1962), especially p. 353.
21. Seymour Martin Lipset, "Working-Class Authoritarianism," in *Political Man, op. cit.*, pp. 101-2.
22. Obviously one cannot assume that attitudes are automatically reflected in behavior, if only because group demands often force people to accept

group command and to set aside personal views. In this regard, I am indebted to Durkheim's observations on the coercive power of group norms:

> So, then, we see here different ways of behaving, thinking and feeling, all of which share this remarkable characteristic of existing independently of the individual mind. These types of behavior or thought not only exist outside of the individual, but they are endowed with an imperious and persuasive power by which they impress themselves on him, whether or not he wills it.

This quotation is taken from a section of Emile Durkheim's *The Rules of the Sociological Method,* quoted in H. Laurence Ross, *Perspectives on the Social Order* (New York: McGraw-Hill, 1963), p. 14.

23. Lipset, *Political Man, op. cit.,* pp. 126-30.
24. Stouffer's study was an important one, but it failed to use a valid technique to compare the views of community leaders and ordinary citizens. Stouffer selected leaders from one universe and ordinary citizens from another. He then generalized as if the two samples belonged to the same universe. More precisely, he drew his sample of community leaders from American cities ranging in size from 10 thousand to 150 thousand, but he selected his cross-section of ordinary citizens from the *entire* population of the United States. His data thereby proved to be both noncomparable and also incomplete since it failed to include community leaders from cities both small and large. For a discussion of this limited sample design and selection, see Samuel Stouffer, *Communism, Conformity and Civil Liberties* (Garden City: Doubleday, 1955), pp. 15-19.
25. Lipset, *Political Man, op. cit.,* p. 109. According to Lipset, this table was computed from IBM cards used by Samuel A. Stouffer in his study, *Communism, Conformity and Civil Liberties, op. cit.*
26. Seymour Martin Lipset, "De Facto Segregation in Berkeley and the Common School Tradition" (mimeographed).
27. See Lipset, *Political Man, op. cit.,* p. 231.
28. *Ibid.,* p. 113.
29. The scapegoat theory became quite popular at the time when many American social scientists were becoming interested in the application of social psychology and empirical methods to the study of race relations. Consequently, for many teachers and students the scapegoat theory was a first social psychological love, the sweetness of which we associate with other first confections such as Veblen's essays on higher education.
30. Seymour Martin Lipset, "Elections: Expression of Democratic Class Struggle," *Political Man, op. cit.,* p. 231.
31. For a discussion of the similarity of their views, see George E. Simpson and J. Milton Yinger, *Racial and Cultural Minorities* (New York: Harper and Row, 1965), p. 103.
32. *Ibid.,* p. 103.
33. My views should not be interpreted to mean that Myrdal has accepted Lipset's attitude on working-class authoritarianism. It would seem, however, that their opinions on class and race are compatible.

34. Simpson and Yinger have summarized their findings in *Racial and Cultural Minorities, op. cit.,* p. 104.
35. *Ibid.,* p. 104.
36. For a sizzling critique of Lipset's analysis of working-class authoritarianism, refer to S.M. Miller's and Frank Riessman's "'Working-Class . . . Authoritarianism': A Critique of Lipset," *The British Journal of Sociology,* 12 (September 1961), pp. 263-77. See also Seymour Martin Lipset, "'Working-Class Authoritarianism': A Reply to Miller and Reissman," in the same issue of *The British Journal of Sociology,* pp. 277-81.
37. Simpson and Yinger, *op cit.,* p. 105.
38. Miller and Reissman have discussed the pertinence of these values in making working-class people more likely to support civil liberties. Lipset would agree that under certain conditions workers do support democracy. However, he is vague on this matter. See Lipset, "'Working-Class Authoritarianism': A Reply to Miller and Riessman," *op. cit.,* p. 278.
39. Harold D. Lasswell, "The Psychology of Hitlerism as a Response of the Lower Middle Classes to Continuing Insecurity," found in Guy E. Swanson, Theodore M. Newcomb, and Eugene L. Hartley, *Readings in Social Psychology* (New York: Henry Holt and Company, 1952), pp. 160-7.
40. Seymour M. Lipset, *Political Man, op. cit.,* pp. 140-49.
41. For a criticism of the increased conservatism in Lipset's writings, see Sidney M. Peck, "Ideology and Political Sociology," *American Catholic Sociological Review,* Vol. 23, Summer, 1962, pp. 128-55.

THREE

The Community and the Sample

Berkeley contains many races, two classes, and plenty of racial antagonisms. On occasion classes use the vote to express themselves on a race issue. Yet seldom have they or other Americans cast their ballots in a fight as significant as the Berkeley Fair Housing election. This conflict had implications for subsequent events in the largest and most swinging state in The Union. For example, the election had a bearing on the occurrence of the Watts Insurrection,[1] for it proved to be a forerunner of how many California whites would repeatedly act to stop blacks at the ballot box when black Americans sought redress for their grievances through parliamentary means. Yet more was involved than the consequences for democracy; what occurred was a fight within the white community which allowed us to examine the effects of class position on racial intimacy.

On Tuesday, April 1, 1963, the citizens of Berkeley, California, participated in a general election. At stake was the office of Mayor (for which three persons contended), Auditor (for which two persons sought the office), School Director (one person ran unopposed), and Councilman (for which ten people contended for four positions).

More important, the ballot contained a referendum measure on race and housing. The ordinance would have prohibited discrimination because of race, color, religion, or national origin when persons engaged in the sale, rental, lease, or other transfer of housing accommodations. In addition, the ordinance would have created a board of inter-group relations, in turn encharged with the investigation, conciliation, and public hearing of complaints on housing discrimination. Unlike most fair housing ordinances, it would have meted out stiff penalties for the violation of these provisions.[2]

The ordinance lost. It failed to carry a majority. Nonetheless, the race was close, for had 1500 of the 43,000 voters cast their ballots in favor rather than against its passage, the result would have been victory rather than defeat for those who favored "fair housing."[3]

The vote was the final product of a campaign marked by considerable controversy. Perhaps it was the hottest fight in California since Upton Sinclair's campaign to end poverty in California—a battle royal conducted during the Great Depression.[4]

The electoral struggle affected almost everyone. Its reporting reached into Bay Area homes, demanded the attention of State pressure groups, elicited comments by federal officials, and alerted foreign news correspondents to the consequences of strife over accepting Negroes as neighbors. Everybody got into the act, including the Democratic Governor of the State. Governor Brown supported the proponents of fair housing, but his backing did not go unchallenged. Powerful groups poured funds into the community. For example, right-wing real estate associations sent money and personnel into Berkeley in order to carry on the fight. One state-wide realty group obtained the backing of most California realtors, perfected an organization exclusively concerned with housing integration proposals, and directed it about the State to kill fair housing ordinances. The group rolled into Berkeley and used its resources to help defeat the housing legislation. This conservative association conducted a spirited campaign, for it viewed the outcome as vitally related to fair housing fights scheduled to be conducted throughout the State of California and elsewhere.[5]

Since the defeat of the Berkeley proposal, we have learned the soundness of the conservative's assumptions. The prophecy was at least partially true. The Berkeley loss had a direct bearing on a subsequent state referendum designed by right-wingers to prohibit legislation which would have outlawed housing segregation. The conservatives also won that fight, and they used many techniques previously tested and found useful in the Berkeley struggle. The Berkeley and California losses had implications for the U.S. as well, for the defeats undoubtedly reinforced a long tradition of racist behavior in many towns found not only in the South but in the North and West. Most important, the elections revealed what many had long suspected; large sections of the working and middle classes had voted against an ordinance that would have created a modicum of housing integration in middle class neighborhoods and thereby generated problems for conservative respectables committed to screening themselves and their children from racial intimacy.

BERKELEY HOUSING AND ETHNIC ENCLAVES

Berkeley "was"[6] a middle-sized city found within a metropolitan area, a very lively one at that. It was a suburb of San Francisco, but the town was more than a "bedroom community." Berkeley was a city within a city, a town whose history long preceded the extensive suburbanization of San Francisco. And like many communities transformed into suburbs long after their inception, the town contained a black minority divided into two groups: the old-timers and the new-comers. During the early 1960s, the old-timers were quiet and respectable. From the point of view of the white business community, the old-timers had emigrated to Berkeley during World War I and the 1920s, had subsequently found niches in the service sector of the economy, and consequently had indicated respect for the *status quo.*

By contrast, the new-comers were judged to be bawdy, brash, and aggressive. Many engaged in crime. Others refused to accept their places in the racial hierarchy and occupational structure. Worse yet, from the point of view of the establishment, the new arrivals outnumbered the old residents and acquired a sophistication and militance quite unlike the opinions associated with the old timers. They were coming of age and developing voting power to make themselves heard on the very problems which had enveloped and degraded blacks. Unfortunately, city officials too frequently responded to black demands with the gusto we associate with the ineffective blunderbuss. We could observe this quality of concern and level of response even though Berkeley black housing and other conditions were relatively worse at the time of the election than they were before the exodus of thousands of blacks out of the rural South and into Berkeley. In this sense, Berkeley was not unique.

When we consider the Northern and Western urbanization of the black city resident, we are struck by the steady increase in the extent and severity of housing discrimination. At one time most of these black subcommunities were small. However, all considerably expanded during and after World War II. They thereby disrupted neighborhoods that were relatively integrated for decades.

Prior to the mass exodus from the South, many Western and Northern blacks lived in or near neighborhoods largely ethnic and traditional in character. They often mixed as acquaintances, if not as intimates, with Poles, Italians, Greeks, and the like, although admittedly most blacks were confined to an all black ghetto.

However, the mass exodus plus housing discrimination eliminated even this modicum of integration when the black populations doubled, tripled, and quadrupled during and after the Second World War. Whites moved out before an advancing black wave. Often they emigrated to subdivisions and suburbs where they erected racial barriers perhaps as visible as the Berlin wall.

For all its cosmopolitan veneer, the San Francisco Bay Area does not deviate from this pattern. Before the war, the black community was miniscule. Perhaps it constituted less than one or two percent of the total population. During the war, maritime, shipping, railroad, shipbuilding, and other industries brought tens of thousands of blacks into the Bay Area. The flow continued after the Second World War and created black demands for housing. However, few authorities did anything to create decent housing for blacks. Builders reserved almost all of the new tracts for whites. Blacks had to settle for homes largely second-rate by white standards. And so forth. Why?

Because we live in a multi-causal universe, we would find it difficult to point to all the causes of racial discrimination on housing. However, we can sort out some of the more visible considerations. We have discussed the values of working-class whites and how their views might clash with uprooted blacks on such questions as housing maintenance, drinking, child rearing, and the like. However, there are other considerations as well. We must take into account real estate boards and real estate brokers. They have used professional pressure and political groups to get their way on matters of where blacks can live. Through the use of large bankrolls and pliant political parties, they have successfully sought to impose their own beliefs on others whenever people have raised the question of race and housing.

Of course, many groups have fought real estate interests on this matter, but they have generally failed, and their lack of success has had an impact on what blacks can become. Jim Crow housing has a strong tendency to produce segregation in education, recreation, religion, and other aspects of their daily lives. Most important, segregation is largely responsible for the ghettoization of urban public schools. The net result is a second-rate education and the consequent limitation of job opportunities even when fair employment laws create them. With discrimination dominating the whole housing market, nonwhites have chosen areas most in need of repair, clearance, and rehabilitation. In these crowded conditions, they have become the chief contributors to crime and delinquency, fire and arson, and other problems so visible to the black person and the white. Consequently, many black Americans have acted in ways which have confirmed the stereotypes of both blacks and whites.

In those few cases where the integrationists have won, we find that the laws often fail to cover certain kinds of housing. More precisely, the laws specifically exempt particular types of housing from the enforcement and provisional sections of the laws. Incredibly enough, many laws specifically allow racial discrimination for some types of housing but forbid it in others. To a member of another planet, this differential treatment of home owners must appear to be incongruous if not ludicrous. If Jim Crow housing is unjust, people should eliminate it, and if laws allow home owners or private clubs to continue to discriminate, what is the justification? Often times there is no rationale other than the notion that individuals can discriminate but corporations can't, thus appealing to public prejudice against bigness while playing up the presumed rights of the individual.

However, even if one were able to successfully rationalize these inconsistencies to a being from the planet Mars, one would still have difficulties when trying to explain what happens in those areas where the law applies. When discriminatory acts occur within a type of housing covered by the law, the average person does not, or cannot, prove such violation. Often he is unaware of the existence of municipal laws, since middle class whites and blacks fail to publicize them in ways which indicate that they exist. However, even if the person is conscious of these laws, he has reason to distrust the law because of its enforcers, many of whom are judged as bigots. Of course, there are many black people who are not skeptical even when they have little reason to expect the enforcement of the law. However, even if such people know and trust the law, as well as its enforcers, they frequently fail to seek justice, because bureaucratic barriers make the application of the law difficult. Too often the plaintiff must acquire expensive legal help and overcome the tangle of complex law, bureaucratic impersonality, and respectable bigotry. This is quite a job, and it costs time and money. The average minority person can anticipate these problems, and he often prefers to live with bigotry than to carry on the expensive fight. Nonetheless, minority group members will on occasion overcome all of these obstacles and obtain legal counsel to guide them through the channels established by the state for personal redress of grievances. Unfortunately, too often when a person makes a complaint, the official city or state agency dismisses it as without foundation. However, in those cases where the plaintiff wins the state finds the defendant guilty of a misdemeanor, while the penalties prove to be relatively insignificant. The net effect is the maintenance of a pattern of housing discrimination.[7]

Hypocritically, when moderate men favor the adoption of housing proposals as laws, these advocates often anticipate such processes. Consequently, they stress the lack of friction which would be commonplace should such proposals become law. These moderate men will sometimes go so far as to justify the passage of such laws by saying that concerned but prudent men can be highly moral yet responsible since race laws can be both effective and mild. From this point of view, the bill's supporters are moral because by participating in the act of law passage, they are doing the right thing; they are chipping at bigotry and promoting progress. From their point of view, this action is better than doing nothing or going to the other extreme. In this regard, moderate men are especially concerned about the consequences of going too fast. They argue: if one pushes too hard against the opponents of integration, their opposition will stiffen and their efforts to halt integration will become successful. However, when moderates fear the actions of radicals, their sentiments are generally unnecessary because almost all American communities fail to contain enough radicals who are in a position to demand and get the use of force to translate laws on segregation into practices of integration. In most communities, there are not enough tough heads to demand enforcement of the penalty provisions of the law, or if there is a sufficient number of radicals present in the community, they cannot bend formal political structures such as the Democratic Party. Without such power, their demands function as safety valves, not political movers.

However, Berkeley might well have been an exception. Its ordinance did contain teeth, provisions which went so far as to promise jail sentences to the recalcitrants. Berkeley also included a radical minority,[8] one quite sizeable by American standards. This minority did not lie outside the Democratic Party. On the contrary, dozens of them held positions within it, and hence they were in situations where they could use both the jaws and the teeth of the ordinance to enforce the law. Berkeley might well have become a deviant case.

Many conservatives anticipated what could happen should the ordinance become law. Had the liberal-left-black coalition won, there was great likelihood of blue-collar blacks breaking out of their ghetto and leap-frogging into working-class districts immediately surrounding the ghetto. Perhaps more relevant, there was little doubt that a sizeable number of *middle*-class blacks would have sought residence in the Berkeley Hills. Berkeley might well have become a classic laboratory on what happens when races meet in a multiplicity of variegated neighborhoods within the same community.

THE SETTING AND THE SAMPLE

Yet the majority of voters prevented the experiment. In order to understand the ordinance vote, we found it useful to take into account the nature of the town, for its class and racial structures provided a testing ground for our ideas on class and intimacy.

The most important thing about Berkeley is its education center. The city contains the seat of one of the largest universities in the world, the Berkeley campus of the University of California.[9] This institution has provided the community with an annual payroll of over seventy million dollars. The payroll has made it the hub of the community's economy. Largely because of the University's pecuniary resources, Berkeley has become a community of intellect. University officials, deans, and department heads, have sought and purchased talent from all over the world. Consequently, it has taken the lead in many fields of intellectual endeavor. The University's personnel have found their way into many community activities as well.

Berkeley, then, has employed the talents of many bright people. Added to this pyramid of intelligence is the cosmopolitanism imparted by the foreign students and campus fringe. Several thousand non-citizens were enrolled, but they were not the only important ingredients in the Berkeley meringue. In addition, Berkeley has attracted thousands of free-lance writers, part-time poets, dissolute painters, hungry photographers, plus numerous others who together have traditionally constituted part of the progressive-left community and recurrently participated in university affairs. They contributed not only their intellectual talents but their political ideas and ribald sexuality as well.

However, one should not attempt to ascribe this cosmopolitanism to the entire Berkeley community, for despite the pre-eminence of the university and its surrounding subcommunity, many townspeople look with wary eye at the house of intellect and its periphery. One could observe the consequences of this suspicion as well. Like all university or college communities, there is the traditional split between town and gown, main street businessmen and university personnel.

Indeed, commercial interests had wholly dominated the political life of the town from the First World War until 1961, just two years before the critical election. At that time, the liberal Democrats edged into a majority on the town's city council. The revolution did not follow, but business interests did confront a potential if not actual check on their activities.

The conservatives derived their power from a number of sources, but most important was the non-university, white population. There were some 35,000 homes in Berkeley, and non-university people were a large majority. Many would have been at home in most suburban communities. Decidedly Northwest European by descent, middle class by fortune, and respectable through group coercion if not personal inclination, they included many elderly and retired citizens.

Adjacent to this gray and chubby phalanx was Berkeley's industry, with its captains, managers, and staff personnel. This population was hidden but significant. When we think of Berkeley, we seldom consider its sizeable industrial base, but we would be unwise to overlook it, if only because of the way in which such wealth has buttressed conservative political interests.

Prior to World War II, Berkeley was a light industrial center. Three hundred companies were located in the city's flatlands. These industries produced a payroll of over forty-four million dollars each year. Those at the helm of this complex found a dozen ways to influence city councils, city planning commissions, anti-poverty agencies, boards of education, and the like. But most important was the way in which these businessmen periodically garnered the voting support and the opinion agreements of the respectables. The coalition appeared to be enough to run the town.

However, a racial shift began during the Second World War, and it has continued to change the demographic character of the community and thereby to erode the political power of the conservatives. Berkeley has undergone a number of racial and population changes since the beginning of the Second Holocaust, although it was not until the compilation of the 1960 census that the pattern proved to be clear. Its figures bothered many people, especially the respectables. Why? Although the Bay Area had grown enormously during the first decade after the war, the Berkeley population declined slightly from 113,805 to 111,363. But more important, the non-white population had grown substantially. It had almost doubled, moving from a little over fifteen percent to twenty-six percent. By 1960, Negroes had come to constitute eighty percent of this non-white population, having chalked up a sixty-four percent gain during the decade. The growth portended a dramatic shift in Berkeley politics.

These changes made many wheel-horses inside the Democratic Party very happy, if only because the overwhelming majority of blacks turned out to be Democrats. These party bosses were made joyous by another event. Blacks replaced many white people of Republican persuasion, most of whom had left for other communities or heavenly pastures.

Negroes did not settle randomly throughout the community, but rather found their way into an area surrounded by a belt of other racial minorities plus working-class whites, many of whom belonged to nationality groups with ethnic stakes in the residential area threatened by Negro invasion. Indeed, the significance of Berkeley's changing population lay not in the mere increase in numbers and proportions but rather in how they carved out black zones surrounded by retreating Asiatics and working-class whites. The net result was the development of three types of residential areas along the racial border: a solid block of black precincts in the South Berkeley area; a mixed but stable area in the western section of the community, and a large, racially mixed and changing zone in South Central Berkeley. Of the three, the last zone proved to be quite significant politically, for it stood as a retreating buffer zone separating all-black from non-black areas. These central Berkeley districts contained a large number of Japanese and Chinese (as well as Filipinos and Indians). In these neighborhoods, they often outnumbered blacks. The ratio of Asians to blacks was as high as twenty to one (while the ratio of whites to blacks was sometimes as great). Obviously, then, these working-class districts by no means excluded whites.

The middle-class whites were heavily concentrated in the northeastern and southeastern corners of the city. Both areas contained few if any blacks; all of the census tracts had less than one percent Negro plus the occasional Oriental. But even this 1960 figure failed to indicate what was happening. Ironically, the Berkeley Hills included the only areas where the black population had actually declined between 1950 and 1960. This black dip accompanied increased liberal protest on matters of race, thereby suggesting an inverse relationship between one and the other. As liberals became more vocal on matters of housing integration, the number of blacks living in liberal neighborhoods decreased. However, one should not be too critical of the liberals in this regard, for they did not hold economic power in the community, and hence were not in a position to translate voiced attitude into real estate practice. By contrast, no such discrepancy between liberal views and racial segregation occurred in Southeast Berkeley, its Claremont district. The area was rock-ribbed Republican and racist by practice if not preference. There one found many business executives, bankers, and the like who worked in San Francisco and who viewed their clusters of Berkeley domiciles as white turfs to be used as resting places for themselves and their children; they had created white dromedary oases located across the Bay and up from the feared flats.

Berkeley, then, was highly stratified. Class-racial strips demarked one area from another, and in this sense Berkeley was no different from all major and minor American cities. If one were to take a trip in Berkeley from the Bay to the top of the Hills—from the chemical plants to the treed summits—the jaunt would have revealed to anyone the strip stratification pattern. The lower classes—as indicated by the disposition of rents and races—drew heavily from minorities, especially blacks, and lived in the Flats (see Figure 1). The middle classes were found overwhelmingly in The Foothills and The Hills. Indeed, as one moved from Central Berkeley to the top of The Hills located in Berkeley's eastern residential districts, the proportion of white middle-class people grew and the percentage of workmen and minorities declined.

THE PEOPLE WE STUDIED

We sampled the Berkeley population so as to include black and white workmen, but we selected white collar residents as well. How did we draw the sample?

As we mentioned, the Berkeley Fair Housing election took place during the spring of 1963. Soon thereafter, a group of young social scientists put together a research team committed to studying the Berkeley voters. By the fall of that year, we had obtained financial support from the Institute of Social Science of the University of California. We were then in a position to start the next phase of the operation.

We began interviewing at that time. By the summer of 1964, we had collected information from 1,008 Berkeley residents. We used a list random sample to select people from fifteen precincts which were chosen on the basis of their racial and class characteristics. We selected several precincts from the ghetto, four from mixed areas, and nine from nearly all-white neighborhoods. Most of the white precincts were overwhelmingly white collar. These areas differed considerably from one another in one important way. Some precincts included large minorities of university people, while the others drew

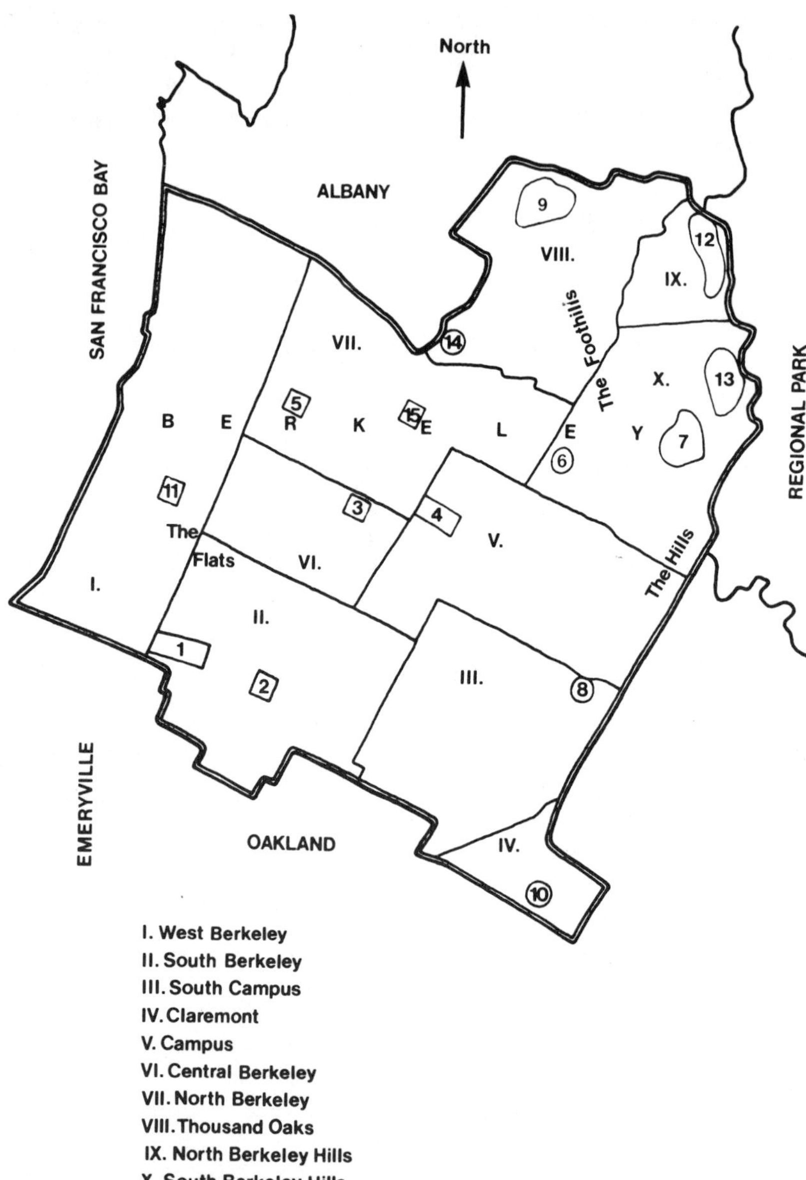

I. West Berkeley
II. South Berkeley
III. South Campus
IV. Claremont
V. Campus
VI. Central Berkeley
VII. North Berkeley
VIII. Thousand Oaks
IX. North Berkeley Hills
X. South Berkeley Hills

Figure 1. Berkeley Precincts Selected by Residential District (Fair Housing Election, 1963)

Precincts in Arabic Numerals, Districts in Roman Figures

most of their members from the non-academic population.

We tried, then, to include a cross-section of the Berkeley population. Yet we were not entirely successful in doing so. Although the sample was completely random within each one of the seven districts, we cannot consider it entirely representative of the Berkeley population, since the precincts themselves were not chosen on a random basis but rather, as we shall see, with other criteria in mind.

Consequently, when we make general remarks about Berkeley, you must keep in mind the limitations of this statement. Our materials only suggest the actual characteristics of the racial, class, and other groups to be discussed.

We can best summarize the sample design by treating it in the following order: (1) the reason for a stratified sample, (2) the place of the research, (3) the time of the study, (4) the selection of the sample, (5) the characteristics of the potential and actual respondents, and (6) the quality of the interviews.

Why Stratify?

As we have already mentioned, it was decided to distinguish between neighborhoods on the basis of race, class, and university ties before selecting representative precincts and interviewing within them.

In order to study these populations effectively we used the technique of stratified sampling. To study something effectively means a number of things, but above all this effort refers to distinguishing between sub-populations that are quite different from one another. When we undertake such a task, we find it useful to conceptualize the community in terms of its multiple components and then to study each, preferably with an emphasis on discovering the diversity of attitudes or behavior. In this way, we scan sub-groups and then stratify. When inaugurating this study, we obviously assumed that race would be an important dividing line, in the sense that when blacks voted, their vote for fair housing should have been greater than the number of whites who did the same. Therefore, it was necessary to interview in both white and black areas. We also assumed that class position of whites should be related to vote, especially if Lipset's comments on working-class authoritarians turned out to be correct. Consequently, we selected both precincts which had (a) large numbers of workman and (b) many white collar people. The same kind of logic underlay our selection of precincts on the basis of university affiliation. We assumed that university affiliation should be significantly related to vote, and hence, we chose many precincts with large numbers of university persons. In the case of comparable non-university people, the problem proved to be less demanding, partially because the white collar population in question was by far the largest group in the city of Berkeley. To sum up, we divided the community into sub-populations called strata. We then selected a sample within each in order to facilitate the testing of hypotheses derived from our theoretical assumptions on the nature of groups discussed.

Where Was the Sample Drawn?

As Figure 1 indicates, we studied districts scattered throughout Berkeley. Among others, we selected two precincts from the ghetto in South Berkeley. We chose another precinct from the central part of the city. This particular area was immediately adjacent to others undergoing change in racial composition, as white residents pulled out for one reason or another. Many of the whites had been older, and hence their exit was partially related to normal attrition due to death and lack of replacement by young whites, almost all of whom preferred to live elsewhere than in the areas occupied by their parents. This precinct, then, contained large numbers of workmen for whom the consequences of housing integration were both immediate and visible.

In this sense, they could view some of the consequences of integration in another precinct, a West Side area, one where the working class was racially heterogeneous. Here, whites, blacks, Asians, native Americans, and others resided together. For many white workmen, integration proved to be a pressing problem. By contrast, we selected a middle-class precinct in North Central Berkeley.

Most of the other precincts were white. But they did differ on the question of university connection. One precinct was located in the Thousand Oaks area, an all-white precinct with a very small university population. To the east of the Thousand Oaks district were the North Berkeley Hills, where the population resembled the Thousand Oaks people, except that there was a larger number of academic types, and their income level appeared to be somewhat higher. Also, it would seem that the population was slightly younger, for the Thousand Oaks area included many retired people. We selected two precincts from this residential district. South of Marin Street, the lower boundary of the North Hills, lay the South Berkeley Hills, an area with a relatively large number of University staff as well as students. However, in most precincts, these two groups still constituted a statistical minority, although their relative numbers had been gradually increasing due to the growth of the University itself. To the immediate west and south of campus were areas with high concentrations of graduate students and lesser faculty. We interviewed in all of these precincts plus one additional area. It was plush, racist, Republican and affluent. Berkeleyans have referred to the bastion of respectable racism as the Claremont area.

As you can see, we ran the gamut of class and racial groups while keeping one eye on the influence of the University, the center of Berkeley intelligentsia, and the other eye on those forces found in the white community which fought for and against fair housing. As we will discover, our concern proved statistically rewarding.

When Was the Sample Drawn?

We selected the sample and conducted most of the interviews during the 1963-64 academic year. More precisely, we completed ninety-five percent of the interviews between September, 1963 and July, 1964. The staff finished the "mop-up" interviews by late summer. Most consisted of those persons who were seldom at home or people reluctant to answer questions. Of these, some were older citizens concentrated in apartment houses; many viewed anybody from the University as odd and treated them accordingly. Consequently, we had to repeatedly contact a majority of these people in order to gain their time and cooperation.

How Was the Sample Drawn?

For a sample that does not purport to tightly represent any particular universe, the sample design may appear to be unduly complicated. Yet, every effort was taken to insure a random sample within each one of the fifteen precincts. Here's how we selected Berkeley residents:

(1) *Selection of Core Areas.* Formal and informal segregation helps survey design. Whites and minorities were sufficiently nucleated spatially to facilitate sampling precincts and transporting interviewers. In Berkeley, one had no trouble locating the black population, since it was found in the predictable areas. They lived in the flats, near the rail lines and expressways, in or near the industrial areas, and the like.

Locating the various whites proved to be relatively easy as well. With few exceptions, white workmen lived in the flats while the white collar population resided in the Hills and foothills. The faculty academics clustered around the campus but preferred the Hills to its north, while the graduate students located equally close to the campus and preferred the flats to the south and the west. In obtaining this information, we relied not only upon government figures but personal observations as well. By pooling the information, it was relatively easy to pick our precincts.

(2) *Preparation for the Drawing of the Sample.* Once we had specified our sampling areas, we proceeded to block-list all dwelling units within each precinct. Volunteers trooped about within and among precincts as they jotted down addresses. Once we had finished this task, we pooled the listings of the precincts and thereby created a larger sample, one both representative and stratified.

(3) *Residents Eligible for the Interview.* We obtained information on certain Berkeley adults but ignored others. After we had randomly selected a dwell-

Table 2. Summary Data on the Total Sample (Sub-Sample Unit = Precinct)

Data on Total Sample	1	2	3	4	5	6	7	8	9	10	11	12	13	14	15	*Total*
Number of Interviews Completed (Total)	59	54	69	48	58	66	71	71	75	55	106	73	71	62	70	1008
By Sex																
Male	50	39	42	32	47	47	61	50	65	41	81	65	55	33	42	(748)
Female	9	17	27	16	11	19	10	21	10	14	25	8	16	29	28	(260)
Language Problems, Not Interviewed	–	–	3	1	–	–	1	–	5	1	1	–	1	–	2	15
Ineligibles (Age, Residential Requirements and/or Citizenship)	25	12	18	45	8	11	9	32	6	17	29	9	6	11	13	251
Non-Dwelling Units	–	–	–	1	–	1	–	–	–	–	1	–	–	–	–	3
Refusals	12	6	49	6	13	18	10	10	12	23	30	17	11	28	13	258
No Such Address	3	–	13	4	1	–	1	1	–	11	2	–	6	1	–	43
Vacant	3	8	18	7	5	4	6	2	3	4	11	1	2	1	4	79

ing unit, the interviewers proceeded to the household and asked the potential source of information a number of screening questions. The interviewer would ask to speak with the male head of household, or, if no male were present, he would try to interview the female bread winner, provided that the person met the age, residence, and citizenship requirements. The potential interviewee must have been an American citizen and 21 years of age at the time of the election. He must also have been a resident of California for one year and Berkeley for six months prior to the election (and thereby met the state and local requirements for registering to vote). As always, many people eligible to register did not, and of those who did, some failed to vote. We interviewed both types of persons. Finally, we excluded from the sample those ineligible to register.

(4) *The Selection of Eligible Citizens.* Separate samples were taken from each of the fifteen districts. We followed standard procedure and used a table of random numbers to carry on the sampling within each population. The use of this technique allowed considerable flexibility in drawing the sample, for we could repeatedly return to our precinct list for additional respondents when it appeared necessary.

Within each precinct we had hoped to interview between forty-five and sixty Berkeley citizens. In most precincts, this strategy proved to be easy enough. However, we had trouble in staying below the upper limits in several precincts, precisely because of the high refusal rates within them. This paradox may be explained as follows: In two working-class areas, we ran into considerable opposition; older people in particular were reluctant to cooperate. This tendency was pronounced among the whites. In both precincts, we decided to compensate for the large number of refusals by selecting the *entire* population within each precinct. We hoped thereby to maximize the possibility of obtaining enough interviews and increasing the representativeness of the sample. In so doing, we obtained more than enough completions, although we suspect that our completions were biased in favor of some groups and against others.[10]

Flexibility proved useful for yet other reasons when carrying out our sample selection. As you might guess, we used the number of eligible contacts located by interviewers in the sample as an important consideration for determining the number of addresses chosen. In the student-faculty neighborhoods, especially, but also within minority areas, many potential interviewees did not meet the residential requirements. Consequently, we had to oversample from these districts in order to obtain enough cases. In the remaining precincts, sample selection was less burdensome, since almost everyone proved to be eligible to register to vote.

When we had gathered a sufficient number of schedules, the "mop-up" operations began. Past refusals, residents just back from trips, hospitals, jails,

Table 3. Interviews Completed, by Precinct, Race, Class, and University Tie (Sub-Sample Units = Precincts)

Criteria for Stratification	1	2	3	4	5	6	7	8	9	10	11	12	13	14	15	*Total*
Race																
Black	48	49	2	1	27	0	–	–	–	–	74	–	–	–	–	201
White	9	4	59	44	23	64	72	69	73	55	31	71	70	61	61	766
Oriental	1	3	5	4	9	2	–	1	2	–	1	2	1	1	9	41
Class																
Miscellaneous	1	4	10	6	3	9	2	13	6	6	6	2	6	9	11	94
Blue Collar	43	36	17	9	34	5	6	2	5	0	78	6	4	14	17	276
White Collar	14	16	39	34	22	52	64	55	64	49	22	65	61	39	42	638
University Tie																
University (staff and others)	2	1	5	6	1	22	14	15	14	7	2	17	13	1	4	125
Students	0	1	10	14	1	7	4	13	1	0	3	1	2	2	4	63
Non-University	56	54	51	29	57	37	54	42	60	48	101	54	56	59	62	820

and mental institutions, individuals who could not or would not speak English–indeed, many levels of humanity–all were repeatedly contacted. Interviews were completed in many instances. We made an effort to minimize refusals and otherwise incomplete schedules by tearing down some of the language barriers separating interviewers who spoke English and certain minority persons who did not. We translated the interview into Spanish and completed approximately five interviews in this manner.

Who Was Actually Included and Excluded from the Sample?

Tables 2 and 3 summarize information on the number of potential interviewees plus basic data on interviews completed. The refusal included eligible as well as ineligible contacts. Table 3 presents basic materials on their racial and class backgrounds plus statistics on university affiliation.

The Interviewing

We should make a few comments on the quality of interviews plus payments made to interviewers. We recruited students enrolled in an advanced course given by the Department of Sociology of the University of California, Berkeley. Few of these students had interviewing experience. We briefly trained and sent them out into the field, where some of them quickly became excellent interviewers. We selected other Cal students as well for the purposes of interviewing. Of these, several had prior interviewing experience, and the quality of their work reflected their previous training.

The Institute of Social Science of the University of California paid for some of the costs of the interviewing, as well as other expenses. However, the key sources of fuel consisted of student commitment to the civil rights movement, the goals of which they viewed as consistent with those of the project.

NOTES

1. The Watts episode is sometimes referred to as a riot. Race riots involve civilian populations using violent techniques against one another. There was little of that in Watts. In fact, if one defines a political insurrection as an uprising against political authority, then the Watts effort constitutes an insurrection. Thousands of Watts blacks engaged the Los Angeles police and two divisions of the National Guard in almost one week of combat.
2. For a first rate analysis of the Berkeley Fair Housing election, see Joe Pimsleur's "Battle in Berkeley," *The San Francisco Chronicle* Volume 26, March 17, 1963. p.3.
3. The word "fair housing" appeared frequently during the campaign and often passed through the lips of ordinance supporters. Obviously, we are

supporters and our search for and use of a neutral rubric would add little to the analysis.

4. Nothing rivals that episode. For a personal account of the End Poverty in California (EPIC) campaign, see Upton Sinclair's, *I, Candidate for Governor and How I Got Licked* (Los Angeles: End Poverty League, Inc., 1935).
5. Subsequently, realty groups led a fight to set up a State of California referendum that would have erased legislation on civil rights. They did, and they won.
6. When we describe Berkeley, we time and again use the past tense because much of 1963 Berkeley cannot be found in Berkeley of 1972.
7. Herbert Hill has given me most of my ideas on this matter. See his "Twenty Years of State Fair Employment Practice Commissions: A Critical Analysis with Recommendations," *The Buffalo Law Review* Volume 14, Fall, 1964, pp. 22-69.
8. The left had a considerable following in Berkeley. When in 1959 a University of California graduate student ran as a Socialist candidate for Mayor of Berkeley, he picked up 21 percent of the total community vote. He did especially well in student and black districts. However, more important was the large number of left-liberals and militants found inside the California Democratic Council (CDC) during the late 1950s and early 1960s. They were articulate on politics and involved in power centers inside the local Democratic Party.
9. For a comparative and excellent discussion of the size, structure and activities of the University of California, see Clark Kerr's *The Uses of the University* (Cambridge: Harvard University Press, 1963).
10. The sample undoubtedly underestimated the number of people opposed to the ordinance, although we made every effort to include these people in our sample. When we sent letters to potential respondents, we notified them of an impending visit but made no reference to race or housing. However, many Berkeley residents associated students, sociology, and the University with forces supporting fair housing and other pieces of reform legislation. These Berkeleyans were reluctant to give cooperation to anybody representing the Little Red School House, especially students, and hence they immediately refused the interview. A disproportionately large number of these people were older women and often single; these people frequently lived in the middle income apartment houses found in zones of racial transition.

FOUR

Class and Status as Sources of Party Affiliation

How people make a living affects just about everything else they do, including politics. Class position partially determines whether their children will survive their first year of life and how long they will live. Class influences what kinds of clothes they will purchase and wear, the kind of beverage they will drink, the quality of food they will eat. Generally, jobs set the limit on people's incomes, hence the kind of homes they can afford. The class character of the neighborhood in turn has predictable consequences on available school resources, hence the level of education and ultimate range of jobs to which the kids may aspire.[1] The class character of a neighborhood has an impact on whether youth will grow up enjoying football, tennis, or polo; hockey, skiing, or yachting. Class position has an effect on the kinds and numbers of books people will read, the magazines to which they will subscribe, and the variety of television programming they'll watch; it is well known for example, that educational television appeals to a "select" audience. Where a person works has a lot to do with the kinds of friends and the forms of recreation he'll choose. And if Kinsey is right, class is even important in as basic a determination as what people wear (or don't wear) in bed. Working–and middle-class people differ on how they view the world. For instance, in describing a disaster such as a tornado, the working class favors the use of concrete terms, while the middle class emphasizes more abstract and analytic descriptions.[2] Not only their favorite categories of thought but the absence of phrases or concepts are predictable, as are people's counterformulations (for example, black power!) against those who oppress them (whitey!). Type of logic and form of argument construction—if Karl Mannheim's analyses are correct[3]—reflect class background. Hence the very cognitive apparatus used to perceive, experience, and deal with reality are to a high degree dependent upon class position. Our "class list" could run on indefinitely. But more to the point, we do know that class background helps shape a person's political choice; in the United States and elsewhere, working-class people have traditionally chosen the party of reform or revolution.[4] By contrast, the middle class is more frequently conservative or reactionary.

Status constitutes the second principal determinant of people's behavior.[5] Where one is positioned on the educational, income, ethnic, racial, and religious ladders has a decisive influence on one's chances of being born alive, reaching adulthood, or living beyond sixty-five years of age, although the Red Man's Revenge—tobacco—and the white man's aerial garbage—smog—promise to become the great equalizers. Until very recently, and to some degree even today, rank in one or more of the pecking orders has helped determine whether one would wear garish clothes—even the term is white middle class—with the proletarian minorities time and again preferring the gaudy variety, while the white Anglo-Saxon Protestant upper classes display a propensity to pattern their dressing apparel after the Oxford elite. The choice of everyday words, one's argot, depends to a high degree not only upon class but ethnic and racial subcommunities. It is sometimes said, for example, that in the United States the working-class poor, especially its racial minorities, return to speaking a "second language" once school is out, and that their vocabulary exudes values judged by the elite as vulgar. Speaking of taste, it is often impossible to obtain a bottle of beer at the average cocktail party given by a university elite, emulators of the powerful. Although many poor blacks and whites may like the full range of drinks, their position in the lower levels of the income pyramid limits sharply their ability to purchase more expensive liquors and wines. The very California Chicanos who tend the growing of expensive grapes generally purchase cheap vino. Nor would a Mexican-American be expected to do otherwise. For a Chicano farm worker to walk into a small-town store and pay three dollars for a quart of excellent California wine would be to risk a censorious glance at the checkout counter. For clearly, when a person is at the bottom of the educational, income, occupational, and ethnic pecking orders, he *should*—so go the small-town folkways—avoid profligate spending habits and select a wine in keeping with his station—that of a potential welfare recipient. Should the Chicano do otherwise, many Anglos would assess his behavior as lacking frugality; perhaps the story would make its way into one of the gossip chains within the Anglo community, especially Kiwanis and Chamber of Commerce circles, a communication net always open to such talk. This conversational material would serve to reinforce stereotypes so useful in sheathing WASP ideology with one more layer of self-righteousness. Both the ideology and sense of self-correctness serve to buttress power relationships that bind the mass of Chicanos to the bottom of the class-status order. In this way, class and status have a dual control function.

But there is political reaction against imposition from above. Low rank honor has a lot to do with how people get exploited—and if the repression is prolonged and unbearable, in the long run the oppressed will get together. They will organize, and they will fight back by whatever means are available. The imposed statuses derive from centuries of colonial-like subordination and serve to maintain prejudice and discrimination. Today the racially oppressed are fighting back in the United States, as evidenced by the growth of the black, brown, and yellow power movements. They are struggling for a better deal; some want a new world. They would prefer to bring about the elimination of class-racial exploitation through reform but if need be, many would tread the revolutionary path.

But can class and status have their double-barrelled drive in a sophisticated community, especially in a setting with high levels of economic security and a long history of fighting discrimination? Wouldn't Berkeley thus be an exception? After all, the city had successfully fought the creation of a second high school, for the decision makers believed that such a school might be located somewhere in the Berkeley hills, where it would draw from the overwhelmingly white upper middle class. Also, Berkeley has traditionally had low levels of unemployment among its blue-collar people, mainly because of its diversified economic base. In that sense, it has never depended on a key industry as has Detroit, Pittsburgh, or Gary; the mass of blue-collar workers do not flounder about looking for work or worrying about layoffs during low points in the country's business cycles. Consequently, Berkeley's working class gives few indications of class consciousness. In Berkeley, union activities are barely noticeable, although a very high proportion of the working-class population is in fact unionized. Although income differences are visible, by East Coast standards, even the poor clearly live in homes and on incomes well above the poverty level.

Until the 1900s Berkeley prided itself as a city without barriers, class or racial. In Berkeley people did the things they wanted to do. Choice not determinism structured their lives. Berkeley was unique—some people said.

Karl Marx was not the first to look with suspicion at such portraits—he frequently called them myths or ideologies. Doubting the wisdom of asserting free will as a source of action and ideas, he also looked to the importance of work relations in determining people's politics—even in communities where economic conditions were stable and where revolutionary activities were consequently absent.[6] Unlike Marx, Max Weber concentrated on status—the ranked position and conferred prestige—of occupations, income levels, nation-

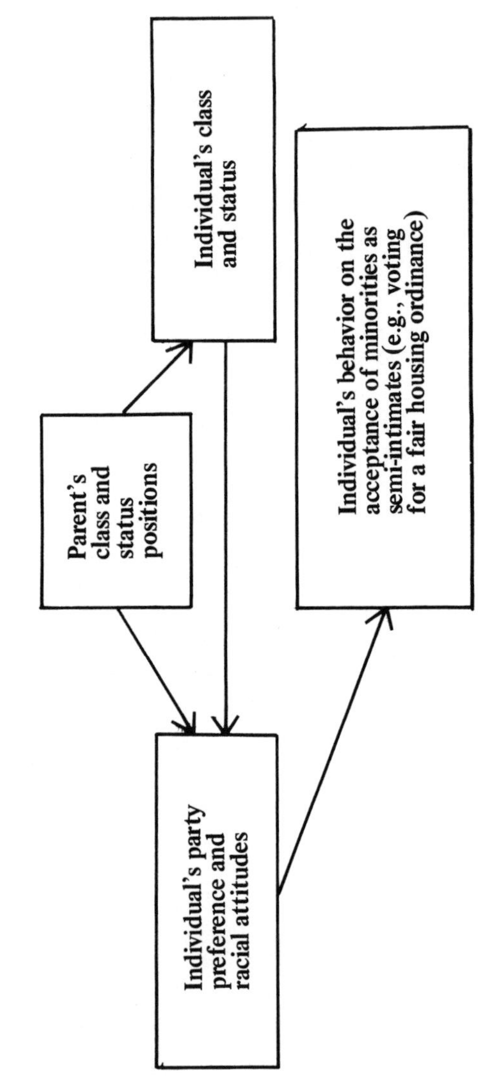

Figure 2. Crucial Determinants of Party Affiliation (and the Acceptance of Minorities)

al ties, as well as races—when accounting for a wide range of human behavior. Weber never viewed status considerations as more or less significant than class. He treated status and class as related to one another and as having a decisive effect on a number of things—including power and hence politics.[7] We shall follow Weber's lead.

THE TWO-GENERATIONAL IMPACT

Both Marx and Weber were well aware of the need to gauge the impact of class position on an intergenerational basis. Status deserved and obtained similar treatment. Marx's analyses of English imperialism in India and white racism in America[8] would suggest that he—like Weber—was aware of group prestige and correlated power and property differences among races. The views of these two giants in sociology would be consonant with the writings of Lipset, Lazarsfeld, Barton, and Linz, who some time ago used cross-cultural statistical materials to demonstrate that class and status positions have been the most significant determinants of party choice.[9]

Time and again they found that working-class Catholics have voted labor and Democratic, especially those having eastern or southern European backgrounds, low income, and less education. In America, working-class blacks have voted along these same lines. In England and Australia, blue-collar Catholics, most of them low-status Irish, have traditionally preferred labor and, of course, almost by definition have had lesser educational and pecuniary statuses. In Sweden, working-class Finns have learned to deal with ethnic discrimination by leaning heavily to the left within their parties, unions, and co-ops. And so on around the world, the same pattern has crystallized and remained. At the other extreme, upper middle-class, white Anglo-Saxon Protestants—the pure WASPS in the United States—have been overwhelmingly conservative, as have their counterparts in England, the Dominions, France, Scandinavia, Germany, Japan, and elsewhere.

Further, if Lipset is correct, two-generational membership in the same class and status categories should be crucial in deciding party preference.[10] Parents' class-status positions plus party choice have been found to be by far the most direct and important determinants of their children's political affiliations (see Figure 2). How this happens is not too difficult to ascertain. Parents generally socialize their kids to accept their political party. The younger ones also inherit their parents' ethnic and religious statuses. And these statuses, plus their group carriers—ones that include their always-teaching parents—help to shape the children's political opinions. That's what happens in churches, ethnic neighborhoods, class-racial schools, workplace associations—parents interpret shared political opinions to the youth. Hence, if we are to discover the antecedents of people's party preferences, we must note the statuses parents have passed on to their children.

DEPRIVATION AND STATUS

When dealing with class, status, and political choice, we are not exploring the uncharted.[11] We have known for quite some time that groups can be distinguished in terms of class-status characteristics, and that they can predictably be linked to their political choices, as in the following four-category model: (1) *consistent underdog;*[12] (2) *inconsistent ethnics;*[13] (3) *consistent elites* (WASP middle class); (4) *inconsistent workers* (WASP working class).

In the case of the *consistent underdogs,* we can observe that the lesser class and status characteristics move these workers to support parties of political change (as indicated in Table 4). Over time, they collectively discover that it is wise to act for their material interests through political parties partisan towards reform, or in some cases, revolution.

In the case of *inconsistent ethnics,* what we have is a middle class group with low ethnic status (as specified in Table 4). An example would be a black or a Jewish white-collar worker. They view the parties of the center and the left as potential vehicles for elevating their group's ethnic status, to make the prestige of this group commensurate with its relatively high class standing. Hence, we are never surprised to find that middle-class blacks, Jews, and eastern (as well as southern European) Catholics, for example, have tradition-

Table 4. The Consistent Underdog and Inconsistent Ethnic: Categories that Press for Progressive Political Change

	The Consistent Underdog	*The Inconsistent Ethnic*
Class	Upper-working or Lower-working	Upper-middle or Lower-middle
Ethnic Status	Lower-medium or Medium	Lower-medium or Lower
Religious Status	Lower-medium or Lower	Lower-medium or Lower
Educational Status	Lower or Medium	High or Upper-medium
Income Status	Upper-lower or Lower-lower	Upper-medium or Lower-medium

ally favored the reform wings of the Democratic Party—the party of Franklin Roosevelt and John Kennedy.

The *consistent elite*—our third category—includes those whose class position and status are high in every possible way; a typical member is middle class, a member of an honorific ethnic group such as the English, Scotch, Scotch-Irish, German (or mixed northern and northwestern European communities and aggregations), a member of a religious group with plenty of honor (for example, Episcopalian, Congregational, or English Catholics), a holder of a university degree, and a high income earner. Many of the persons in this category would qualify as WASPS in the broadest sense—white, middle-aged, Anglo-Saxon, Protestant, and middle class. Historically we know their predominant political choices: Republican, satisfied, stand-pat. Since many who "have" want to "keep," this group hopes to repel those whom they often judge to be leftist renegades, and the best way to accomplish this goal is through support of a well-financed, conservative party—one, parenthetically, with a history of ethnic traditionalism sufficiently rigid to help guarantee *their* class retention of wealth, power, and prestige.

Table 5. The Consistent Elite and Inconsistent Worker: Categories that Press for Conservative Political Change

	The Consistent Elite *(WASP middle class)*	*The Inconsistent Worker* *(WASP working class)*
Class	Upper-middle or Lower-middle	Upper-working or Lower-working
Ethnic Status	Upper-medium or Lower-medium	Upper-medium or Lower-medium
Religious Status	Upper-medium or Lower-medium	Upper-medium or Lower-medium
Educational Status	Upper-medium or Lower-medium	Upper-lower or Lower-lower
Income Status	Upper-medium or Lower-medium	Upper-lower or Lower-lower

Table 6. Intergenerational Background (including Ethnicity) vs. Party Preference

	Father's Occupation: Blue-Collar (no Farmers)						*Father's Occupation: White-Collar*					
Party Preference	*Respondent's Occupation: Blue-Collar*		*Respondent's Occupation: White-Collar*				*Respondent's Occupation: Blue-Collar*		*Respondent's Occupation: White-Collar*			
			University[1]		*Non-University*				*University*		*Non-University*	
	N NW[2]	*S E*[3]	*N NW*	*S E*	*N NW*	*S E*	*N NW*	*S E*	*N NW*	*S E*	*N NW*	*S E*
Democrat	(18)[4] 55%	(5) 55%	(12) 57%	(3) –	(33) 37%	(11) 48%	(12) 43%	(5) 50%	(52) 52%	(13) 52%	(100) 37%	(22) 71%
Republican	(7) 21%	(3) 33%	(7) 33%	(1) –	(47) 53%	(9) 39%	(10) 36%	(1) 10%	(30) 30%	(5) 20%	(138) 51%	(5) 16%
Independent	(8) 24%	(1) 11%	(2) 10%	(1) –	(9) 10%	(3) 13%	(6) 21%	(4) 40%	(18) 18%	(7) 28%	(31) 12%	(4) 13%
Total	(33) 100%	(9) 100%	(21) 100%	(5) 100%	(89) 100%	(23) 100%	(28) 100%	(10) 100%	(100) 100%	(25) 100%	(269) 100%	(31) 100%

1. Includes Students
2. North and Northwestern European
3. Southern and Eastern European

Finally, there are the *inconsistent workers* (WASP working class), persons high in nationality, prestige but low in class honor. A number of considerations dictate a conservative political choice for many of these workers. For one thing, they attempt to resolve the contradiction between the low prestige of their class and the high prestige of their ethnic group by identifying with the presumed class to which they aspire—sharing the Republican politics of the middle class. An example of the inconsistent worker would be an English-American tool-and-die maker who supports the Republican party.

To summarize, then, there are two clusters of class and statuses pushing for the politics of progress and change and two doing quite otherwise. In each case, class is important, but only in relation to status. At least that's what we believe to be the case.

What this four-part distinction does is recognize that people are tribalized along ethnic lines as well as organized in terms of class. Further, when we combine status and class, it is obvious that we view certain kinds of status consistency (more accurately, status-class inconsistency) as extremely important. As a number of studies[14] have indicated, among the inconsistent ethnics are many who act in ways incongruent with their middle-class positions, but consonant with their own ethnic group demands for equality, as suggested by Table 4. At the other extreme, among working-class people who also belong to a high status ethnic (and/or religious) group, a disproportionately large number deny the low prestige of their class position by presenting themselves to others in terms of that status group having the higher prestige. They do so in part to obtain preferential treatment in day-to-day contacts with others.[15] In the context of affirmation of superiority, they would celebrate the honorific (however petty) middle-class standards most evident within their high prestige ethnic and religious groups by giving credence to the most conservative opinions and choices. Voting conservative becomes a way of indicating one's ethnic superiority despite one's subordinate class position. In effect, a disproportionately large number of inconsistent workers should support a conservative political party, as suggested by Table 5.

WHAT HAPPENED IN THE BERKELEY 1963 ELECTION

Generally, the findings relative to the four class-status categories just outlined supported our expectations, although there were some intriguing exceptions, many of which we can best discuss by observing the inter- and intragenerational impacts separately. Table 6 emphasizes the significance of parental influence, especially father's occupation. Of those who were working class on a two-generational basis, thereby reflecting the impediments to mobility in a stratified society, a disproportionately large number proved to be non-Republican by choice. In the case of the eastern and southern European ethnics, a relatively large number should have supported the progressive party. They did. Although these proportions proved to be sizeable, the percentages were similar to northern, northwest, and central Europeans, groups with higher ethnic status. Yet we can see where our predictions went wrong. Much to our surprise, very few "WASP workers" preferred the Republican party. Briefly, we found that a large proportion of high ethnic status workers affiliated with the Republican party only when they derived from the middle class. By contrast, two-generational workers of high ethnic status origins, whether Protestant or Catholic, were decidedly Democratic. Apparently our hypothesis about the "inconsistent worker" is applicable only to workers of middle-class backgrounds–the so-called "skidders."[16] Reared in the white-collar world, their parents impress upon many of them the need to align themselves with the party of genteel respectability. At least that would be our brief interpretation of these results.

At the other extreme, when persons were consistently white collar, non-University, and northern European, the preferences were heavily Republican, as indicated in Table 6. In the case of the non-University "pure WASP," the conservative preference clearly revealed itself; of the 55 such persons in our study, there were 13 Democrats, 38 Republicans, and 4 Independents. From another vantage point, we observed that of those who were Republican, a very large number came from the WASP, white collar section of the population. Hence, we would be foolish to stereotype the middle class. Our sample contained people with a rich variety of status characteristics. For example, white-collar Jews[17] turned out to be non-Republicans in most cases, as did Catholics, especially those from southern and eastern Europe[18] Clearly then, we do not want to give the impression that membership in the middle class is a sure indication of conservative party preference, especially among those with non-Protestant backgrounds.

Although we have established the significance of intergenerational phenomena, especially the importance of father's occupation, the lack of a convincingly large number of cases has hampered our effort to combine the characteristics of two succeeding generations. Consequently, at this point we would like to focus on crucial determinants while omitting the class characteristics of respondents' fathers. In doing so, we would be foolish to suggest that the fathers' class and status characteristics are not relevant for this part of our analysis; on the contrary, we must keep in mind that these attributes are *crucial* in specifying class-status determinants of sons' and daughters' political views, since the parent's background largely determines the distribution of people within the labor force, the crucial source of their political preference. As John Porter points out:

> In every society there are established mechanisms by which members are sorted out and assigned to particular social tasks. Often this process is based on biological or inherited characteristics. In most societies there

> are, for example, male roles and female roles. Sex has always been an initial basis of sorting and assigning people to their appropriate tasks. Hence in this particular society, few women occupy positions of power because it is not "appropriate" that women should. Colour is another important biological characteristic which has been used as a basis of sorting people out.
>
> In addition to these very obvious biological differences social characteristics have also been used in this assignment of people to social tasks. Religion, ethnic affiliation, educational experience, social class, and other such characteristics are often treated as biological attributes even though they are socially rather than genetically acquired.[19]

Let's turn to Table 7 and observe the combined significance of class and University affiliation on the Berkeley vote. We find that a progressive party did well within the working class and University white-collar populations, in that order. By contrast, the white-collar, non-University category turned out to be relatively conservative, especially among northern Europeans (see Table 8). As expected, the eastern Europeans proved to be overwhelmingly Democratic irrespective of class and university tie.[20] Table 9 brings together ethnicity and religion among white-collar, non-University populations–thereby taking into account subgroups for which we had enough cases to carry on a convincing analysis–and we find the expected: Catholics of eastern European origins led Catholics of northern European background, who in turn stood out ahead of others in registering with the Democratic party.[21]

Table 7. Class Position, University Tie, and Party Preference

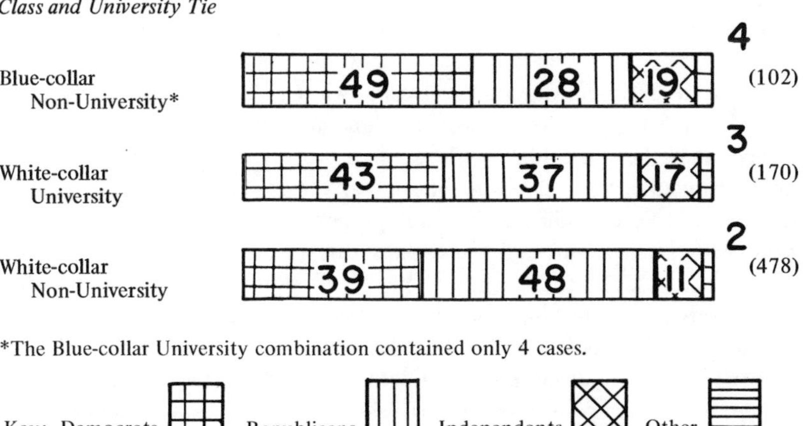

*The Blue-collar University combination contained only 4 cases.

Table 8. Ethnicity, Class, University Tie, and Party Affiliation

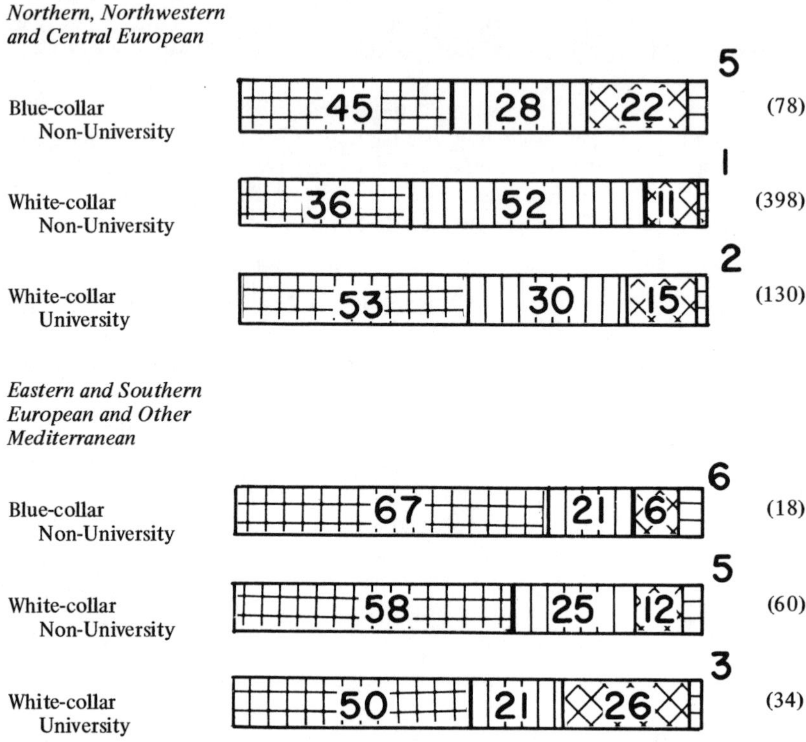

Key: See page 63.

If we once again confine our analysis to white-collar, non-University voters and add the matter of education to ethnic and religious considerations, we observe that the more highly educated in every group identified relatively more frequently with the Republican party (see Table 10). Interestingly, additional analyses indicate that this propensity was most obvious among those who perhaps suffered the most status anguish from the discrepancy between their social and pecuniary honor; of those who were white-collar, non-University, Protestant, higher educated *but low incomed,* 38 viewed themselves as Democrats and 108 as Republicans. We suspect that of those who fell in the larger (Republican) category of status inconsistents, a large number would complain most bitterly about the malingering practices of the poor who supposedly do not pay taxes but are supported by public welfare.

Table 9. Ethnicity, Religion, and Party Affiliation (White-collar, Non-University Only)

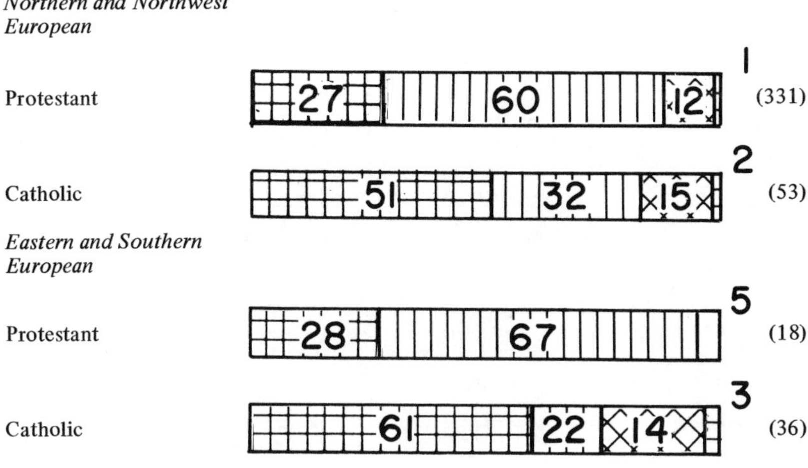

Key: See page 63.

Among complaining WASPs, Republican preferences stemmed not only from collective political beliefs—they were surrounded by associational Republicanism—but the desire to support a party they believed would drive the "lazy" ones off the welfare rolls. This vanquishing of the poor would supposedly lower taxes for the beleaguered lower-middle classes. Consequently, it would increase the living standards of those who would like to maintain a consuming style more in keeping with the upper-middle class, so obviously the modal form of the greater WASP, middle-class community.

CONCLUSIONS

Our information is consistent with our expectations on the double impact of class and status groups. Specifically, voters turned out to be overwhelmingly Democratic when they were consistently working-class on a two-generational basis as well as members of lesser status groups. Their political affiliations were obviously in keeping with their class and status group interests. In supporting the local party of reform, they were backing the organization that has traditionally acted in their interests, admittedly not as a class party with a class program but as a reform organization concerned with alleviating the problem facing working-class ethnic and religious groups. At the other extreme, when people belonged to the high prestige class and status groups in the community, they generally supported the party of economic conservatism

Table 10. Ethnicity, Religion, Education, and Party Affiliation (White-collar, Non-University, Northern, Northwest, and Central Europeans Only)[1]

	Party Affiliation[2]			
	Democrats	Republicans	Independents	
Protestant				
Lesser Educated	29	63	8	(56)
Better Educated	24	66	10	(182)
Catholic				
Lesser Educated	70	15	15	(13)
Better Educated	35	45	20	(20)

1. The number of eastern and eastern and southern Europeans (and other Mediterraneans) was insufficient to analyze through the use of bar charts. However, we should note that only *one* of the lesser educated Catholics (N = 11) in this category preferred the Republican party, while 3 of the better educated (N = 8) did the same.
2. The "other" preferences have been omitted.

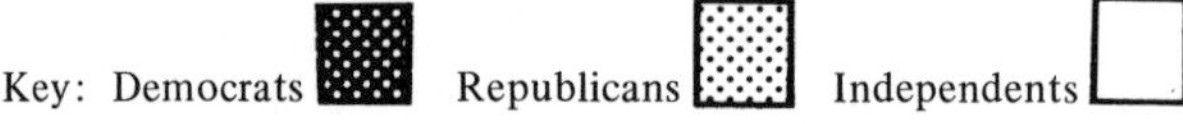

and racial traditionalism, the party that has time and again stood for the retention of the *status quo* in pecuniary, racial, and religious affairs. In so doing, the Berkeley voters acted in terms of their own group interests.

More difficult are the interpretive problems associated with matters of status crystallization, since analyses generally suffer from nonspecification of rank combinations that are most pertinent in producing a desire for change. We have stressed the ethnic- (religious-) class combinations as crucial, with low ascribed ethnic honor coupled with high class prestige leading to large proportions favoring the party of change. They favor this political choice in an attempt to resolve the major contradictions associated with class and status in our society. Supposedly if and when someone does well in terms of occupational success—arrival in the middle class—he should be able to live where he prefers, eat what he wants, educate his children where he wishes, and promote his children into areas of occupational success without being prejudged on the basis of ethnic and religious background. But many persons cannot exert this freedom because their low as well as ascribed ethnic, religious, and educational statuses bring discriminatory actions obviously sponsored by those white, Anglo-Saxon, Protestant, middle-class people at the top of the system. Through interaction with these pedigreed WASPs, the ethnic inconsistents—such as white, Anglo-Saxon, Protestant, middle-class professionals—learn not only of their own status inconsistency, but the consequences of the contradiction between the ideology of success and the practice of ethnic and religious discrimination for people like themselves. There are a number of ways in which the ethnic inconsistents can attempt to resolve the problem, one of which is to personally favor a political party that works for the elimination of discrimination. Another is to urge others like themselves to do the same. Thus collective political demands arise for progressive party commitment to the elimination of ascribed status as the basis for judgment.

These efforts, these demands, by no means fell upon an unresponsive Democratic party organization in Berkeley, for if nothing else, the University-dominated party favored the elimination of discrimination for those urban minorities having both urban *savoir faire* and correlated incomes.

In keeping with at least part of our interpretation, Lenski has commented:

> . . . There is some limited evidence that . . . persons of inconsistent status are more likely to support liberal and radical movements designed to alter the political *status quo* than are persons of consistent status. The classical case of this has been the strong support which successful Jewish merchants and professional men have given such movements in every part of the world. Similar examples can be found among economically successful members of other ethnic, racial, and religious minorities. In fact, political sociologists have shown that such individuals are much less likely to support established conservative parties than are persons in the same occupational class who are members of the majority group. Thus, voting studies show that with class position held constant, Catholics are more likely than Protestants to support liberal or socialist parties in Protestant nations, while Protestants are more likely to support such parties in Catholic nations.[22]

There is little we can add, besides this final point.

You will recall that our hypotheses on Berkeley voting choices in the 1963 election were based upon non-University studies. These research efforts have revealed, for example, that union membership was a significant source of party preference. If research derived from non-University communities[23] has application to our study—that is, even in overwhelmingly white-collar Berkeley—then union membership should help determine party preference. In keeping with this expectation, union membership did make a difference, both in the Catholic and Protestant blue-collar groups.[24] Interpretatively, it would seem that among Catholics (and lesser ethnics), blue-collar union membership reinforces an inherited political tendency expressed through a religious group which nationally and historically has been decidedly working class in membership, pro-union by inclination, and economic reformist in character. Among Protestant (and more privileged ethnic) workers, union membership has countered middle-class, politically conservative Protestantism.

Despite our general approach—and many of our generalizations seek an undeserved level of generality—we would admit that Berkeley is unique. But then, so are Madison and Oshkosh, Wisconsin. Nonetheless, we suspect that Berkeley, Madison, and Oshkosh have a lot in common, namely the predictable impact of class-status characteristics on the political choices of their citizens. In this respect, Berkeley may well be not too different from those non-University towns where social scientists have gathered the basic findings on the significance of class and status.

NOTES

1. Myron Brenton recently analyzed the growing cost of higher education for the middle class and assumed that the working class was by and large out of the race for achieving a college or university education. He observed:

   > Though higher education is becoming less a privilege for the wealthy and more a right for everyone, it should be noted that the disadvantaged—despite scholarship and community action programs designed to help them—are not in college in significant numbers. U.S. Office of Education statistics show that only 4.6 percent of the campus population is Negro. At the moment, for groups with very low incomes, failure to be academically prepared and motivated for college is more of a problem than finding the money to pay for it.

   See his "The Higher Cost of Higher Education," *The New York Times Magazine,* April 21, 1968, p. 32.

   Other persons in the past arrived at similar conclusions about our educational system. See, for example, Robert S. Lynd and Helen M. Lynd, *Middletown* (New York: Harcourt Brace, 1929), pp. 185-7. See also Harold M. Hodges, *Social Stratification* (Cambridge, Mass.: Schenkman, 1964), pp. 260-1. Most relevant is Joseph A. Kahl, *The American Class Structure* (New York: Rinehart, 1957), especially pp. 281-9.
2. For an encyclopedic discussion on the class impact in a variety of areas, see Harold Hodges, *op. cit.,* especially pp. 1-38, 62-6, 78-100, 113-94.
3. See Karl Mannheim, *Ideology and Utopia* (New York: Harcourt Brace, 1936), pp. 271-9.
4. T. B. Bottomore has discussed the continued impact of class on people's politics in his *Classes in Modern Society* (New York: Pantheon Books, 1966).
5. See Hodges, *op. cit.,* pp. 217-18 for a preliminary discussion on status politics.

6. For a summary view on this point, see John C. Leggett, *Class, Race and Labor* (New York: Oxford University Press, 1968), pp. 8-42.
7. Weber's best discussion of this problem occurs in his "Class, Status and Party," in H.H. Gerth and C. Wright Mills, *From Max Weber* (New York: Oxford University Press, 1953), pp. 159-95.
8. See Karl Marx, *The Civil War in the United States* (New York: International Publishers, 1961); Karl Marx, *The First Indian War of Independence* (Moscow: Foreign Languages Publishing House, 1960); Karl Marx, *On Colonialism* (Moscow: Foreign Languages Publishing House, 1960).
9. See Seymour M. Lipset, Paul F. Lazarsfeld, Allen H. Barton, and Juan Linz, "The Psychology of Voting: An Analysis of Political Behavior," in Gardner Lindzay's *Handbook of Social Psychology,* Volume 2 (Cambridge: Addison Wesley, 1954), pp. 1135-50. More recent confirmation of Lipset *et al.* basic assertions can be found in the writings of Angus Campbell, Phillip Converse, and Samuel Eldersveld, among others. Angus Campbell and Homer C. Cooper used a probability sample of the entire United States to study the 1954 congressional elections and found that while Protestants were split between Democrats and Republicans, Catholics and Jews tended to vote Democratic. See their *Group Differences in Attitudes and Votes* (Ann Arbor: Survey Research Center, 1956), p. 23. Angus Campbell, Phillip E. Converse, Warren E. Miller, and Donald E. Stokes have observed that although the working-class base of the Democratic party is proportionately tiny by comparison to the blue-collar underpinning of labor parties such as Norway's, nonetheless the Democratic party is relatively dependent upon the voting support of the blue collar, lesser educated. The Democratic party also contains the largest proportion of those blue-collar workers who identify with the working class. (We found this to be the case in our study, although class identification in Berkeley was not of great significance, in part because of the middle-class, economically stable character of the Berkeley community.) See their *Elections and the Political Order* (New York: John Wiley, 1966), pp. 255-7. The same authors in an earlier study–*The American Voter* (New York: John Wiley, 1960), p. 302–used a U.S. sample and found that members of union households, union members, Negroes, and Jews were overwhelmingly Democratic in the 1948, 1952, and 1956 presidential elections; Catholics gave the Democratic candidates somewhat less support, especially in the Eisenhower elections. Samuel Eldersveld observed that working-class people, especially the proletarianized ethnics–Poles, for example, whom he studied in Detroit during the 1956 congressional elections–were disproportionately concentrated at all levels of the Wayne County (Detroit) Democratic Party. See his *Political Parties: A Behavioral Analysis* (Chicago: Rand McNally, 1964), pp. 54-7, 60-1, 84-5, 92-3, 212-15, 506-7. Oscar Glantz's Philadelphia study of the 1952 presidential election concluded that Protestants were disproportionately Republican and Catholics were heavily Democratic. See his "Protestant and Catholic Voting Behavior in a Metropolitan Area," *Pub-*

lic Opinion Quarterly, 23 (Spring, 1959), pp. 73-82. Robert Alford makes similar observations in his "The Role of Social Class in American Voting Behavior," *Western Political Quarterly,* 16 (March 1963), pp. 180-94. Benton Johnson studied Eugene, Oregon, in the late 1950s and found that the Protestant Fundamentalist working class were disproportionately Republican while liberal middle-class Protestants were more heavily Democratic, thereby reducing the class voting differential both within the larger Protestant community and the metropolitan area at large. See his "Ascetic Protestantism and Political Preference," *Public Opinion Quarterly*, 26 (Spring, 1962), pp. 35-46. J.S. Roucek has convincingly contended that John F. Kennedy's 1960 political victory stemmed largely from his ability to put together the old F.D.R. coalition (labor, city machines, liberals, Negroes, some farmers, and the South, plus Catholics) of voters, at the center of which were the disadvantaged class and ethnic groups. See his "The Vote of the American Minorities in President Kennedy's 1960 Election," *Politics,* 26 (March, 1961), pp. 33-42. Also see Charles Glock and Rodney Stark, *Religion and Society in Tension* (Chicago: Rand McNally, 1965), pp. 185-226; Gerhard Lenski, *The Religious Factor* (Garden City: Doubleday, 1961), pp. 120-91.

10. Two types of evidence support this contention: first, the classical community studies concerned with class and status group structures; second, the more recent survey research explorations. In the case of the community observations, Robert and Helen Lynd's efforts on Middletown would constitute an illustration of the classical community study undertaken during the 1930s. See their *Middletown, op. cit.,* p. 415, and *Middletown in Transition* (New York: Harcourt Brace, 1937) pp. 175-6, 201, and 204. Most pertinent would be Seymour M. Lipset and Hans Zetterberg's "Social Mobility in Industrial Society," in Seymour Lipset and Reinhard Bendix, *Social Mobility in Industrial Society* (Berkeley: University of California Press, 1959), pp. 69-72. More recently, H. McClosky and H.E. Dahlgren presented information confirming the hypothesis that the indoctrination, retention, or shift of party loyalties is related to family and other primary bonds. However, Republican voters appeared to conform more strongly than Democrats to family influence. See their "Primary Group Influence on Party Loyalty," *American Political Science Review* 53 (September, 1959), pp. 757-76. Eugene S. Uyeki and Richard W. Dodge arrived at similar conclusions on the general impact of parental partisanship on the political perspectives of their children. See their "Generational Relations in Political Affiliation and Involvement," *Sociology and Social Research,* 48 (January, 1964), pp. 155-65. Also relevant is Eldersveld's tabular observation on party ideology and the father's political preference and activity. See his *Political Parties, op. cit.,* pp. 212-14.
11. The Lynds' *Middletown in Transition, op. cit.,* pp. 358-72, was one of the first studies to systematically appraise the relationship between class

position and voting, in this case, the 1936 presidential election. Also see Alfred W. Jones' similar findings in the same election in his *Life, Liberty, and Property* (Philadelphia: Lippincott, 1941), pp. 315-17.

12. See Gerhard Lenski, *Power and Privilege* (New York: McGraw-Hill, 1966), pp. 64-5, 71. Also see John C. Leggett, *Class, Race, and Labor, op. cit.,* pp. 1-18, 96-130.
13. For a summary and well documented statement on the much researched matter of status crystallization, see Gerhard Lenski's *Power and Privilege, op. cit.,* pp. 86-8.
14. Lenski, *ibid.,* p. 87.
15. Lenski, *ibid.,* has phrased the matter in the following way:

> . . . an individual with inconsistent statuses or ranks has a natural tendency to think of himself in terms of that status or rank which is highest, and to expect others to do the same. Meanwhile, others who come in contact with him have a vested interest in doing just the opposite, that is, in treating him in terms of his lowest status or rank.
>
> One can see how this works, and the consequences of it, by imagining the interaction of a Negro doctor and a white laborer in a situation where neither the racial nor occupational status system alone is relevant. The former, motivated by self-interest, will strive to establish the relation on the basis of occupation (or perhaps education or wealth), while the latter, similarly motivated, will strive to establish the relationship on the basis of race. Since each regards his own point of view as right and proper, and since neither is likely to view the problem in a detached, analytical fashion, one, or both, are likely to be frustrated, and probably angered, by the experience.
>
> The practice of "one-upmanship," as this pattern of action has sometimes been called, is so common in everyday life that most who indulge in it hardly give it any thought. The net effect, however, is to create considerable stress for many persons of inconsistent status. As a result, such persons are likely to find social interaction outside the bounds of the primary group (where others tend to be like themselves) somewhat less rewarding than does the average person.

16. For a full discussion of the skidder and his propensity to be traditional and conservative, see the last section of Chapter 5.
17. A number of the studies have commented on the propensity of Jews to vote for liberal and progressive parties and candidates even when they had become middle class. In our Berkeley data, we found that of the 25 Jews observed, only four preferred the Republican party, while the overwhelming majority suppored the Democratic organization. This distribution occurred despite the fact that almost 90 percent of the study's Jews turned out to be white collar. These findings are by no means unusual. Maurice G. Guysenir studied a predominantly Jewish ward in Chicago in 1952 and found that Jews voted very heavily for Stevenson. No matter how he analyzed Jews, they sided with this Democratic party candidate. However, Guysenir found one significant difference within the Jewish community; he observed that Jews with high socio-economic status voted less often for Stevenson (62 percent) as compared to middle (73 percent)

and low (95 percent) socio-economic status categories. See his "Jewish Vote in Chicago," *Jewish Social Studies,* 20 (October, 1958), pp. 195-214. Joseph S. Roucek analyzed a 1964 U.S. Gallup poll which indicated that the Jewish community comprised one of the most Democratic religious groups in the U.S. electorate; Democrats outnumbered Republicans 4 to 1. See his "The Role of Religion in American Politics," *The Journal of Human Relations*, 11 (Spring, 1963), pp. 350-62. In 1960, Angus Campbell and others also observed that Democratic Jews outnumbered Republican Jews 4 to 1. They argued that:

> This appears to be largely a consequence of the Depression and subsequent events during the Roosevelt period. During the 1920's the vote in heavily Jewish districts of the eastern metropolises ran as high as 80 per cent Republican. Although vote is not the same as party identification, it can scarcely be doubted that the orientation of this group toward the two parties was substantially altered during the 1930's. We may surmise that the rise of the Nazi dictatorship in Germany and the opposition of the Roosevelt Administration to it must have played an important role in this change.

See Campbell, *et al., The American Voter, op. cit.,* p. 159.

18. Few treatments of Catholics make the necessary nationality distinctions. Still, they are useful. See, for example, Joseph S. Roucek's secondary analysis of "The Role of Religion in American Politics," *op. cit.,* pp. 350-62. He observed that in 1954 almost one-quarter of the U.S. population was Roman Catholic, and that of these a very high proportion was Democratic. Oscar Glantz reached similar conclusions in his study of Philadelphia during the early 1950's. See his "Protestant and Catholic Voting Behavior in a Metropolitan Area," *Public Opinion Quarterly,* 23 (Spring, 1959), pp. 73-82. Robert Alford analyzed the role of social class, regionalism, and religion. Focusing on presidential voting behavior as measured by public opinion surveys taken between 1936 and 1960, he gauged class voting by subtracting the percentage of nonmanual workers voting Democratic from the percentage of manual workers voting for the same party. Among his findings were (1) that class voting rose to its highest point in 1948; (2) that the move to the right during the Eisenhower elections did not erase the class differential in voting patterns so common in the 1930's; (3) that class voting is highest in the west central region of the U.S. and lowest in the South; and (4) that class voting varied much more among Catholics than among Protestants and was lowest (for the Catholics) in 1944 and 1960, when large numbers of middle-class Catholics swung behind the Democratic party candidate. Bernard Cosman compared Negro with white Protestant and white Catholic voting in Louisiana, and he found that Nixon did best in the 1960 presidential election in non-Catholic parishes with few Negroes. See his "Religion and Race in Louisiana Presidential Politics," *Southwestern Social Science Quarterly,* 43 (December, 1962), pp. 235-41, and J.S. Roucek, *op. cit.,* pp. 33-42. Angus Campbell and others in 1960 observed the

steady erosion of Democratic party strength inside the Catholic community as it became increasingly middle class in composition. See their *The American Voter, op. cit.*, p. 36.

19. John Porter, *The Vertical Mosaic* (Toronto: University of Toronto Press, 1965), p. 264.
20. We found that class-religious categories affiliated as expected: blue-collar Protestants were 36 percent Democratic (D), 39 percent Republican (R), and 23 percent Independent (I); white-collar, University Protestants were 34 percent D, 49 percent R, and 15 percent I; white-collar, non-University Protestants were 26 percent D, 65 percent R, and 9 percent I; blue-collar Catholics were 70 percent D, 20 percent R, and 7 percent I; white-collar, Catholic, University people were only six in number–two D, three R, and one I. White-collar, non-University Catholics were 48 percent D, 34 percent R, and 16 percent I. The remaining–never more than 3 percent in each case–consisted of those with other party preferences.
21. Sam Eldersveld went beyond the usual analysis of Catholics and dwelt at length on the significance of ethnicity inside the Catholic world. He found time and again that an eastern European Catholic group–Polish Detroiters–studied in the 1956 election included a disproportionately large number of Democratic party supporters; further, these Poles were found in unusually large numbers at all levels of the Democratic party; Detroiters of Catholic-Irish background gave considerably less support to the Democratic party. See his *Political Parties, op. cit.*, pp. 56, 57, 85, 93.
22. See Lenski, *Power and Privilege, op. cit.*, pp. 87-8.
23. Illustratively, Campbell and Cooper (*op. cit.*, p. 28) studied the 1954 congressional elections and observed that union membership was highly correlated with Democratic vote. Eldersveld's study of the 1956 congressional, state (Michigan), and U.S. vote (*op. cit.*, pp. 83-93, in particular) demonstrated time and again the impact of the union on voting preference and choice. Oscar Glantz's 1952 study of Philadelphia came up with the same findings on union impact. See his "Class Consciousness and Political Solidarity," in *American Sociological Review*, 23 (1958) pp. 375-83.
24. Among blue-collar, unionized Protestants only, 48 percent were Democratic (D), 22 percent Republican (R), 26 percent Independent (I), and 4 percent other. By contrast, blue-collar but nonunion Protestants were 21 percent D, 51 percent R, and 21 percent I. Among Catholic manual workers, 74 percent of the unionized were affiliated with the Democratic party, 21 percent with the Republican party, and 5 percent were Independent. In the comparable, nonunion category, it was 58 percent D, 17 percent R, 17 percent I, and 8 percent other.

FIVE

Class, Party Preference, and the Fair Housing Vote

Class position helps determine political identification which in turn partially transcends class tie when people act on racial questions, as in the 1963 Berkeley election. Blue-collar experiences should help create Democrats, while Democratic party affiliation should prompt many to vote in favor of a fair housing ordinance.

Oddly enough, even the experts have overlooked this possibility, including Lipset. Although Lipset has led the way in analyzing the impact of social class on voting commitment—indeed, he has presented what is perhaps the most extensive and useful review of the impact of class on political attitudes—he has neglected to consider how political loyalty relates to a racial vote.[1] Had he done so in his study of "political man"[2] or elsewhere, he might have discovered how, if at all, affiliation with political parties helps determine voting choices in fair housing and similar elections. For example, in California, voters register as Democrats, Republicans, or Independents. What has been the impact of these political ties on race relations?

Our remarks on party affiliation should not be interpreted to mean that class differences are irrelevant *within* political groupings. On the contrary, class differences on racial justice should be apparent, especially within the party of reform. There, the leadership resides inside the middle class and sets policy on matters of race. These middle-class reformers are more likely to act in favor of race legislation than are working-class people. Nonetheless, we should observe that when working-class people affiliate with the party of gradual change, more of them should be supporters of racial equality than in either class within the Republican Party, the key carrier of economic conservatism and racial traditionalism. In this sense, party affiliation should prove more significant than class and reflect the tone of the parties.[3]

When we assay the implications of our opinions for Lipset's theory on working-class authoritarianism, we observe how our approach differs fundamentally from his position. First, we focus on behavior, not attitude. The object of our analysis is to find out what people do, not what they say. Second, we view class as a significant source of political loyalties, but not as a primary cause of choice on racial matters; our intent is to explore the tie between political loyalty and choice on racial acceptance, a consideration overlooked by Lipset.

Let us develop this point, but before doing so perhaps we should keep in mind Lipset's views and examine the statistical significance of class and status phenomena as they bear on a fair housing vote. Then we can move to an analysis of political party preference. If we find that both class (as well as status considerations) and party preference are related to people's voting choices, we can then examine the impact of class on vote while taking into account the significance of party preference. This part of our analysis completed, we will consider the effect of party preference, keeping in mind class and status considerations.

CLASS EFFECT: THE BLUE-COLLAR VOTE

For the purpose of analysis let us assume that blue-collar workers include a relatively large number of authoritarians. (We will examine this assumption in Chapter 8.) Furthermore, let us hypothesize that these attitudinal tendencies lead a disproportionately large number of them to vote against fair housing.

Our analysis substantiates these expectations (see Table 11). Clearly, blue-collar ranks contained a relatively small number who voted in favor of fair housing–20 percent for the proposal, 46 percent against; one quarter did not vote. Among middle-class Berkeleyans, 38 percent cast their lot for having blacks as neighbors, while 44 percent lined up against fair housing; slightly less than 20 percent did not vote. These differences are statistically significant and *consistent* with Lipset's views.[4]

THE STATUS IMPACT: EDUCATION AND INCOME

How about the status considerations of education and income? On the whole, our information (Table 11) also falls in the same direction, although the data are not as clear-cut as in the case of class. Consider education: Only two categories, high school graduates and Ph.D.s (or equivalent), failed to vote as expected. (This failure stemmed from considerations explored in the last part

Table 11. Class, Status, and Fair Housing Vote (Whites Only)

	For Ordinance	Against	Did Not Vote	N
Class				
Working	20	56	24	(N=109)
Middle	38	44	18	(572)
Education				
Grade School (1-8)	11	64	25	(44)
Some High School (9-11)	26	62	12	(47)
High School Grad	17	58	25	(100)
College (1 M.A.)	33	48	19	(371)
M.A. (and higher)	61	19	20	(108)
Ph.D. (or equivalent)	44	40	16	(96)
Income				
Low ($0 - 3,999)	28	33	41	(115)
Medium ($4,000-- 7,999)	35	42	23	(179)
High ($8,000 +)	38	49	13	(430)

Key: For Ordinance (dark shading), Against (light shading), Did Not Vote (blank) of the chapter.) On the whole, however, the information proved to be substantially and predictably related to education.

What was true of education was also true of income, although the statistical differences were not as great as one might expect. Low-income people had the smallest portion (28 percent) voting in favor of the ordinance, while medium-and high-income Berkeleyans scored as expected—when we consider only the percentages in *favor* of the ordinance. On the other hand, if we note the percentage of voters *against* the ordinance, we can observe that low-income whites had the *smallest* proportion voting *against* the proposal—32 percent of the low earners, 42 percent of the medium, and 49 percent of the high earners. It might be safe to say then, that this piece of information on income and vote raises certain questions about the Lipset position. Consequently, we might benefit from observations on the connection between vote and considerations other than just class and status.

PARTY PREFERENCE

How was party affiliation connected to the fair-housing vote? Interestingly, party choice also worked out as expected (see Table 12). Among whites only, 15 percent of the Republicans voted for the ordinance; over four times as many lined up against it; and almost one-fifth failed to vote. Once again among whites, 54 percent of the Democrats favored the ordinance; 27 percent went against it; and 19 percent did not vote. Within the independent camp, the voting pattern fell half way between the two other (and larger) categories.[5]

These findings may pique some readers, for there would appear to be an inconsistency between these and the results discussed earlier on class and status. What was the apparent contradiction? Clearly, the white collar, better educated, and to a lesser degree, the high income categories contained more

Table 12. Party Preference and Vote (Whites Only)

Republican	15	67	18	(313)
Democrat	54	27	19	(328)
Independent	32	38	30	(105)

Key: See page 77.

than their share of supporters for fair housing; the data thereby reinforce our image of liberalism as permeating the middle class. Clearly also, Republicans were overwhelmingly against the ordinance. However, the information on party and vote moves us to pause and question self-celebration within the middle class on this matter, for the Grand Old Party has traditionally included a relatively *large* number of middle class, *better* educated, *high* income people—categories supposedly aligned *with* those forces in *favor* of the ordinance. How can one resolve this contradiction?

Class, Status, and Party Preference

Let us consider the impact of class and status while keeping in mind the prior significance of party preference. If we look at Table 13, it becomes apparent that class and status did *not* constitute important considerations: (1) there were more *blue*-collar Democrats (25 percent) than *white*-collar Republicans (15 percent) voting in favor of the ordinance; (2) there were *fewer* working-class (45 percent) than middle-class (71 percent) Republicans voting *against* the proposal; (3) only within the Democratic Party does the relationship between class and vote hold; here, the middle class (61 percent) far outdistanced the working class (25 percent) when it came to voting in favor of the proposal. In other words, when we consider the relationship between class and vote and simultaneously take into account the significance of party preference, class ceases to be significant. But the incidental significance of class in determining vote does not prove the relevance of party membership.

Put more precisely, if class considerations failed to relate to vote as expected, perhaps party affiliation will suffer from the same shortcoming. Indeed, when one examines the prior significance of class, the information

Table 13. Party, Class, and Fair Housing Vote (Whites Only)

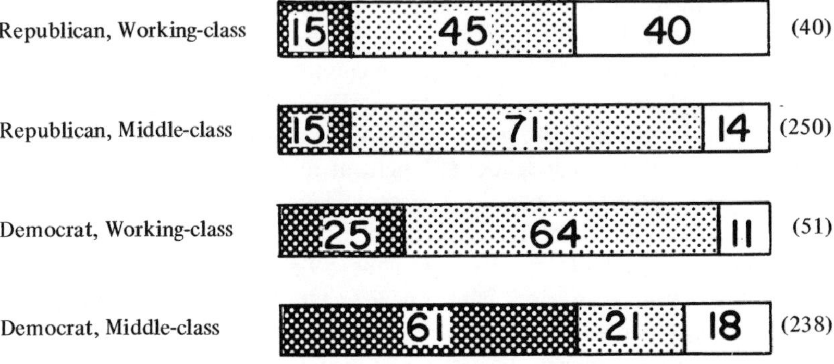

Key: See page 77

proves fascinating (see Table 11). Let us examine the data more closely, for they demonstrate that class considerations did *fail* to dispel the importance of party preference:[6] (1) within the blue-collar world, for every Republican who voted for the ordinance, three voted against it; (2) among blue-collar Democrats, for every one who voted for the ordinance, almost three opposed it; (3) among the middle-class Republicans, the vote was overwhelmingly against the ordinance; for every Republican who favored it, over four lined up as expected; (4) among comparable white-collar Democrats, almost the opposite was true. Obviously, then, party preference proved to be more significant than other considerations; it remained related to vote even when one examined the pertinence of class. In this statistical sense, party affiliation proved more powerful than class.

However, what may be true of class may not be true of the status considerations noted earlier. Perhaps education and personal income prove relevant when one takes into account the significance of party choice. However, Table 14 would indicate otherwise.

The relationship between education and vote disappears when one interprets the significance of party tie: (1) A higher proportion of the lesser educated Democrats voted for fair housing than was the case among most Republican categories; only among college educated Republicans (but no doctorates) were there relatively large numbers who favored the ordinance. (2) The lesser educated Republicans sometimes included more voters in favor of fair housing than was the case among the better educated Republicans–for example, among Republicans with some high school, 13 percent voted in favor of the ordinance and 74 percent cast their lot against it, and among Republicans with Ph.D.s, M.D.s, D.D.S.s, and L.L.D.s, 9 percent lined up for the ordinance and 79 percent against it. (3) This is not to say that education is without significance among the *Democrats;* on the contrary, education has a profound and consistent impact. As one moves from the lesser educated through the medium to the better educated, there is a serial-like increase in the proportion for the ordinance, except at the highest level of formal schooling, where fewer of the Ph.D.s and their counterparts scored for the ordinance than in the next lowest level. Among Democrats, the statistical differences are great, ranging from grade school (14 percent) in favor, 68 percent against) through some high school (31 percent in favor, 54 percent against), high school (33 percent in favor, 40 percent against), college, up to M.A. (59 percent in favor, 23 percent against, college, M.A. plus (84 percent in favor, 6 percent against), and Ph.D. and its equivalent (59 percent in favor, 18 percent against). Education, then, does have a near linear effect, but only within one of the two major parties.

Education has an impact, but it is screened by party affiliation. Let us re-examine Table 12 and be more precise on this matter. If one takes into

Table 14. Education, Political Party Preference and Vote (Whites Only)

Lesser Educated

Party Preference	*Education of Voter*											
	Grade School (1 – 8)				*Some High School (9 – 11)*				*High School (12)*			
	F	A	DNV	Total	F	A	DNV	Total	F	A	DNV	Total
Republican	(0)	(8)	(5)	(13)	(2)	(11)	(2)	(15)	(3)	(28)	(6)	(37)
	0%	62%	38%	100%	13%	74%	13%	100%	8%	76%	16%	100%
Democrats	(4)	(19)	(5)	(28)	(8)	(14)	(4)	(26)	(13)	(16)	(10)	(39)
	14%	69%	17%	100%	31%	54%	15%	100%	33%	40%	27%	100%

Better Educated

	College (Up to M.A.)				*College (M.A. plus)*				*Ph.D. and Others*			
	F	A	DNV	Total	F	A	DNV	Total	F	A	DNV	Total
Republican	(31)	(122)	(26)	(179)	(9)	(15)	(10)	(34)	(3)	(26)	(4)	(33)
	17%	68%	15%	100%	26%	45%	29%	100%	9%	79%	12%	100%
Democrats	(73)	(28)	(23)	(124)	(48)	(3)	(6)	(57)	(30)	(9)	(12)	(51)
	59%	23%	18%	100%	84%	6%	10%	100%	59%	18%	23%	100%

Legend: F = For housing ordinance
A = Against housing ordinance
DNV = Did not vote

account the prior significance of education, then it becomes clear that party preference operates in a predictable manner at all educational levels: (1) Among the least educated, *not one* of the thirteen Republicans eligible to take part in the election voted in favor of the ordinance; on the other hand, 14 percent of the Democrats voted for it. (2) If one examines those with some high school, almost the same percentage differences separate Democrats from Republicans. (3) Among high school graduates, exactly the same pattern occurs, while the percentage gap widens. (4) Within the lesser college category and among those without a master's degree, the hiatus becomes even wider, with 59 percent of the Democrats and only 17 percent of the Republicans voting for the ordinance. (5) Among those college graduates with an M.A. but not a Ph.D., the Democrats (84 percent) far outdistanced the Republicans (26 percent) on the vote for fair housing. (6) Finally, a 50 percent difference separated Democrats from Republicans with Ph.D.s or their equivalent.

Nevertheless, the class-status hypothesis might have stood up had we considered personal income when examining the pertinence of party affiliation. Perhaps, for example, personal income operates independently of party identification. However, Table 15 suggests otherwise. If we make a distinction between low and high earners[7] and examine only whites, our results clearly indicate that personal income operates in an inconsistent manner. Among Republicans, a larger proportion of low-income than high-income people were *in favor* of fair housing. Just the opposite tendency occurred among Democrats. However, as you will recall, both patterns are consistent with our information on occupation and education.

Table 15 also indicates that party affiliation had a greater effect than income. You will observe that low-income Democrats (42 percent) more than

Table 15. Party, Income, and Fair Housing Vote (Whites Only)

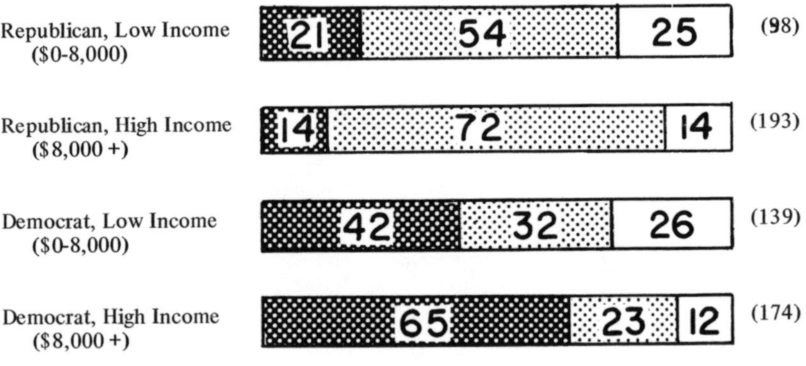

Key: See page 77.

low-income Republicans (21 percent) voted for the ordinance, while a 50 percent difference separated high-income Democrats (65 percent) and Republicans (14 percent). Once again, we see the minimal significance of a status consideration.

Party choice proves important. It is so significant that it helps to explain why high school graduates (see Table 11) included *fewer* in favor of fair housing than was the case among those with some high school education. When we recall Table 11 and focus on those with a high school diploma, we can observe that a disproportionately large number—almost two-thirds—were Republicans and that few (three out of 31 voters) cast their lot for the proposal. Consequently, we now know why the result on high school preference took such a nonpredictable form—a great many high school graduates turned out to be Republicans.

Ph.D. and Party Preference

However, our figures fail to explain why fewer Ph.D.s and equivalents should support fair housing than those only slightly less educated, for the Democratic Ph.D.s (and equivalents) outnumbered the Republicans almost 5 to 3. How, then, can we account for the unexpectedly large number of Ph.D.s who voted against fair housing? In trying to answer this question, we would be remiss to overlook the simultaneous significance of *types* of higher degree obtained and political party preferred. If one distinguishes among Ph.D.s, L.L.D.s, D.D.S.s, and M.D.s, the results prove fascinating (see Table 16). Two important observations can be derived from the data: (1) Ph.D.s—followed by law school graduates—led over other advanced degree holders in voting against the ordinance. (2) Democrats leaned heavily to one side while Republicans pressed noticeably in the opposite direction. Of these two points, perhaps party preference would seem most pertinent. Among Republicans with a Ph.D., for example, *only one out of 19,* or 6 percent, voted for the ordinance. On the other hand, 21 of the 37 Democrats did so. We might approach the figures on Ph.D.s in yet another way. Among Republicans, for every one who voted for the ordinance, fourteen cast their lot against it. Among Democrats, for every five who voted for it, one lined up against fair housing. If we examine the data on voters holding law, medical, and dental degrees, the same pattern occurs, although the number of cases tails off significantly.

Perhaps one more point is worth noting. We can observe how professions help color attitude, especially among Democrats. Within this group, more lawyers, dentists, and M.D.s were against the ordinance than was the case among professionals with Ph.D.s. In this regard, the differences are not great but discernible. Of course, we do not have many cases in Table 16, especially for physicians and dentists; hence, we do not wish to mislead the reader into believing that this information constitutes convincing evidence. Our data only suggest the actual distribution.

Table 16. Type of Higher Degree and Vote on Fair Housing (Whites Only)

Type of Higher Degree		Vote on Fair Housing*			
		For	Against	Did Not Vote	Total
Ph.D.	Rep.	1	14	4	19
	Dem.	21	4	12	37
L.L.D.	Rep.	1	4	0	5
	Dem.	5	3	0	8
M.D.	Rep.	0	6	0	6
	Dem.	3	2	0	5
D.D.S.	Rep.	1	2	0	3
	Dem.	1	0	0	1

*Because of the few cases involved, we have not calculated percentages.

Perhaps most surprising would be the lack of impact of increased education within the Republican population, especially among those with higher degrees. Our information would strongly suggest that education among Republicans does *not* increase progressive action but perhaps makes most of them more sophisticated in concocting verbalisms directed against the idea of having blacks as neighbors. Although there were exceptions–education would seem to have made them more agile in this regard–they spelled out in no uncertain terms why they voted against the proposal when asked "Why did you vote the way you did?" Here are their verbatim replies:

> [*Self-employed dentist*] No one is going to tell me what to do with my own property. I believe Negroes ought to have rights to use public facilities–but I feel I should be allowed to do what I please with my own property.

> [*Research Associate in Physiology, University of California*] I don't want anybody to tell me what to do with my property–whom to rent to, and the like. I'm scared to death of Negroes. They are a primitive race, and they just run wild. Race revolution is one of the tenets of the Communist Manifesto. It's Communist inspired. I hope they don't get any Negroes up here [the Berkeley Hills] because it will be ruined. I don't mean civilized and cultured people. The Negroes are 200,000 years behind the rest of the human race. Savages.

[*Self-employed physician*] I felt that house owners had the right to select their own buyers. Coercion should not be used.

[*Self-employed dentist*] Property values would go down. Also, you can't legislate equality. Man has a right to do as he wishes with his property.

[*Retired surgeon formerly employed at a large midwestern university*] I voted against it because of the section that restricted the preference of whom my wife could rent rooms to if I passed away. However, I do feel that apartment and actual boarding house owners should integrate.

[*President of a large mining company*] The proposed ordinance took out of the hands of the courts the power that they deserve and put the power in the hands of a committee. It took away some individual rights.

[*Retired physician*] I felt that it was against the American plan of dealing with private property as you see fit. I'm not a segregationist, and I don't feel that others are bigoted simply because they voted against the ordinance. I voted against the ordinance–not so much as a partisan thing–because I wanted to be loyal to my neighbors. Also, I feel that a person should sell to whomever he pleases. You should know whom you're selling to–I'm not against Negroes, you understand. . . .

[*Professor of Electrical Engineering, University of California*] Number one –the penalty clause. I just couldn't see it. Furthermore, I don't like this guy Chamberlain. Even if he is a physicist and prize award winner at the University, I think he's an egotistical little guy and politically we're on opposite sides of the fence.

[*Attorney and Professor of Law, University of California*] I voted against the penal provisions, making it a misdemeanor for a property owner to exercise his freedom of choice in considering prospective buyers or renters. I don't think a person should be fined or given a jail sentence for this. I don't feel a person should be legally forced to stand before a conciliation board and be faced with possible conviction for exercising his rights as a private property owner.

[*Self-employed physician also doing research for the University of California*] There are two bad things–the prison and the fine. If I didn't accept a colored man, it would mean prison and a fine. That's what's wrong with the Rumford Act. It's wrong. It's an invasion of one's personal rights. The better class Negroes didn't want it.

[*Biochemist employed by the State Health Department*] Because I think people have a right to dispose of property the way they wish.

[*Self-employed consulting chemical engineer*] I voted against it because it is bad legislation. It is impossible to legislated acceptance and tolerance.

[*Self-employed M.D.*] It's not a democratic thing; it forces something down people's throats. The ordinance takes away people's rights. I want to be able to sell my home to whom I want. My neighbors are dear to me. I don't want to put Negroes between them. The ordinance takes away our liberties and puts everyone in the same category. It destroys individuality. I like Negroes, for I was raised with them but not on a socially equal basis. But I don't think there should be any mixing at all of Negroes and whites in a neighborhood. I think neighborhoods should be all white or black, but not in between. When you get mixing, you get intermarriage. Furthermore, once a white steps down, he is as good as black. Of course, I wouldn't put in a Negro as president either or as president of a school board as just happened. I think it's a white man's country and feel a little bit like a South African white. I wouldn't do anything if a Negro moved in across the street, but I would try to buy the house out from under him. I just don't want them in the neighborhood. I don't feel it's right.

[*Retired, self-employed dentist*] It's an infringement on rights; it's one step along, then something else. I wish to choose my neighbors by selling to whom I wish.

[*Executive for a mining corporation*] I think that many people felt it was a violation of their property rights. It was a violation of private rights.

[*Professor of Anthropology, University of California*] I think this kind of legislation should be on a state basis, not local and in a community such as Berkeley.

[*Retired director of Elementary Science Project, University of California*] I do not deny the rights of the Negro but I don't think government should meddle in private affairs. I don't want government in the private sector.

[*Professor at the University of California*] The ordinance is wrong in its conception. I'm not in favor of the ordinance as written. It is against individual rights in trying to protect the rights of others.

[*Retired college teacher, University of California*] It doesn't offer protection to private property rights. Also, it's an encroachment of free speech. Some processes are allowed to the plaintiff that are not allowed to the defendents; the ordinance provided unequal representation in the due process clause.

[*Self-employed consulting geologist*] Human rights leave me cold. I don't expect anybody else to provide for me, the hell with everybody else. People are soft-headed because of 40 years of socialism. Being soft-headed is being concerned about others at one's own expense. Soft-headedness arises because people have nothing or have a lot, for example, F.D.R. and Wallace [Henry Wallace, the 1948 Progressive party candidate]. I voted against the ordinance as a matter of principle; I believe in the preservation and handling of what you own should be up to you. One segment of the community shouldn't be elevated to a preferential position. I feel that law enforcement shouldn't be in the hands of a kangaroo court. Law would be in the hands of those not burdened by a sense of law or an idea of property. The administration of law should be in the hands of the courts, not in the hands of an amateurish city council.

[*Self-employed attorney*] I think the ordinance constitutes an unnecessary infringement of property rights. I did *not* vote against Negroes. If you lose ownership rights, you lose personal rights. Human rights are not more important than property rights. We must not restrict freedom in any form as long as you don't impinge on the rights of others.

[*Consulting engineer and Professor Emeritus, University of California*] It wasn't a good fair housing ordinance. One should, if he owns or sells or rents, be able to choose whom he should sell or rent to.

[*Self-employed lawyer*] The ordinance involves criminal responsibility. It's too drastic.

[*Retired Professor of Plant Pathology, University of California*] I didn't like it. It forced you into a straight-jacket. It's a step toward government regulation of everything. It's very restrictive.

[*Self-employed attorney*] Personally, my neighbors would not want me to sell to anyone whom the neighbors would not approve of—colored or white. I did not approve of a *law* limiting selling to someone the neighbors didn't like or accept. Also, the rights of personal property and the privilege of the final decision of whom to sell to belongs to the owner.

[*Professor of Virology, University of California*] I felt the ordinance took away basic property rights, and I don't think any law should be passed that has that effect. Also, this was mainly a city issue and the ordinance wouldn't affect the state as a whole. Perhaps if it had been a state-wide issue and would be effective on a broader level, such a proposal might be more feasible.

[*Retired Professor of Education, University of California*] I didn't feel it was fair.

Several peculiar themes emerge. First, property rights take precedence over other things. Second, it's not that these Republicans disliked blacks, it's that they disliked laws that throttled their individual liberties, especially those of property relationships. Third, and this theme runs counter to the second one, it's not that they disliked fair housing legislation but thought state rather than local laws would be more appropriate.

UNION MEMBERSHIP, DOWNWARD MOBILITY, AND THE LAW OF EVOLUTIONARY POTENTIAL

If Republican white-collar professionals sounded like skilled justifiers of the racial *status quo*, what kind of noises did blue-collar people make, especially Democratic rank-and-file trade unionists?[8] More precisely, how is union membership related to fair housing? How do our findings fit our previous remarks on downward mobility, the law of evolutionary potential and working-class authoritarianism, keeping in mind that we expect union impact to be of slight significance in this overwhelmingly white-collar community?

When discussing the significance of union impact, we must make minimal distinctions. Without attempting to be exhaustive, we offer the following questions to illustrate our point:

(1) Does union membership make an individual more likely (than the remainder of the population) to vote for fair housing?

(2) In the blue-collar world where more unions exist and have a demonstrated impact on politics, do union members support or oppose fair housing?

(3) Inside each of the two major parties, what is the significance of blue-collar unionism?

(4) What is the joint importance of blue-collar unionism and working-class consciousness within both major political organizations, but especially the Democratic party?

(5) Among blue-collar union members, is there a difference between (a) those who descend from the middle class into the working class and consequently suffer a loss in prestige and those who (b) grow up in the working class and remain in the blue-collar world? In other words, does unionism have an impact on the skidder as well as the nonskidder, and if so, can we discern the effect in both major parties?

(6) If unionism does prove to be significant in one or more of these contexts, why should this be the case?

(7) How do our empirical findings match our general expectations (see Chapter 7) on the law of evolutionary potential?

Many writers have avoided making the necessary distinctions among types of unions, referring instead to discriminatory actions of American unions in general.[9] With a few notable exceptions, these analysts have ignored the differences between craft and industrial unions and neglected the positive contributions of industrial labor organizations.[10] Specifically, many observers have arrived at valid conclusions on the behavior of craft union leaders, but they have applied these generalizations to all organized labor in general—all leaders and all rank-and-file—thereby lumping together different forms of unions, varieties of leaders and rank-and-file memberships.

Perhaps most questionable is an analytical hesitance to distinguish between the actions of labor leaders and the choices of rank-and-file members. This conceptual laxity is reprehensible, for there is no one-to-one correlation between the views of leaders and ordinary members. Considering just the logical possibilities, there are at least four alternatives: (1) a leader who discriminates (in his voting habits) and a rank-and-file member who does not; (2) the reverse; (3) leadership and membership both discriminate; (4) both do not.

Let us elaborate on the first possibility. It would seem that many union leaders can discriminate while many white rank-and-file—admittedly a minority—go their own way and promote equality. This rank-and-file category should emerge, especially among the better educated workers, partially because of a humanist sympathy for the underdog, and partially because of a general view rooted in attachments to liberating groups and experiences.

This propensity appeared in many of the replies given by blue-collar whites who belonged to unions and who voted for the Berkeley Fair Housing ordinance. Here's how they—almost all Democrats—justified their votes:

> [*Retired metal worker*] That's the way I thought I should do it. People want places to live. People should be able to live where they want. *Why do you think most people voted against it?* Too much money, I guess. They don't like the colored. People with a lot of money don't like to mix with other races.
>
> [*Machinist*] We feel like it's right. How would God feel about such a thing. We're all weak when it comes right down to it. *Why do you think most people voted against the ordinance?* People just have an inner fear—fear of intermarriage. I often wonder if my children were young again how I would feel there.
>
> [*Assistant foreman in a cemetery*] Everyone needs a chance in life for the good things. A fair-housing law is a way of giving Negrooes that chance. They can get better education and more self-respect. I am certainly for that.
>
> [*Retired refinery worker for Standard Oil*] You have to live with them. *Why do you think most people voted against it?* I don't know why they don't make up their minds to live with them. I'm surrounded by colored; they live all around me. I don't know why they don't make up their minds to live with them.
>
> [*Machinist for Kaiser Aircraft and Electronics*] In the long run it's better for the economy and race problems. Such legislation is possible as a helpful force toward solving race problems.
>
> [*Longshoreman—from Georgia*] The ordinance provided for something which was necessary in Berkeley—a beginning step. *Why do you think most people voted against it?* The basic reason was prejudice and misinformation. Many who voted against it thought it was more sweeping than it actually was—they thought it meant taking people of another race into their homes.
>
> [*Retired ship carpenter*] Well, the reason for having laws interfering with people is that even for good things it is necessary to have law enforcement. I felt it was a worthy and good thing to have restrictions for that purpose. If it is considered a sacrifice, the sacrifice should be considered an achievement about property rights. I feel very strongly about the least destruction of property whether I own it or not. I think the sit-ins of CORE was the wrong thing to do. It was like a miniature mob violence. It can get out of control and does harm. That should be related to the sacredness of property and people's rights everywhere. I always put, as I have said, the people's rights foremost. *Why do you think most people voted against it?* Because their hearts are too hard. The solution of the races lies in the heart of the

people. They felt property rights came first. I feel the opposite—the people come first.

[*Ink maker for a printing company*] I feel that if somebody wants to move in next to me, I don't care—I live in a neighborhood with various races. We're pretty happy around here.

[*Ski repairman*] It is unfortunate that something like that is necessary but since it is, then there should be a law. It is a poorly written law, however.

[*Printer*] I favor integration. The gradual method doesn't work, however; it has to be legislated.

[*Retired printer*] People have the right to live where they please.

[*Gardener and landscaper*] I believe the colored people are sufficiently educated to know the law and when they're breaking it.

[*Warehouse foreman*] I believe in equal rights.

[*Truck driver*] I voted for it because it was a fair ordinance.

Union Impact

As we have already indicated, working-class people should be most likely to support a fair-housing proposal not only when they belong to a union but also affiliate with a reform party. The political organization should prove relevant because it carries and espouses beliefs that are potentially acceptable among its members. These party notions should find greatest acceptance among workmen who carry certain class views. More precisely, unionized Democrats should both identify with the working class and vote for fair housing. Unionized workmen should be more likely to support egalitarian action on race when they belong to a party that calls for civil rights legislation, and when they hold views that move them to identify with a class that contains large numbers of minorities. Presumably, identification with the working class will sometimes be associated with sentiments of intraclass solidarity, and these views should cross-cut racial and ethnic groups. This mental connection will not be uncommon to all workmen who identify with their class, for there are many who view themselves as members of the working class but reject minorities, as we shall see.

Membership in a union should be an important consideration in analyzing a vote on fair housing among blue-collar people from both working- and middle-class families. When a person leaves the middle and joins the working class, his friends and relatives define the move as lamentable and inform the person about his misfortune. During these moments of apparent concern, the individual views himself as less of a person than he might otherwise be. In effect, he defines himself as having less prestige because of the opinions of "significant" others. In some instances he is likely to criticize himself for personal failure, while at the same time irrationally blaming his dim destiny on those powerless, letarianized, racial minorities who have allegedly connived to deny him his proper position and status. With this mentality, the skidders should stand out in terms of opposition to proposals such as a fair-housing ordinance.

But unionization should counter this tendency for skidders to deprecate and reject minorities, especially when there are indications that they simultaneously: (1) come from both middle-class and reformist families (Democratic, Socialist, and the like); (2) give indication of high educational achievement (at least by working-class standards); and (3) belong to unions with high evolutionary potential.

Unfortunately for this analysis, Bay Area unionism in 1963 included few such organizations. In most cases, we had arrived a good 30 years too late. By the early 1960s, the few Bay Area unions were relatively undifferentiated, unspecialized, and uncoordinated, although the industrial unions were more democratic in this regard than the craft organizations. Hence, an egalitarian position on race could not be written on a blank piece of union stationery, for fear of being soiled by years of racial indifference at best, and racial intolerance at worst.

In our sample, almost all unionists belonged to old-time groups such as the carpenters', printers', and teamsters' organizations. A handful were in the industrial unions. The relative paucity of workmen in groups such as the longshoremen and auto unions, especially in Berkeley, makes it statistically impossible for us to differentiate between those who belonged to traditional unions (craft and teamsters, for example) and newer ones (the auto and longshore groups, among others). Hence, we must observe that most of the unionists were much alike, that is, members of relatively elaborated unions in terms of organization. Yet, for the purposes of analysis, we can define unionists as if they belonged to organizations having a high degree of evolutionary potential—in reality, a propensity to be racially egalitarian—on the question of minorities, even though this democratic tendency cannot be found in most of them. The reader might reject our classification—one that combines unionists in both types of unions—for it biases our results. That objection would be understandable. There is a bias, but it runs contrary to the acceptance of our hypothesis on the law of evolutionary potential. In effect, when we include craft unionists and teamsters in our category of unionists, we are stacking the cards *against* the acceptance of this chapter's key hypothesis and this book's favorite assumptions.

With this bit of necessary methodology as a backdrop, we can now proceed to the pertinent questions and results. In part because of the statistical detail involved and paucity of cases sometimes presented, we have placed the statistical evidence in Appendix A.

The Union Vote

(1) *Setting aside the blue-white collar distinction for a moment, do we find that union membership makes its members more likely to vote for fair housing than the rest of the population?*

If one considers unionists in both the blue-collar and white-collar worlds, the answer is "no." Table A-1 (Appendix A) indicates the differences involved. Within the white union world, 29 percent and 46 percent voted for and against the ordinance, respectively. Among white nonunionists, the same vote was 36 percent and 44 percent.

Yet our analysis is too simple on this point, for the information in Table A-1 fails to address itself to the heart of the controversy on unionism and race, namely, does union membership make a difference inside the working class?

(2) *In the blue-collar world, where most of the unionists are and where they are expected to count in politics, do union members stand out as supporters of fair housing?*

It is difficult to answer this question, for we lacked the number of cases to conduct a convincing inquiry. Still, the statistical distributions are indicative. If we examine only the voting unionists within the working class, we find that 14 out of 40 favored the proposal, while 8 out of 33 nonunionists voted for fair housing (see Table A-2). The differences are present but hardly significant.

Yet even if one views these differences as significant, one can still wonder about the results. Perhaps we obtained them because an unusually large number of unionists happened to be Democrats. Had we controlled for party preference, the relationship between union membership and vote might have disappeared.

(3) *Inside both major parties, what is the significance of blue-collar unionism?*

If we examine Table A-3, we can only conclude that unions have the least impact upon unionists who belong to a political organization *opposed* to housing integration, for personal affiliation with groups having conflicting values seldom leads to forthright action for those involved. And what is true of individual affiliation would also be true of categories or groups articulated with collectivities having contradictory values on controversial matters such as race.

Specifically, one of the 11 Republican unionists voted for the ordinance, while 4 out of the 20 nonunionists cast votes for the proposal. The reader might be skeptical about these results, for the number of cases is small, especially among the unionists. Still, the evidence might well be indicative of how Republican unionists voted on fair housing, at least within the blue-collar sector of Berkeley.

On the other hand, union affiliation had its greatest impact among those unionists who belonged to a party committed to support fair housing. Almost one-third of the Democratic trade unionists voted for it.

Given the findings discussed in the earlier chapters, it would seem that the majority of white blue-collar workers will pull for a fair-housing bill under the following circumstances: (1) their parties and unions press them to support racial acceptance; (2) they live beyond the pale of organized religion; (3) they have at least a high school diploma. To sum up, group ideas command the most obedience when they converge on a category of persons. At the same time, noninvolvement in discriminatory organizations facilitates support for a racial minority, especially among workmen having a wide range of formal education.

We are not saying that these and other necessary sources of racial acceptance come to bear simultaneously, nor with equal force. We are not judging their serial connections and uneven weights. This knotty problem we leave to future thought and research. We are simply suggesting some of the factors to be taken into account when trying to assess the sources of working-class support on one dimension of racial intimacy.

As yet, we have said nothing about *class identification* and its significance among blue-collar unionists in the Democratic party. Hopefully, this social-psychological dimension should create a few votes for fair housing.

(4) *What is the significance of blue-collar unionism and working-class identification in the Democratic party?*

Unfortunately, we almost run out of cases for this part of our analysis. Yet it would be unwise to overlook the distribution shown in Table A-4. When blue-collar, Democrat unionists identified with the middle class, 7 out of 27 (25 percent) voted for the proposal; when they identified with working class, 3 out of 8 (37 percent) lined up for fair housing. Class identification would therefore seem to be of some significance, however minimal. On the other hand, if we look only at nonunion members, identification with the working class seems irrelevant. In this category, a very small number of blue-collar people supported fair housing, and those who did viewed themselves as middle class. Of course, we are not saying that blue-collar identification with the middle class moves *all* of these particular persons to vote for such an ordinance. This kind of statement would misconstrue what we said and misinterpret what we have found.

At best, these results dimly suggest subpopulation preferences, for it is clear that we have run out of cases in this part of our analysis and no doubt exhausted the credulity of the reader. Nonetheless, our scanning of the empirical materials has proved useful, for we have presented evidence that suggests the importances—however minimal—of union affiliation.

We can now ask how unionism contributed to the views of those who are mobile.

(5) *Among blue-collar people, does union membership make a difference when people move from the middle into the working class and consequently suffer a loss in prestige? In other words, does unionism have an impact on the skidder,*[11] *and if so, can we discern its effect in both major parties?*

Before we answer this question, perhaps we should distinguish among four types of people assessed in terms of their mobility experiences; (a) *middle-class stationaries*; (2) *upwardly mobiles*; (3) *working-class stationaries*; (4) *skidders*.

(1) The middle-class stationary is one from middle-class parentage and is himself in the white-collar world. The literature on class and mobility would suggest that this level should contain the fewest number of prejudiced people. We would add that previous theory and research overemphasizes prejudice and neglects action, be it discriminatory or otherwise. (For an example, see our discussion in Chapter 8 of an authoritarian personality.) Previous work on mobility may on occasion make the distinction between thought and act (an example would be the work of Bettleheim and Janowitz, materials to be discussed later in this chapter), but most materials continue to focus on ethnic attitudes, ignoring discriminatory behavior and overlooking party affiliation. Still, in spite of our justifiable carping, we would expect this aggregate to line up heavily for fair housing, provided we ignore the salience of party preference.

(2) The upwardly mobiles do not have a clear-cut record. The information on this type is uneven. There is some evidence to indicate a high incidence of antisemitism among those who rise from the working to the middle class. This is partially understandable, given the keen competition between Christians and Jews for prestige occupational positions. On the other hand, upwardly mobiles may well identify with the underdog, as when a disproportionately large number support reform and revolutionary parties, as upwardly mobiles have quite frequently done according to data assembled by Lipset and Zetterberg.[12] Consistently enough, the literature on race also demonstrates that upwardly mobiles contain fewer bigots than the cluster dropping down into the blue-collar world from the middle class. The literature not only compares the upwardly mobile favorably with the skidder but finds more tolerance among them than within the working class, partially because of the civilizing effect of education upon occupational climbers who attach themselves to political organizations committed to the advancement of minority interests.

(3) The working-class stationaries are at least second generation blue-collar —what most people have in mind when they talk about "the working class."

They are born into the blue-collar world, and they stay there. To put it more precisely, most working-class kids grow up, take manual jobs, and stick with them for most of their lives. In this sense, they qualify as stationaries, having remained in the same class as their fathers.

Their class ties, hence their traditionalism on matters of race, should lead many to vote against fair housing. Stationaries should contain a high proportion of people opposed to fair housing. In this respect, only one group should surpass the working class stationaries–skidders.

(4) About the skidder, the literature is fairly clear cut. Bettleheim and Janowitz have observed the variety of ways in which downwardly mobiles express their conservatism. They have also discussed why skidders should score in this manner:

> Downward mobility is seen as a sociological process which has effects on psychological processes connected with personal control. We are aware, of course, that psychological processes contribute to mobility, particularly to mobility different from dominant societal trends. But the underlying rationale was that downward mobility as a social process would increase feelings of subjective deprivation and insecurity, which would contribute to hostility and prejudice. Likewise, from a psychological orientation, the sociological variables would lend understanding to the context. We believe the same approach would be relevant for a range of social behavior broader than ethnic intolerance.[13]

Bettleheim and Janowitz's materials leave little doubt as to where we should place the downwardly mobiles on the question of fair housing; they would seldom favor it.

Interestingly, the literature on racial prejudice bypasses the simultaneous impact of the unions, party preference, and mobility. Hence, we may find some surprising results.

To sum up, when we rank people by the four types of mobility experiences described above, they should score high and low on fair housing in this order: (1) middle-class stationaries; (2) upwardly mobiles; (3) working-class stationaries; and (4) skidders (or downwardly mobiles).

With the exception of our material on working class stationaries, the evidence does work out as expected (see Table A-5): (1) middle-class stationaries voted almost one-to-one for the proposal; (2) upwardly mobiles went approximately 10 to 7 against it; (3) working-class stationaries voted 6 to 1 against it; and (4) skidders voted 2 to 1 against the fair-housing ordinance.

The last finding may seem unusual. We had expected the skidders category to contain the fewest number supporting fair housing. But if we consider blue-collar workers only, an uneven distribution of Democrats may account for the high number of fair-housing supporters among the skidders as well as the low number of supporters among the stationaries. And what is true of blue-collar people may also be the case inside the white-collar world. Perhaps the white-collar stationaries came out on top because so many of them happened to be Democrats.

Is this the case? When one controls for party preference, several startling things do happen, occurrences that can only be of some importance for the literature on downward mobility (see Table A-6): (1) Among middle-class stationaries, there are wide differences between Democrats and Republicans. (This evidence suggests that our data are either unique or that previous research on downward mobility has neglected the connection between political affiliation and ethnic-racial behavior.) (2) The differences between working-class stationaries and skidders become less when we consider Democrats only. (3) Among Republicans, the gap between stationaries and skidders widens. However, we cannot make a convincing estimate because of the small number of cases.

Perhaps these results would fail to be altogether convincing even if we were to have more data, for we have neglected to take into account the pertinence of union membership. When we view its salience (see Table A-7), several things happen: (1) Unionism fails to be significant in accounting for the views of white-collar Democrats. These findings should not surprise us, since University people happened to be the hard core of fair-housing supporters within the white-collar, Democratic world, and only a fraction of University Democrats belonged to a union. (2) However, among Democrats in the blue-collar world, unionism did appear to be important, for union skidders and stationaries scored highly, with skidder Democrats having the highest percentage for fair housing. (3) Among Republicans, unionism apparently counts for little. (4) If we consider nonunion Democrats (both white and blue collar), mobility status proves to be irrelevant. If we consider only workers classified in rows 11 and 12 of Table A-7 we can observe the absence of support for fair housing. This particular result might seem surprising, for the Democratic party is supposedly the party of change and progress on matters of race legislation, especially inside the blue-collar world. (5) While mobility status may have been relevant among nonunion Republicans, the paucity of cases precludes making any interpretive remarks.

Yet we are struck with a point that runs counter to our general expectations.

Unionized Democrat skidders still contain a relatively large number who voted for fair housing. One wonders about these results, if only because education appeared to be extremely significant among Democrats. If this were the case, and if a combination of liberating circumstances should prove to be most effective in creating a fair-housing vote, shouldn't the amount of formal education override mobility status among the unionized in the party of reform? In that case, if we consider only unionized Democratic skidders (and nonskidders) then: (1) among the least educated (both skidders and stationaries), relatively few should have voted for fair housing; (2) among the better educated, skidders should not differ from stationaries; (3) fewer of the least educated skidders should have favored fair housing than was the case among educated stationaries.

If we examine only the skidders among the least educated, unionized, blue-collar Democrats, we find that 2 voted in favor and 4 went against the proposal (see Table A-8). Within the other significant category—the better educated—the vote was 4 to 4.

When we observe the impact of education among the blue-collar stationaries, we find a similar and predictable effect: (1) within the least educated category, the vote was 3 to 1 against (as opposed to 2 to 1 against within a comparable category of skidders); (2) among the better educated, the vote was 2½ to 1 against the ordinance (as opposed to 1 to 1 within the corresponding skidder category).

Among the better educated, skidders and stationaries did not differ. If we compare the least educated skidders with the better educated stationaries, the skidders (2 to 1 against) come out ahead of the better educated stationaries (2½ to 1 against). Why the skidders should continue to remain ahead on this matter may be partially explained by the party affiliation of their parents, a subject we will take up in our interpretation of the results.

Summary Remarks

Because of the small number of cases involved in this analysis, we advance our concluding and interpretive remarks with considerable doubt. However, if the statistics in any way reflect population characteristics, we owe it to ourselves and to the readers to make an effort. In this attempt, we will discuss only what appear to be major points and disregard for the moment the number of cases involved in each instance.

If the law of evolutionary potential has application to matters of union membership, then it should affect the vote on acceptance of racial minorities as semi-intimates. In this discussion we observed that we could make the necessary assumptions about union membership on the privilege of backwardness, but only with considerable trepidation. Having done so, however, we applied them to the vote. The results confirmed our expectations, but union significance proved to be less than overwhelming—a finding hardly at odds with the fact that many craft unionists were included in the category of union members supposedly taking advantage of the privilege of backwardness.

We then coupled union membership to downward mobility and observed that party preference and unionization were of greater significance than mobility.

Among Democrats who were both skidders and union members, a disproportionately large number voted for fair housing. These findings would be consistent with our ideas on traditionalism if we could assume that a relatively large number of these skidders derived from families that were both middle class and liberation-progressive. This assumption about the presence of antitraditionalism within the family of origin would seem warranted, since parental party preference is known to be a crucial determinant of sibling political orientation.[14] Of those skidders who were Democrats, many presumably came from Democratic (or Socialist and the like) families. Democratic middle-class families may well have had kids who became working class but retained the antitraditional views of their parents, especially when these skidders belonged to industrial unions. Since these results are less conclusive than the findings presented earlier, this chapter's concluding comments will dwell only on class, status, and party.

CONCLUSIONS

Within this chapter we have emphasized and demonstrated the importance of political party preference and questioned the pertinence of single generational class and status considerations in our attempt to assess why the people of Berkeley voted the way they did on a fair housing ordinance in 1963. Specifically, occupational, educational, and income differences proved important only when we ignored the significance of political affiliations—the important factor in the vote. When one took this variable into account, it turned out to be more important than class tie and status rank. More Democrats than Republicans favored fair housing at every class, educational, and income level. Democrats went for fair housing more than Republicans; for example, among the better educated (Ph.D.s and their equivalent), the numerical differences separating Democrats from Republicans were startling to the extreme.

During the 1950s, many theorists pontificated on the significance of education. Presumably, the better educated overwhelmingly favored the acceptance of blacks as neighbors, while the less pedigreed—the great unwashed with stumbling vocabularies and overriding prejudices—invariably acted against blacks. Our study allows us to dismiss this stereotype, for we have demonstrated how even the *least* educated Democrats (and some of the lesser educated Republicans) were more in favor of fair housing than was the case among many categories of better educated Republicans. Education apparently made these particular elites more facile traditionalists on matters of race.

But party preference was only one major consideration in the 1963 Berkeley fair housing election, for our world is one where multiple considerations combine to determine how people make choices. In this regard, we would be foolish to overlook the influence of institutions whose activities have traditionally had some bearing on matters of race. We will next consider the importance of university affiliation and religious ties.

NOTES

1. Actually, there are two such analyses: ,Seymour M. Lipset, Paul F. Lazarsfeld, Allen H. Barton, and Juan Linz, "The Psychology of Voting: An Analysis of Political Behavior," in Gardner E. Lindzey, *Handbook of Social Psychology*, Volume II (Cambridge: Addison-Wesley, 1954), especially pp. 1134-50; Seymour Martin Lipset, *Political Man* (Garden City: Doubleday, 1960), especially pp. 131-309.
2. Lipset, *ibid.*
3. Of course we are not saying that party affiliation is the only significant consideration, nor are we saying that the combined impact of political and class positions is less than party tie considered by itself. A multi-variable analysis would reveal quite otherwise, as we shall see.
4. When we use the term statistically significant, what we have in mind is the standard test of significance and the probability of the results occurring by chance at the .05 level or less.
5. The independents scored this way throughout the analysis. They almost invariably located between Democrats and Republicans. However, because of the few independents in the sample, we were unable to develop a refined statistical analysis that might have allowed us to weigh the importance of four or five considerations as they simultaneously related to vote.
6. A particular class position may help to create preference, but it cannot dispel its importance once it takes form, as we indicated earlier.
7. The more refined, three-way categorization failed to reveal any departure from this pattern.
8. As we have already implied in Chapter 2, Bay Area union leaders remained quiet on the fair-housing issues.
9. See William Peterson and David Matza's essay on working-class authoritarianism for an analysis that fails to make this distinction, "How Democratic Are the Working Classes?" in *Social Controversy* (Belmont: Wadsworth Press, 1963), pp. 220-1.
10. An exception would be Herbert Hill's "Labor Unions and the Negro" in *ibid.*, pp. 221-33. Another first-rate effort is Julius Jacobson's *The Negro and the American Labor Movement* (Garden City: Anchor Books, 1968).
11. For an excellent review of the empirical studies concerned with downward mobility and prejudice, see Bruno Bettelheim and Morris Janowitz, *Social Change and Prejudice* (London: The Free Press of Glencoe, Collier-MacMillan Limited, 1964), pp. 25-49. Also see Harold Wilensky and Hugh Edwards, "The Skidder," *The American Sociological Review* 24 (April 1959), 215-31.
12. See Seymour M. Lipset and Hans L. Zetterberg's "Social Mobility in Industrial Society," in Lipset and Bendix, *Social Mobility in Industrial Society* (Berkeley: University of California Press, 1959), pp. 66-9.
13. See Bettelheim and Janowitz, *op. cit.* p. 26.

14. For a thorough review of the classical empirical materials (and theories) on parental political views and sibling political orientations, see Seymour M. Lipset, *et al.*, "The Psychology of Voting: An Analysis of Political Behavior," *op. cit.* pp. 1143-6. In this regard, the most pertinent information is as follows:

> The long-term significance of family environment on political behavior may be seen in the various studies which indicate that between two-thirds and three-quarters of the voters in the United States vote for the same party that their fathers have voted for . . . Part of this relationship of course, may be explained by factors other than family influence, for most individuals possess the same politically relevant traits as their parents, such as class or religion. The Elmira Study attempted to deal with this problem by comparing people with a given family background who were in a social category that conflicted with their background, such as middle-class people of Democratic parentage, or workers with Republican fathers. In each case, the father's politics proved to be as important a determinant of present vote as the larger social group. In a study of a national sample of graduates, Haveman and West (1952) found that upward mobile graduates, (those earning high income) who came from Democratic families either tended to remain Democrats or, if they broke with family traditions, reported themselves as "independents." Those with Republican backgrounds were much less likely to change at all. Similar findings are reported for samples of the total population (Mayer, 1952). This study also indicates that the extent of political loyalties in the family depends on the political climate of the community.

Ibid., pp. 1144-5. Unfortunately, our study did not ask questions on parental political preference.

SIX

The Uneven Impact of Institutions: The University and the Church

Social institutions support the *status quo* yet foment change.[1] Nowhere is this contradiction more apparent than in the field of race relations.

In the United States, university administrations and trustees have traditionally stood as a bulwark of genteel racism, covered with a moderate veneer. In discussing race relations, the university elite have generally relied upon mild rhetoric and public relations programs. When they *have acted,* they have time and again concocted quotas, segregated dormitories, tolerated fraternities, maintained white faculties, and favored white office workers. These practices and views indicate where the administrative heads were at—where they have stood on matters of race—although universities have in the last decade begun a major face lifting job, perhaps more visible in the realm of reception secretaries than organizational structures. In the last several years, student activists have forced many university elites to take the first steps in democratizing their institutions. To the accompaniment of (if not in all cases solely because of) almost continuous student pressure, some of these administrators give indications of grudgingly accepting the twenty-first century.[2]

Yet the university is not all of bent coin. Many faculty members and students have demanded change and acted accordingly, not only on campus but in nearby communities.[3] There, institutions do a less adequate job of hiding their traditionalism. Especially is this true of organized religion in America. Its all-white parishes and congregations lend credence to the remark that Sunday morning is the most segregated moment in the American weekly round, for not even the university has stratified the population so magnificently on the basis of race. Religious parishioners and to a lesser degree local church leaders act to maintain "lily-white segregations"—sometimes sprinkled with Negro respectables often lighter skinned than many tanned Caucasians. In this sense, white congregations have the potentiality of becoming "token congregations."[4]

To many laymen these remarks might seem unfair, for they neglect the wide range of tolerance among churches; further, our views apparently disregard the actions of many militant ministers, priests, and rabbis. Again, we would be remiss to overlook the attitudes of Unitarians and Quakers as opposed to such groups as Baptists and Mormons. Likewise, some would correctly contend, many priests and ministers have led in the liberation struggle launched by minorities.

Hence, a blanket generalization is unfair and incorrect. These counter-remarks would move us to qualify our views, for when we discuss the faithful we must obviously make a distinction between the influence of organized religion *as a whole* and the impressions made by religious denominations and selected leaders *in particular.*

All these considerations force us to examine the pertinence of university affiliation and religious ties, both their presence and absence. Berkeley is (and was) a good place to examine these phenomena, since the community contains not only town folk but a large number of academic people and practicing nonparticipants found well beyond the pale of organized religion. Given these large minorities, we should take advantage of the opportunity to contrast these two populations with ordinary citizens.[5] Since university and nonreligious populations are traditionally more egalitarian than their respective nonuniversity and religious counterparts, we would expect the humanistic clusters to contain more people favoring fair housing.

UNIVERSITY TIE

Analysis of our data on the 1963 Berkeley election (see Table 17) indicates that 30 percent of the non-University and 55 percent of the University employees voted for fair housing, while 53 and 25 percent, respectively lined up against the proposal. Among students, 39 percent were in favor, 14 percent were against, and 47 percent did not vote. These findings justify our expectations. Perhaps the only surprise is the low proportion of students who voted for fair housing. This low turnout occurred partially because, though a large number of students were eligible (to register and) to vote, their mobility interfered with their doing so. Among the other University personnel—the faculty and staff—there were some differences in vote, a consideration to receive more treatment in the last part of this chapter.

Table 17. University Tie and Fair Housing Vote (Whites Only)

No University Tie	30	53	17	(583)
University Employed (Faculty and Other Staff)*	55	25	20	(116)
Students	39	14	47	(59)

*Other staff, less than 5% of subtotal.

Key: See page 77

On the whole, if one compares Town and Gown communities, the results are not too surprising.

UNEVEN RELIGIOUS IMPACT

What was the importance of religion? The impact was uneven, although initial analysis had suggested otherwise.

To begin, we must distinguish between those with a minimal attachment to organized religion and those who have no such ties.[6] It then becomes clear that personal affiliation through preference has a predictable impact (see Table 18). Twenty-eight percent of those with a religious preference and 48 percent of those *without* opted for fair housing, while 55 percent and 28 percent, respectively, voted against it. Apparently having a preference is of some importance—for black as well as white people.

But this analysis oversimplifies, for it overlooks the significance of participation among those who have a religious choice. One would expect a higher proportion of church attenders to vote against the ordinance. In general this happened. Compare the data in Table 16 for those who seldom if ever attend and those who go to church once a month or more often; the results are clear:

(1) Of those involved in organized religion as frequent participants, only about one-quarter voted for the ordinance.

(2) Among those who had a preference but attended church only a few times a year, a mere (and surprisingly) 20 percent voted for the ordinance. (Why this should be the case we shall discover in the last part of the chapter.)

(3) The category of adults who have a preference but never attend church provided a larger percentage of ordinance supporters.

Table 18. Religious Preference and Fair Housing Vote (Whites Only)

Religion: Preference and Attendance				
Preference				
Have Preference	28	55	17	(498)
No Preference	48	28	24	(258)
Attendance				
Once a Week	28	55	17	(155)
Few Times a Month	27	53	20	(45)
Once a Month	29	51	20	(51)
Few Times a Year	20	62	18	(139)
Never	35	43	22	(105)
Not Affiliated	48	28	24	(105)

Key: See page 77.

(4) Those without preference had the highest proportion in favor of the ordinance.

Yet even if organized religion serves as a socializer of racism or as a repository of racists, among white there should be a few differences among religions or denominations. What was the case? If one examines Table 19, it becomes immediately apparent that organized religion as such in Berkeley did not line up as one homogeneous block against fair housing. Within the Catholic camp, there were over three times as many against the ordinance as in favor. Among Protestants, the difference was only two-to-one against, while among Jews the

Table 19. Religion and Fair Housing Vote (Whites Only)

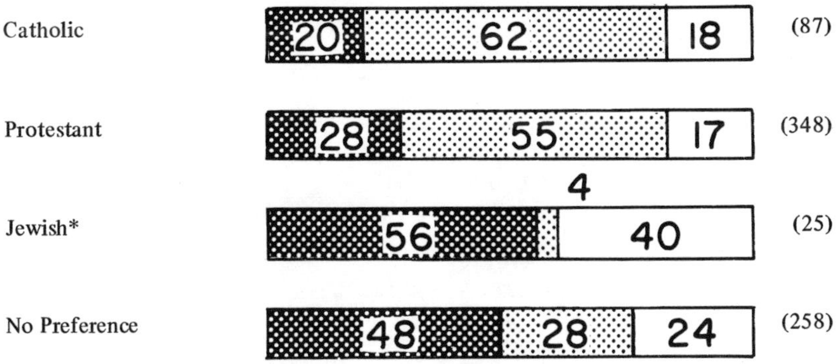

Catholic	20	62	18	(87)
Protestant	28	55	17	(348)
Jewish*	56	4	40	(25)
No Preference	48	28	24	(258)

*Many of the 40% who did not vote were students.

Key: See page 77.

trend was just the opposite; of the 15 Jews who voted in the election, only one went against the ordinance.[7]

A critic might argue that we should not use blanket statistics on Protestant voting, for many studies have indicated how Protestants differ among themselves on matters of attitude and action. For example, when Glock and Stark studied a cross-section of whites in four Bay Area counties,[8] they observed a tendency for certain Protestant groups to contain a disproportionately large number who held that discrimination against other races would definitely prevent salvation. Among the major denominations–Congregationalists, Methodists, Episcopalians, and Disciples of Christ, followed by Presbyterians –there were more favoring this belief than was the case among Lutherans and Baptists. Interestingly, the sects scored quite highly.[9]

Our analysis of the Berkeley situation follows roughly the same pattern, although the findings on sects proved to be at variance with the above information. Nonetheless, our data are consistent with what is generally known about the racial conservatism of these fundamentalist groups (see Table 20).[10] In short, most of our information confirms Glock and Stark's evidence.

We might go one step beyond Glock and Stark and cluster our religious groups into three gross categories: Liberal (Congregational, Methodist, and Episcopalian), Moderate (Disciples of Christ and Presbyterian), and Conservative (Lutheran, Baptist, and Sects), and then compare the results on the 1963 Berkeley fair housing vote.[11] When we do, the findings clarify the range of differences among Protestants. The results are significant, from 7 to 5, 3 to 1,

Table 20. Denominational Vote for Fair Housing (Whites Only)

Particular Denomination or Sect	*Vote on Fair Housing*			
	For	*Against*	*Did Not Vote*	*Total*
Congregationalist	(18) 36%	(25) 50%	(7) 14%	(50) 100%
Methodist	(10) 29%	(20) 57%	(5) 14%	(35) 100%
Episcopalian	(19) 34%	(25) 45%	(12) 21%	(56) 100%
Presbyterian	(14) 24%	(36) 61%	(9) 15%	(59) 100%
Lutheran (both American and Missouri Synods)	(5) 16%	(19) 61%	(7) 23%	(31) 100%
Baptist (both American and Southern)	(0) –	(5) –	(4) –	(9) 100%
Christian Science	(1) %	(5) %	(2) %	(8) 100%
Latter Day Saints	(1) 8%	(8) 67%	(3) 25%	(12) 100%
Unitarian	(11) 42%	(11) 42%	(4) 16%	(26) 100%
Society of Friends	(5) %	(0) %	(0) %	(5) 100%
*Sects**	(2) 11%	(12) 63%	(5) 26%	(19) 100%
Miscellaneous Protestants	(14) 28%	(27) 54%	(9) 18%	(50) 100%
Total	(100) 28%	(193) 54%	(67) 18%	(360) 100%

*Includes one Disciples of Christ

Table 21. Liberal, Moderate, and Conservative Religious Groups and Fair Housing Vote (White Protestants Only)

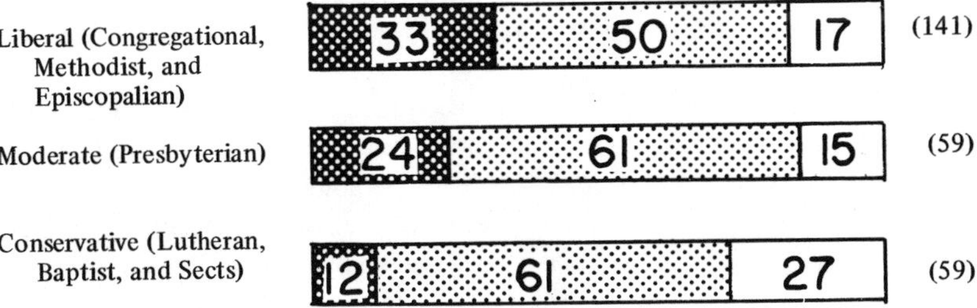

Key: See page 77.

(and) 5 to 1, respectively, *against* fair housing (see Table 21). When we couple this finding to our previous results, the combination suggests that religious tie, University affiliation, and party preference—when treated simultaneously—should be demonstrably related to racial partisanship. This relationship should hold both inside the working and the middle classes. Keeping in mind our earlier arguments, we would add that party preferences should prove relevant as a force acting for or against black interests.

The findings do work out as expected (see Table 22), especially in the election; the ratio was almost 5 to 3 in favor of fair housing. Although we

Table 22. Party, University Tie, Religious Preference and Fair Housing Vote (Working-class Only)

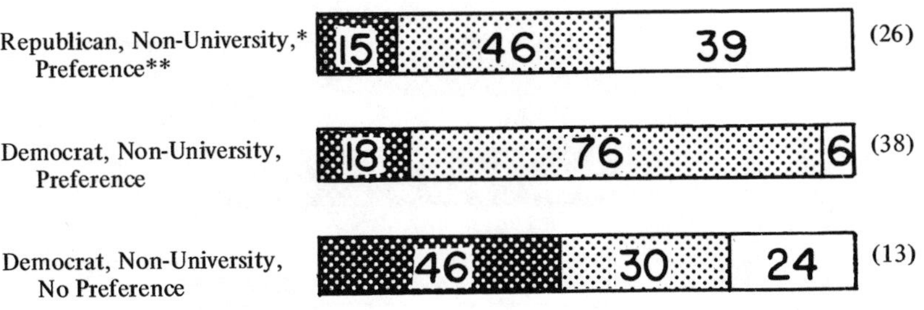

* There were no University working class respondents, either Republican or Democrat.
** Republican, Non-University, No Preference (N=5).

Key: See page 77.

would be unwise to speculate on the significance of this figure because of the paucity of numbers, the data do suggest how we might increase racial acceptance among working-class whites, at least inside the Democratic party—namely, minimize the number of true believers and maximize their opposite.[12]

Should we venture to make such a recommendation for the white-collar world as well? Let us forego this temptation until we have considered comparable Republicans and Democrats. Table 23 demonstrates the overwhelming impact of party preference, the supplementary effect of University connection, and the lesser importance of religious preference. Religious choice proved to be of some relevance, especially within the Democratic party.

Whatever the impact of religious preference, and it would appear to be of ephemeral significance in this context, it is clear that in this election the

Table 23. Party, University Tie, Religious Preference, and Fair Housing Vote (Middle-class Only)

Republican, Non-University, Preference	13	74	13	(168)
Republican, Non-University, No Preference	14	76	10	(37)
Republican, University, Preference	32	48	20	(25)
Republican, University, No Preference	(1)	(6)	(2)	(9)
Democrat, Non-University, Preference	53	33	14	(88)
Democrat, Non-University, No Preference	65	19	16	(75)
Democrat, University, Preference	65	13	22	(23)
Democrat, University, No Preference	74	5	21	(38)

Key: See page 77.

"preference category" contained relatively few who opted for racial equality.

SOME CLARIFICATIONS

Yet some of our information is inconsistent with data given earlier (Table 16). You will recall that relatively few people voted for the ordinance when they were among those who attended church only a couple of times a year. How can we account for these findings? We counted the number of Republicans (78) and Democrats (39) in this group.[13] The count explained the seeming inconsistency on low church attendance and small vote for fair housing. This category of infrequent church attenders was heavily loaded with members of a party overwhelmingly against fair housing.

Still, these findings fail to give us a refined view of how these considerations affected Berkeley's "upper crust," the town's elite, the ones toward whom "the great unwashed" should look for moral guidance on racial affairs–if the adulatory elite theory is correct, and if elite statements on their alleged "racial responsibility" deserve our respect.[14]

Let us examine only the white middle class (white collar) who are better educated (a B.A. degree, its equivalent or higher) and medium or high incomes ($8,000 or more in 1962 for the head of the household.) Although this statistical categorization would include more than those ordinarily defined as an elite–our inclusion would subsume many upwardly moving mobiles within the middle class–the use of this large umbrella does give us sufficient cases to carry on the analysis.

When we gauge their voting choices, as indicated in Table 24, what do we find? Sizable statistical differences–indeed, voting polarization–occurred among Berkeley's more well-heeled. Democrats acted differently from their Republican counterparts, irrespective of University tie and church attendance. Striking are the statistical differences between these Democrats and Republicans. In some cases the differences reached 60 percent! Given these findings, it would be absurd to generalize to the well-to-do as having some kind of consensus on race.

THE LARGER PICTURE

These findings should not be surprising, for they are compatible with what we already know about universities and religions. Universities contain intellectuals who have favored economic and racial change. Over the decades, the central tendency has been clear. University intellectuals have generally located themselves to the left of this country's population on matters of economic reform and civil rights.

With this tendency in mind, Lipset has discussed "the historical leftism of American intellectuals," and his analysis is similar to ours:

Table 24. Party, University Tie, Church Attendance, and Fair Housing Vote (White, White-collar, Better Educated, Medium and High Incomes)

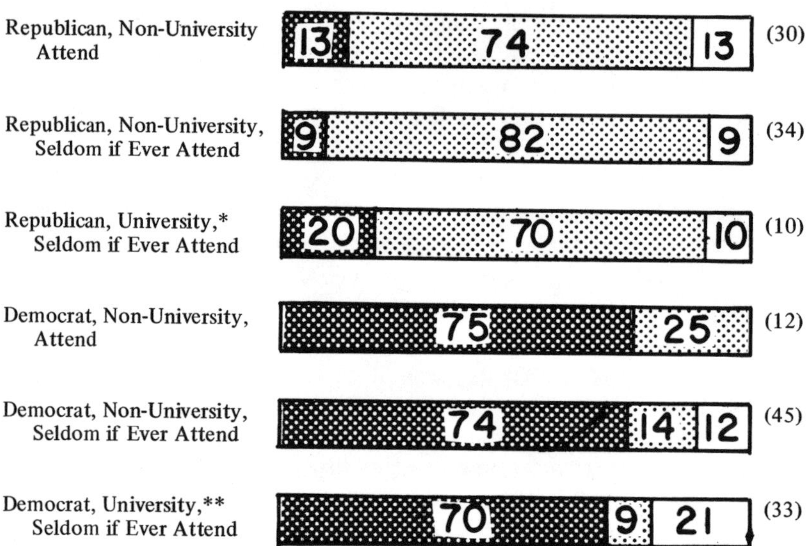

* Republican, University, Attend, N=2.
** Democrat, University, Attend, N=6.

Key: See page 77.

In 1937, a Chicago survey reported pro-New Deal sentiments among 84 per cent of professors of social science and 65 per cent of natural science faculty members, as contrasted with 56 per cent among manual workers, 16 per cent among lawyers, physicians, and dentists, and 13 per cent among engineers. Roughly similar results were obtained on attitudes toward various socioeconomic issues. Amost two decades later, interviews conducted by Paul F. Lazarsfeld and Wagner Thielens, Jr., two Columbia University sociologists, of a systematic national sampling of over 2,000 social scientists teaching in American universities in 1955 revealed that three-quarters were Democrats and that two-thirds had voted for Stevenson in 1952, a year in which close to half of the manual workers and members of trade unions swung to Eisenhower. And, like the 1913 and 1933 studies of religious belief, the survey found that the more distinguished professors showed a much higher proportion of liberals.

One interesting indicator of the philosophy of the academic community is the consumer's co-operative movement. Urban co-ops, except for those with strong ethnic links like the many Finnish ones, scarcely exist outside of academic communities, and the prosperity they enjoy there bears witness to the academic world's hostility toward private business. Palo Alto (Stanford University) and Berkeley (University of California) have large co-ops, but efforts to maintain such stores in other parts of metropolitan San Francisco have repeatedly failed. Similarly, Ithaca (Cornell University), Hanover (Dartmouth College), the Morningside Columbia University area in New York City, and the Hyde Park district in Chicago where the University is located, all have established co-operatives.[15]

We are not saying that all university intellectuals lean to the left and favor equality. The universities have always included defenders of conservatism and traditionalism,[16] and our study included many University staff who voted against the fair housing ordinance. Of these, a disproportionately large number—especially among the Ph.D.s—came from the hard sciences.[17] But the statistical differences between them and the social scientists were small. Perhaps of more significance was the propensity for a sizeable minority of hard scientists to lodge themselves in the Republican party—although the overwhelming majority of hard scientists were Democrats—and for Republican academics to contain a majority who voted *against* fair housing.

To sum up, crucial in accounting for the division among academicians was their political location, either inside the party of genteel conservatism or the organization of patient reform. Of University personnel registered as Republican voters, the overwhelming majority voted against fair housing. Just the opposite was true of University Democrats.

Yet our analysis of University tie, party preference, and racial acceptance was incomplete until we observed the added importance of religious preference and involvement. These results increased our general knowledge of the relationship between religion and race. As you will recall, we found that when people had a religious preference, a disproportionately large number voted against fair housing. Relatively few white Christians favored the ordinance, although there were differences among the Protestant denominations on this matter.

How unusual are these findings? Apparently they are not at odds with the evaluations of many theologians. In fact, when a religious scholar connects Christian creed with continued segregation and then comments on what we call "token congregations," we have reason to take heed:

> Yet today, despite the fact that there is "scarcely a major denomination that has not declared itself in favor of integration," there has been little actual desegration in the Protestant churches in America. Quantitatively, the record of the Roman Catholic Church with its power to outlaw segregation in its schools and churches by episcopal edict, despite the reluctance and resistance of its laymen, has been considerably better than the record of most Protestant denominations, and we must ask at the proper

> time what is implied by these contrasting records. To be sure there are a number of interracial churches to which Christians point with wonder, with pride, and, sometimes, with misgivings. But in the main such integration as has taken place thus far in Protestant American Christianity has fallen into one or more of the following limited patterns: (1) situations in New England and the upper Midwest where the Negro population is small and of relatively high cultural order and where the presence of one or two Negro families has meant the difference between an exclusive and inclusive church; (2) situations in large cities or academic centers where there is available a sufficient population of intellectual, social, and religious liberals to sustain an interracial church; (3) integration from the top, beginning with official church pronouncements and continuing with the appointment of Negroes to official boards and staff positions but not reaching down to the local church; (4) integration on the fringes, beginning with such church-related organizations as the American Bible Society, the World and National Councils of Churches, the Y.M. and Y.W.C.A., and, locally, on the edges of the church in such groups as the Boy Scouts of America, the Girl Scouts, the United Church Women, the Inter-church Athletic Leagues, etc., yet never entering the core of the real church; (5) integration in communities in transition where the Negro population is growing and the white population is rapidly diminishing and where the interracial church will by all practical definition soon become a Negro church attended by a few remaining whites; (6) a few churches which were deliberately organized to attract and serve a racially mixed constituency. In a word, there is little evidence that the local white churches are as yet taking seriously the resolutions and pronouncements of their respective official bodies. There are areas of the country in which this condition may change rapidly in the next decade, but there are also areas where the segregation of Negroes from the white churches will survive long after the public schools have been completely desegregated and will then die a slow and painful death.[18]

Even when tokenism has become the pattern, many Christians, northern ones included, have declared themselves on the question of racial intimacy by advocating totally segregated schools. In the late 1950s Gerhard Lenski focused on religion and race (in the Detroit metropolitan community) and discovered that:

> White Protestants and Catholics were the most likely (34 per cent) and Jews the least likely (8 per cent) to advocate segregated schools. These figures are partly a reflection of the differing percentages of southern-born whites in the various groups. Fifty-five per cent of southern-born whites favored segregated schools, compared with only 30 per cent of those born elsewhere. Since 90 per cent of the southern-born whites were Protestants, this obviously affected the percentage of Protestants favoring segregated schools. When the comparison is limited to those born outside

the South, the three groups rank as follows in terms of the percentage of persons advocating segregated schools:

White Catholics	33 percent (N=215)
White Protestants	27 percent (N=210)
Jews	8 percent (N= 26)[19]

After weighing these results, we might conclude that the most relevant consideration in Lenski's study was the narrow difference separating the two major categories of Christians, although white Catholics led in favoring segregated schools. Approximately one-third of the white Christian community spoke in favor of Jim Crow schools, although there were more northern Catholics than northern Protestants who voiced support for this practice.

In a second observation, the Christians failed to speak for the Jews on this matter of segregation, for Jews contained only a small percentage in favor of this racist pattern.

Perhaps of interest is the way in which our findings on religious differences almost mirrored Lenski's results. In our study:

(1) A very large number of both Protestants and Catholics lined up against fair housing, while the percentage difference between them was both small and predictable.

(2) Only one Jew voted against the ordinance.

(3) So we might safely conclude that a mixed but expected Christian voting pattern failed to find a reflection in the Jewish community.

When we examine Lenski's study of Detroit, we see another similarity, that the more involved, more devoted Christians were also the most conservative on a variety of topics, ranging from political choices through toleration of political deviants to attitudes toward race.[20] We found like results.

Nor were Lenski's and our findings unique. Lipset has used crosscultural data to demonstrate the relationship between religion and conservatism:

> In all of the above countries, Jews, although relatively well to do, are politically the least conservative denomination, a pattern which holds as well in many non-English-speaking Western nations. Electoral data in Austria show that the Jewish districts of Vienna, although middle class, were disproportionately Socialist in many elections before 1933. A study of voting in Amsterdam, the Netherlands, also indicated that the predominantly Jewish district of that city was a strong Social Democratic center. The leftist voting patterns of the Jews have been explained as flowing from their inferior status position (social discrimination) rather than from elements inherent in their religious creed.[21]

CONCLUDING REMARKS

Like Lipset, we had some success in observing the significance of university connection and religious preference in the 1963 Berkeley election. More precisely, we were able to note how denominational affiliation helped shape the race vote within the Protestant world. We demonstrated how our findings complement current research—in this case, recent studies conducted by Glock and Stark as well as Lenski.

We were also struck by the differences among the white, white collar, better educated, and high income voters. In this group, the differences between University Democrats and town Republicans (especially Democratic and Republican nonchurchgoers) were almost as great as those that separated Democratic from Republican Ph.D.s, another elite group (analyzed in Chapter 5).

These two sets of findings were complementary, for Ph.D. Democrats and upper crust Democrats were anything but mutually exclusive populations; there was a great deal of overlap. The same was true of Ph.D. and elite Republicans. So our findings should not come as a surprise, except among those who might accept the following belief:

> . . . there is no really conservative tradition in America, a condition common to many former colonies. American democracy was born in a revolution against a foreign oppressor and rejected the claims of inherited privilege. And Americans regardless of party, class or religious persuasion, believe in their revolutionary creed—unlike those Europeans who live in societies with ancient aristocratic class structures and established churches, where the forces of conservatism never really accepted the legitimacy of equalitarian democracy even when imposed by revolutions.[22]

A conservative tradition may be absent from American society—but a traditional and sizeable core does exist within the upper echelons of our middle class.

And many of its more religious persons, especially among party conservatives, have struggled to withhold equality. Today the critics of religious traditionalism are many, both black and white. Some of these people are angry. Like James Foreman, they demand that white churches reimburse black and brown people for the billions stolen from minorities through various forms of imperialistic exploitation. To say the least, these black militants would find it hard to accept Lipset's celebration. Other black critics take less militant stands than Foreman but similarly point to the economic—that is, capitalistic—basis for religious endorsement of racism:

> The Reverend Channing Phillips, a Negro, of the United Christ Church of Washington, D.C., said that if the church was to fight racism it must move away from the "false base of pietism" and become an institution not only of love but also of power that does not reject violence. . . .
>
> "When a society does not permit restructuring power that produces justice through economics and political maneuvers, then the church ought not to shy away from aiding and abetting the development of the only power available—which is the power of violence," Mr. Phillips said in an address yesterday.

Racism will not be dealt with effectively until it is realized that economics is a primary motive, he asserted.

"As the capitalistic system has moved to seek new resources and consumers under its horribly efficient technology, it has developed racist ideologies to support its stated objectives," Mr. Phillips said. He spoke scornfully of what he called the "insanity that allows economic expenditures for conquering space to have priority over conquering racism."

"The principle of American blacks demanding reparations is right," he said.

He did not express confidence that the church would help the blacks with these claims. "The church has a penchant for letting economic factors silence moral requirements," he said. "Therefore no miracles ought to be expected."[23]

A Black Panther was more to the point:

"You can wait-in or sing-in all you want, but power comes from the barrel of a gun."

This was the message carried to Sunday-morning worshippers yesterday at the Washington Square Methodist Church, and the speaker was David Brothers, deputy chairman of the New York State chapter of the Black Panther party.

He was one of four Panthers who expounded the party's philosophy to about 200 young worshippers, most of them clad in hippie garb.

"Violence," Mr. Brothers said, "is as American as cherry pie. You put a .38 on your hip and you get respect."

At the beginning of the service, the Rev. A. Finley Schaef, minister of the church at 133 West Fourth Street, said he had invited the Panthers to speak "because they are people and we are like them."

Mr. Schaef then offered a prayer "for children everywhere so that they may grow up in peace."

After a ballet interlude, Zayd Shaker, deputy for information of the Panthers, New York State Chapter, read the party's 10-point platform.

These included demands that all black men be exempt from military service, that those in jail be released, that blacks be tried by juries selected from the black community, that police brutality and the "murder of black people" be brought to an immediate end and that all blacks "should arm themselves for self-defense."

During the question-and-answer period following the service, both Mr. Brothers and Mr. Shaker denied that the Panthers intended to "blow up stores or churches."

They insisted that they would inflict no damage on places were "poor white people" were working or worshipping.

"We believe in a proletarian dictatorship," Mr. Shaker said. "We are not racist. We are engaged in a class struggle."

Asked by one worshipper what the role of "concerned whites" should be, Mr. Shaker replied, "Make the revolution in the mother country."

> Panther philosophy views black communities as oppressed "colonies" of the United States.[24]

Clearly, many whites and blacks are taking the egalitarian values of early Christianity seriously. They act to liberate blacks from the economic controls of current-day capitalism and fetid white traditionalism. Catholic priests and nuns now rot in prisons for their direct efforts to free blacks and browns from fighting in Vietnam. These Catholic freedom fighters have not only upset judges but challenged bishops and cardinals. The black militants can count on the continued support of these white allies in the black struggle against white religious racism. In carrying on this fight, the blacks can also look to the support of others, those with the freshness of youth and the freedom from institutional involvement.

NOTES

1. Many sociologists focus on the way in which institutions maximize social control but seldom deal with the way in which institutions work inadvertently for social change as well. See, for example, Erving Goffman's *Asylums* (Garden City: Doubleday, 1961), especially pp. 3-124. Also see Ronald Freedman, Amos H. Hawley, Werner S. Landecker, Gerhard E. Lenski, and Horace M. Miner, *Principles of Sociology* (New York: Henry Holt, 1956), pp. 188-92. By contrast, Nikolai Bakharin's classic, *Historical Materialism,* an important work republished recently [(New York: Russell and Russell, 1965), pp. 239-401 suggests an approach that dwells not only on social groups and their mutual adjustments but also on the contradictions within and amongst them. In his discussion of "The Contradictory Character of Evolution, External and Internal Equilibrium of Society," we can dwell on his insights and learn to refocus our perceptions when we observe institutions:

   > . . . Every structure involves internal contradictions; in every social class form, these contradictions are very sharp. Bourgeois sociologists, while recognizing the mutual relation of the various social phenomena, do not understand the internal oppositions of these social forms. In this respect the entire school founded by the originator of bourgeois sociology, Auguste Comte, is very interesting. Comte recognizes the relation between all the social phenomena (the so called "consensus") in which its "order" is expressed. But the contradictions within this "order," particularly such as lead to its inevitable destruction, do not receive his attention. On the other hand, for the advocates of dialectic materialism, this phase is one of the most essential, perhaps *the* most essential phase. For, as we have seen, the contradictions in any given system are precisely the "moving" element, leading to an alteration of forms, to a characteristic transformation of species in the process of social evolution or social decline.

2. One is struck by the paucity of black academicians within the best universities. Frequently, white administrators account for this situation by

pleading that they could not hire blacks since they have failed to qualify. This we know to be incorrect. E. Franklin Frazier, for example, turned out first-rate studies on social change, family structure, and race, but he never obtained a tenured position at a big university such as the University of Chicago. Robert Hutchins, former Chancellor at the University of Chicago, recently noted that when he tried to appoint a well known Negro to a position within the Department of Sociology at Chicago, the departmental chairman opposed it, protesting that the departmental members would not accept the appointment of a Negro. Subsequently, the departmental members heard of this excuse falsifying their views and signed a petition urging the chairman to hire the Negro in question. The chairman ignored the petition and refused to hire the black man.

A recent nationwide study (1967) of university trustees pointed to the conservative and oftentimes reactionary attitudes of these decision makers. Especially was this true of academic freedom, the right to a higher education, their pro-business orientation, and the university decision-making process. See Rodney T. Hartnett, *College and University Trustees: Their Backgrounds, Roles, and Educational Attitudes* (Princeton: Educational Testing Service, 1969), especially pp. 13-37.

3. An example would be student involvement in the New Left programs focusing on civil rights and peace activities, commitments also supported by many faculty at such schools as the University of California, Stanford, the University of Chicago, Harvard, and the University of Michigan.
4. The "token congregation" would include a small percentage of blacks drawn mostly from the upper middle classes. The select few would range from one to five percent, but not more, if only because a larger representation might move many whites to attend another church.
5. Although university and college people are but a minority of the total population in an advanced industrial society, their community's growth in numbers would seem to be greater—when taken together—than that of the remainder of society. In the United States, the university and college population has more than tripled in the last 25 years, while the remaining nonstudent population has not.
6. Gerhard Lenski did a very detailed analysis of attachment to organized religion and the consequences of psychological and organizational ties for conservatism, which he measured along political as well as religious dimensions. Generally, he found that when the Detroit population (1957) was committed to support organized religion, these religious enthusiasts contained a disproportionately large number who turned out to be conservatives, a point we will consider at greater length in the latter part of this chapter. Gerhard Lenski, *The Religious Factor* (Garden City: Doubleday, 1961), pp. 157-67.
7. These findings were completely consistent with those found by Lenski. *Ibid.*, p. 148.
8. Charles Y. Glock and Rodney Stark, "Is There an American Protestantism?" *Trans-Action*, 3 (November/December, 1965), p. 13.

9. Perhaps there was a confounding variable in the distributions but conversations with the authors failed to indicate their awareness of what it might be.
10. A sound treatment of American sects can be found in Liston Pope, *Millhands and Preachers* (New Haven: Yale University Press, 1942), especially Chapter 7.
11. Admittedly, had we placed the Lutherans among the moderates, the gap between them and conservatives would have been greater. But we didn't. We thereby stacked the cards *against* ourselves and reduced the size of the percentage difference between conservatives and moderates.
12. This last remark is made half in seriousness and half in jest. Actually, as we noted, the few cases prevent our making the kind of strident recommendation that our own predispositions might favor, partially because we are unaware of antecedent and concommitant considerations that move blue-collar people to remain beyond the pale of organized religion.
13. In this case, we use the word "group" to avoid repetitious use of the word "category." We are discussing a statistical aggregate more closely approximating a category than a collectivity with an objective structure and common values.
14. What we reject are the views of those sociologists who hold that the lower classes must look to a "responsible elite" when taking their cues on the civil rights and the civil liberties of minorities. Some writers have misquoted Samuel Stouffer on this matter. Lest we forget what this fine sociologist did say, let us reacquaint ourselves with one of the final passages of his famous study on civil liberties:

    > Even though the local community leaders in all roles studied are more tolerant than the cross-section of people in their own cities or in the nation as a whole, this finding is not necessarily a basis for complacency about leaders' own attitudes. To some people the leaders may appear surprisingly tolerant—or even dangerously so. But to other observers who have a different level of expectation or standard of judgment the leaders themselves are disappointingly less tolerant than might be hoped. The prospect has rosy or somber hues, depending on the spectacles worn. Even an anxious devotee of civil liberties who may be a wearer of darkened glasses would rejoice, however, to see the leaders ahead, not behind, the rest of the people from his point of view. The big question is: Will they *lead?* And lead even better in the future than in the past? This volume cannot answer this question. Only people in their communities can answer it—by their actions in the years ahead.

    Here and elsewhere, Stouffer claims that community leaders must take the lead, that they have the responsibility and the education to do so. However, he does not say that the lower classes should emulate them, or that the educated automatically act as guardians of civil liberties and civil rights. Were he able to view our information on education, income, and political party preference, we are sure that he would accept our distinctions and that he would recommend changes inside the party of his own preference, that Grand Old Party which deserted blacks one hundred years after it called for their emancipation. See Samuel Stouffer, *Communism, Conformity and Civil Liberties* (Gloucester: Peter Smith, 1963), pp. 235-6.

15. See Seymour Lipset, "American Intellectuals: Their Politics and Status," in *Political Man, op. cit.*, pp. 314-15.
16. Most relevant would be Lipset's discussion of "The Move to the Right" among American Intellectuals. See his *Political Man, ibid.*, pp. 340-4. Lipset is not the only interested party. Among others, C. Wright Mills has commented on "The Conservative Mood," in *The Power Elite* (New York: Oxford University Press, 1959) pp. 325-42. Many of these analyses were more pertinent to intellectual thought and action during the 1950s—when elite theory proved acceptable to the politics of adjustment—than to the early 1960s—when Pareto, Mosca, Michels, Schumpeter, and the like found fewer supporters. They have given way to writers more attractive to young intellectuals highly concerned with race, reform, and revolution. The current crop would include Frantz Fanon, Malcolm X, Ché Guevara, and Mao Tse-tung.
17. The hard sciences include those we associate with the physical sciences—physics, chemistry, and geology—and the life sciences—biology, physiology, and zoology. It would obviously exclude such fields as sociology, economics, social welfare, political science, the classics, foreign languages, mathematics, as well as psychology, a borderline case.
18. Kyle Haselden, *The Racial Problem in Christian Perspective* (New York: Harper and Row, 1964), pp. 32-3.
19. Gerhard Lenski, *op. cit.*, p. 148.
20. *Ibid.*, especially Chapter 4, pp. 120-91.
21. Seymour Lipset, *Political Man, op. cit.*, pp. 243-6.
22. *Ibid.*, pp. 320-1.
23. See "Action by Churches on Racism Is Called Urgent by McGovern," *New York Times*, May 22, 1969, p. 39.
24. "Panther Official Tells Methods, 'A .38 on Your Hip Gets You Respect,'" in *New York Times*, May 26, 1969, p. 30.

SEVEN

White Tradition and the Law of Evolutionary Potential

THE CAKE OF WHITE CUSTOM

Even if we assume that we have identified key forces opposed to racial reaction, we must nonetheless continue our analysis and isolate those other considerations deemed relevant. Having done this, our next task will be to weigh their importance with respect to political affiliation.

Let us now consider some favorable arguments concerning those people long associated with institutionalized racial traditionalism: the home owners; the unruffled generation; and the older residents. Many are presumably beyond the pale of liberating processes such as membership in a civil rights generation, a category relatively unsullied by the blandishments of adaptation to institutions.

When the family, the school, and the church inject beliefs, values, and norms into the cortical areas of a population on an intergenerational basis, we refer to the groups as *institutions* and to their messages as *traditions.*[1] Institutions pass down philosophies, however flat and hypocritical they may be. These persuasions include views on property, and here our analytical effort begins.

Private Investment and Home Ownership

Property and vote should be related.[2] When the form of property is a private home, the owners strive to protect the domicile from a number of presumed threats, including property devaluation and social desecration through occupancy by a "lesser" race[3] or ethnic group.

By contrast, owners of investment property have often acted quite differently to maximize economic gain. For them, devaluation of property might prove profitable when they can control its value on the housing market—a black "invasion" could result in greater profit than usual if the real estate speculator can control the processes involved.[4] We are not especially concerned here with practices such as block-busting, nor are we moved by the significance of investment property with respect to the question of race, at least not in this chapter. Rather we are dealing with the first consideration, home ownership.

Presumably, when lesser ethnics move into a neighborhood that contains the usual gamut of people associated with the acceptable pattern of urban ethnicity and home ownership, home owners view intruders as objects that tarnish the neighborhood and thereby devalue their property. What occurs is a collective rejection, one in which home buyers and owners lead the way, for they strive to protect neighborhood "property values." In this sense, they differ from the renter. Everything else being equal, the renter will not be primarily concerned with racial influx. If he doesn't like the alleged despoliation of his neighborhood, he can leave and not worry about the matter of home investment, since he does not have a material interest to maintain. He experiences the privilege of nonownership. For this reason, not being strongly opposed to local integration, he may be more susceptible to accepting arguments made by groups favoring various racial groups living in the same neighborhood. Consequently, home renters should include many who favor racial integration on the neighborhood level.[5]

Generational Impact

Racial traditionalism should be most acceptable to those who are part of a generation that failed to witness a racial insurgence, when they were growing up.[6] If one considers generational groupings, it is useful to distinguish among the *unruffled*, the *liberation*, and the *civil rights* generations.

In a general sense, the unruffled generation would be one in which an age cohort has come of age—that is, individuals who have passed through a period of late adolescence and early adulthood as members of a superordinate racial group when it was the rule for a racial minority (such as black Americans) to accept its subordinate place in the community scheme of proper distribution of races. In United States history, blacks were at the bottom and whites were at the top both during and prior to the 1920s. More important, violence as well as custom then deemed that caste relations should mark all ties between whites and blacks. With the exception of escapist movements, black masses during the early twentieth century failed to create a major liberation move-

movement,[7] as it was called during the 1930s. To be more precise, that generation's ranks should include an unusually large number of ordinance supporters.

The liberation generation should contain proportionately fewer in favor of fair housing than the *civil rights generation.* In many settings, these younger people would become overwhelmingly in favor of racial equality and remain so; as a civil rights generation they became political at that moment when a civil rights struggle began to assume *massive* proportions, as in the United States during the late 1950s. In that particular context, the civil rights groups and racist institutions tangled. For a variety of reasons, many young people identified with—and vicariously participated in—civil rights struggles directed against schools, churches, businesses, and unions. For some of the youth, participation was direct, involving commitments, demonstrations, arrests, prosecutions, persecutions, and the creation of consciousness. This consciousness proved to be multifaceted, for it included not only a sense of generational identity (all those under 30 as opposed to all of those older) but a rejection of traditional formulas (advanced by establishment liberals, labor, and conservatives), plus an acceptance of direct action.

It would seem that these younger people—those under 30 in 1963—should contain a relatively large number who favored fair housing.

The Older Residents

Everything else being equal, the young are unusually adept at sponsoring and accepting social change, especially when their adoloscent political experiences prompt them to do so. The new residents should also carry views at variance with those of established persons. Here the population divides along the dimension of length of residence, with many of the newcomers acting as harbingers of change, especially when they turn out to be young males without property. Why?

After spending some time in a community, one learns how older residents—people who have been in the town for a long time—earn prestige partially on the basis of the class and racial content of the community. When a town is almost entirely upper working and middle class as well as white, it acquires medium to high prestige. Its residents contrast it favorably with other towns. They identify with the area and acquire honor themselves, especially when they compare themselves invidiously with those living in communities having less honor. The end result takes the following form: regional members develop a hierarchy that ranks communities on the basis of class-racial prestige.

Town honor is lessened when the percentage of minority members increases and the city fathers cannot stop its expansion. The loss of honor looms as most significant among residents who have lived in the community for a long time. The old-time residents react vigorously for they are the ones most committed to evaluating various communities along traditional lines and to staying in the community. This commitment to live in the town heightens a sensitivity to calibration of prestige among communities. Both length of residence and degree of commitment lead them to discern any action that might diminish town prestige. A fair housing ordinance would have exactly this effect, for it would facilitate the settling of racial minorities in a high prestige community and thereby begin its honorific decline. This reranking process might appear acceptable to newer residents, but among the neighborhood people with high seniority, the influx of new residents would seem reprehensible. Consequently, the old-time residents would contain many opposed to a fair housing ordinance.

Expectations and Results

We are now in a position to summarize our materials on the pertinence of several considerations associated with tradition. When we examine the *mores* on race and make assumptions on their key carriers, the following groups and categories loom large as barriers to the acceptance of a fair housing ordinance:

(1) *home owners,* most of whom presumably correlate black invasion with the physical deterioration of neighborhood and the decline of neighborhood prestige;

(2) *the unruffled generation,* most of whom are committed to a racist perspective;

(3) *the long-term residents,* many of whom recall the days when the town did not have a race problem, since Orientals and blacks knew and kept their place.

On the whole, the findings prove consistent with what we thought would happen (Table 25). In the case of home ownership, for example, we found that white home owners voted 2 to 1 against the proposal; home buyers split, renters voted almost 4 to 3 for the fair housing ordinance. Of course, this comparison is based only upon those who voted. The renters did include a very large number of nonvoters, in part because of the large number of students in this category.

The rest of Table 25 also provides considerable support for our expectations. Generational membership seemed to be of considerable importance, at least at first glance. The unruffled generation voted over 2 to 1 against the ordinance, the liberation cluster went almost 7 to 5 in favor; the civil rights generation gave 3 to 1 support to the ordinance, among those who voted. We might wonder whether these results stemmed from the predictable impact of age *or* generation. The classical age hypothesis holds that irrespective of generation, younger people invariably favor change, but as they grow older, they shy away from youthful commitment and become attracted to conservative and traditional formulas. Hence, there would be an inverse relationship be-

Table 25. Traditional Considerations and the Berkeley Fair Housing Vote

Traditional Considerations	*Vote on Fair Housing*			
	For	*Against*	*Did Not Vote*	*Total*
Home Owners	(111) 30%	(221) 60%	(38) 10%	(370) 100%
Buyers	(66) 45%	(64) 44%	(15) 11%	(145) 100%
Renters	(79) 34%	(59) 25%	(95) 41%	(233) 100%
Other	(4) –	(0) –	(2) –	(6) –
Traditional Generation (50+)	(112) 28%	(237) 59%	(52) 13%	(401) 100%
Liberation Generation (30-49)	(123) 45%	(96) 36%	(50) 19%	(269) 100%
Civil Rights Generation (21-29)	(26) 31%	(10) 12%	(48) 57%	(84) 100%
New Residents (1-5 years)	(53) 36%	(25) 17%	(71) 47%	(149) 100%
Short Term (6-10)	(41) 42%	(34) 35%	(21) 23%	(96) 100%
Medium (11-20)	(84) 47%	(71) 40%	(23) 13%	(178) 100%
Long Term (21+)	(77) 27%	(183) 64%	(28) 9%	(288) 100%
Life Residents (since birth)	(7) 16%	(30) 68%	(7) 16%	(44) 100%

tween age and vote for fair housing. We will soon examine this generation-age controversy at length.

Not only did our findings on generational membership work out as expected but so did those on length of residence, if one accepts the argument on the significance of tradition. A larger number of newer residents were in favor of the ordinance. Among those who had lived in Berkeley for one to five years, the plurality was 2 to 1 in favor, while the six to twenty year category voted 6 to 5 for the proposal. In the case of the old-timers, there was a statistical reversal, with the long-term and lifetime residents voting 2 to 1 and 4 to 1, respectively, against fair housing.[8]

Of course, we may have obtained these results because of the peculiar distribution of Democrats in the different categories; perhaps a relatively large number of them can be found within the new resident population. If so, our results would be spurious.

And perhaps what is true of length of residence might also be the case when we consider home ownership and generational membership, factors which we will now examine.

Party Preference?

When we take into account the importance of party affiliation, we note that home ownership is of some significance, but largely among Republicans. With the Democratic population, we find the absence of a clear-cut relationship (see Tables 26, 27, 28).

Table 26. Party, Home Ownership, and Fair Housing Vote

Republican, Home Owners	15	77	8	(191)
Republican, Buyers	19	65	16	(54)
Republican, Renters	13	42	45	(62)
Democrat, Home Owners	51	37	12	(140)
Democrat, Buyers	66	26	8	(70)
Democrat, Renters	49	18	33	(113)

Key: See page 77.

Yet even among Republicans the findings do not offer strong support for the proposition that home ownership *per se* helps to differentiate owners from buyers and renters, even though it is transparent, as we have already indicated in our discussions of Ph.D. Republicans,[9] that many of them seemingly value the sanctity of private property and vote accordingly.

By contrast, Democrats would seem to deemphasize the sanctity of home ownership and stress human rights. This tendency is most noticeable among the better educated, particularly the Ph.D.s and their equivalents–most of them home buyers–as indicated by the following verbatim comments on why they voted for the proposal:

> [*Self-employed physician*] I voted for the ordinance because I'm a liberal. I thought the ordinance was fair; I felt that the evils in it would be remedied later.

> [*Self-employed dentist*] Some people voted against the ordinance because they feared that property values would decline. I think that this belief rests upon a false premise.

> [*Chemist employed by Standard Oil*] I think that the race problem is the chief domestic problem in the United States. The situation is desperate, and I'm willing to buy something new. Of course, I don't think that racial peace will come from political action, but we must try.

Table 27. Party, Generation, and Fair Housing Vote

Republican, Unruffled	13	76	11	(195)
Republican, Liberation	20	60	20	(94)
Republican, Civil Rights	15	20	65	(20)
Democrat, Unruffled	46	39	15	(157)
Democrat, Liberation	65	20	15	(133)
Democrat, Civil Rights	50	3	47	(36)

Key: See page 77.

[*Attorney employed by a lumber and mill employees assocation*] I'm not prejudiced. I don't have fears of any penalty which could be imposed. *Why do you think most people voted against it?* The reason most people give is dislike for the excessive penalty, but the real reason is because they are race prejudiced, but won't admit it.

[*Self-employed attorney*] I firmly believe in it for my part. I once tried to rent to members of a minority group and had trouble from some of my neighbors. Even though I was born in Texas, I am against prejudice.

[*Attorney employed by a Berkeley law firm*] I believe it's proper and needed social legislation. It's one part of change coming about whereby Negroes are going to receive equal treatment. And law, by its very nature, is needed to legislate morals, and, as a matter of fact, law does legislate morals. *Why do you think most people voted against the ordinance?* There are many, many reasons. There was misunderstanding of the issues involved. The ordinance doesn't say you have to accept all Negroes.

[*Assistant Professor of Mathematics at the University of California*] I voted for the ordinance because it is an important issue, and people should be able to live where they want regardless of skin color.

[*Self-employed attorney*] I thought it was a fair thing. Everyone who pays taxes has the right to live where he wants to live. *Why do you think most people voted against the ordinance?* Because the solid voters in Berkeley were Caucasian home owners.

Table 28. Party, Length of Residence, and Fair Housing Vote

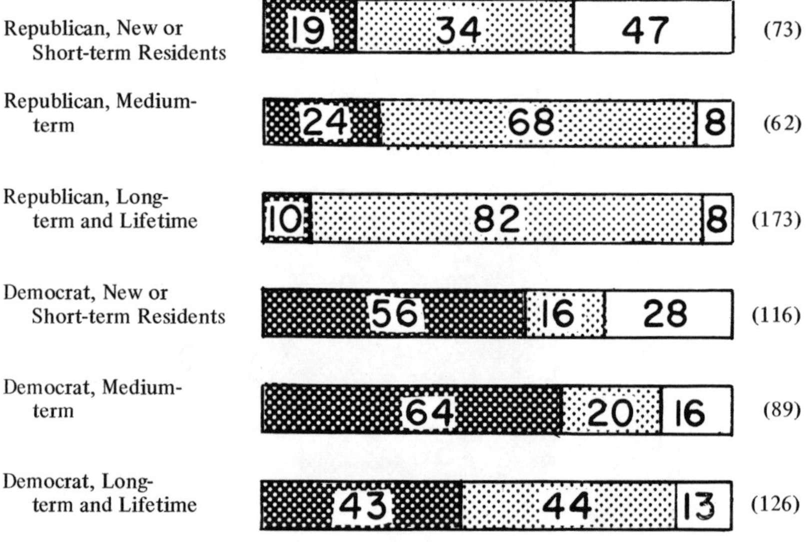

Key: See page 77.

[*Professor at the University of California*] I thought the moral question of allowing Negroes the opportunity to break through the unfair barriers against them far outweighed the property rights of homeowners or any other rights.

[*Professor of Sociology at the University of California*] I am generally for measures opposed to discrimination. I agreed with the arguments for it.

[*Professor of Spanish at the University of California*] I voted for the law just because it's fair to minority groups. It's time to get wise in Berkeley. *Why do you think most people voted against the ordinance?* Because they didn't understand what it was about. The issue was beclouded by the real estate people.

[*Professor of Education at the University of California*] Part of my beliefs includes the rights of anyone to own a home wherever he wishes. *Why do you think most people voted against the ordinance?* Economic fears. They felt it would affect their property values and their rental values.

[*Assistant Professor at the University of California (female)*] I feel strongly that the Negro has gotten a poor deal here and the fair housing law would have helped him. They need jobs; but you have to start somewhere, and this was a good bill and a good place to begin. *Why do you think most people voted against the ordinance?* I campaigned for the ordinance in my area. They were worried about the economic loss, personally. An area of open housing would be bad for investments. They question the rights of minorities. These reasons are probably rationalizations for their prejudice. The papers gave it bad publicity which would reinforce opposition to fair housing.

[*Retired Professor of Economics at the University of California*] All people should have equal opportunity to housing.

[*Professor of Psychology at the University of California*] I am not in the least afraid of a drop in real estate values. *Why do you think most people voted against the ordinance?* People are afraid of a drop in real estate value.

[*Professor of Mathematics at the University of California*] Equal rights are more important. The country must establish equality for all citizens.

[*Professor at the University of California*] We voted for the law because we're interested in social justice.

[*Self-employed physician*] Moral reasons.

[*Professor at the University of California*] It should be illegal to refuse to sell someone a house because he is black.

[*Self-employed attorney*] It was a good measure.

[*Professor of Psychology at the University of California*] I thought it was the right thing to do. It was a better alternative in view of my beliefs.

[*Teacher at the Pacific School of Religion*] I believe in civil rights. There should not be discrimination in the sale of property on the basis of race, creed, or color. Passing the ordinance would have been a constructive thing.

[*Attorney employed by the Kaiser Foundation*] The discrimination problem is serious, with housing an important element. Passage of the bill would have produced an atmosphere which could solve the problem. *Why do you think most people voted against the ordinance?* To many Berkeleyans, Negroes pose an economic and social threat which can be best resisted (from their point of view) by taking positions and performing actions not likely to help the Negro's advancement.

[*President of a Lutheran theological seminary*] I voted for the ordinance on the principle of the accordance of the law of the land as delivered by the Supreme Court—and, having no racial prejudice that I can discover. I roomed with an American Negro in Delhi. Part of my conviction as a Christian is that racial matters should be cared for without discrimination. *Why do you think most people voted against the ordinance?* Well, I think it's self interest and the feeling that fair housing and similar things perhaps are pushed too hard. It is reaction to aggressive concerns of Negroes and liberal movements on their behalf.

[*Doctor of Psychiatry at Cowell Hospital*] Racial equality is important. I believe in one world.

[*Dentist in private practice*] I voted for it on the basis of the primacy of individual rights. It is a civil rights question.

[*Teacher at Saint Mary's College*] It is a matter of justice, necessity, and the fact that it was one of the first approaches toward the solution of some racial problems. *Why do you think most people voted against the ordinance?* They thought it was a violation of the Bill of Rights, and they had a distorted idea of how this resolution, if passed, would be implemented. They feared the jail penalty. Even the so-called "enlightened" ones had this fear.

[*Professor of Economics at the University of California*] I'd like to see this on the state books. Realtors are responsible for keeping segregation. We should strike at this power. *Why do you think most people voted against the ordinance?* I think that most people have one reason for being able to do what they believe is protecting their property value. Many others are out and out against others using their property. Neighborhood pressure is also important.

[*Attorney employed by the State of California*] I worked hard for its passage; I felt it was a just, right law.

[*Professor at the University of California*] I voted for the ordinance because it was consistent with the American ideal of equal rights for all. One doesn't have the right to discriminate just to save personal liberty or choice of neighborhood acquaintances.

[*Self-employed physician*] It is the moral thing to do. All people should be free to live where they want to live.

[*Professor of Political Science at the University of California*] I'm not prejudiced, and I'm not stupid. It is important that the school system becomes a mechanism for equal opportunity in a democratic society.

[*Self-employed attorney*] Equality of treatment in housing, education, and employment is basic to a free society. Racial discrimination is an evil; it is immoral.

[*Engineer at Aerojet*] I have a basic conviction that there should be no discrimination.

[*Professor of Social Welfare at the University of California*] I believed in the philosophy behind it; I didn't think about its constitutionality.

Among highly educated Democrats—even the home buyers and owners—human rights took precedence over property privileges. That was the modal pattern. These same persons were in many cases members of either the liberation or the civil rights generation, new or short-term residents, and they acted accordingly (see Tables 27 and 28).

Generation Versus Age

But are generations as important as they appear? What seems to be a generational phenomenon may only be an age grade regularity. Young people are always more progressive than older folk. Hence, a curious observer might say that we obtained these results on generations because of an inverse relationship between age and support for the ordinance and not because of the significance of generational impact. The formula is simple: as age increases, civil rights support declines. In this sense, the skeptical critic might argue that the age factor would prove to be marked even when we simultaneously control for party affiliation and sex. From this point of view, were we to treat age level by examining it at ten-year intervals, it should prove significant, even taking party preference and sex into account.

That's what happened. When we scrutinize Tables 29 and 30, we find that it is impossible for us to reject the age counter-hypothesis. There is a neat, stepping-stone relationship between increased age and heightened opposition to the ordinance. Presumably, had the generational hypothesis been correct, the age subdivisions within each generation would have been identical or nearly so. What happened? Within the liberation generation (ages 30-49), the category (40-49) contained a relatively large number who voted *against* the ordinance.

Perhaps we can find yet another way to phrase our reaction to the differences within the *liberation* generation. Let us look at Table 29 once again. We can observe that the 30-39 age category voted approximately 3 to 1 for the ordinance, while the 40-49 group went 2 to 1 for the proposal. Roughly the same pattern emerges when we make comparisons within each generation.

Table 29. Party, Sex, Age, and Fair Housing Vote (Democrats Only)

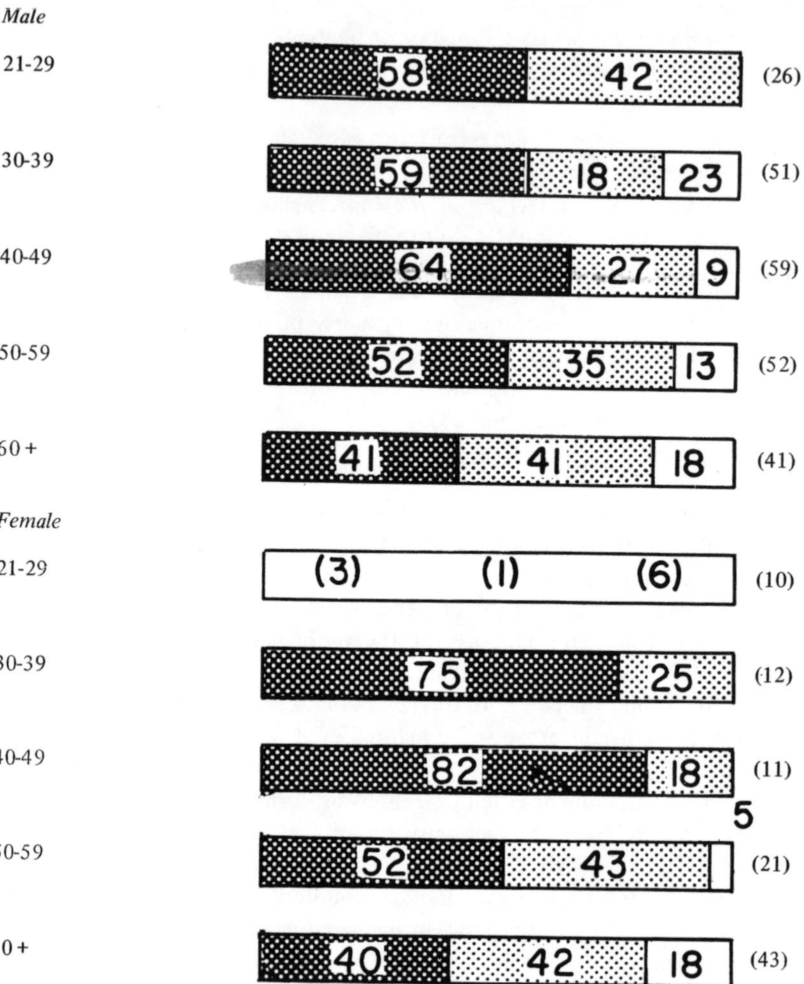

Key: See page 77.

Yet to dismiss the generational hypothesis at this point would be unfair. Some might argue that although aging erodes a generational bias, the age factor fails to eradicate the effects of generational membership. To test this proposition, we would have to observe and follow three successive cohorts through time. Subsequently, we could make comparisons which would hold the age factor constant. Given this control, if successive generations were to

Table 30. Party, Sex, Age, and Fair Housing Vote (Republicans Only)

Male				
21-29	20	13	67	(15)
30-39	16	52	32	(25)
40-49	20	63	17	(46)
50-59	11	78	11	(54)
60+	11	80	9	(84)
Female				
21-29	(0)	(2)	(3)	(5)
30-39	(2)	(5)	(2)	(9)
40-49	31	62	7	(13)
50-59	27	60	13	(15)
60+	14	71	15	(42)

Key: See page 77.

demonstrate similar declines with age but indicate consistent differences among generations at all age levels, then we would be in a position to tentatively accept *both* the generational and age hypotheses. However, as our ahistorical data now stand, we lack this kind of intergenerational material. As a result, we can neither accept nor reject the generational hypothesis, at least not in the eyes of those who support a generational approach. These critics

Table 31. Generation, Age, and Vote on Successive Fair Housing Ordinances:
A Speculative Distribution on Impact of Generation and Age

	Age Group	*% Voting for Fair Housing Ordinances*				
		1923	1943	1963	1983	2003
Unruffled Generation	*21-29*	25				
	30-39		20			
	40-49		17			
	50-59			14		
	60+			12		
Liberation Generation	*21-29*		30			
	30-39			28		
	40-49			24		
	50-59				22	
	60+				18	
Civil Rights Generation	*21-29*			45		
	30-39				40	
	40-49				35	
	50-59					30
	60+					28

would demand the kind of material suggested by Table 31. It indicates the distribution of statistical information that would support our speculative remarks.

To obtain such information we would have to reorient our research approach; but should such information become available, we would be on our way to obtaining data with the kind of historical breadth so necessary if we are to rescue sociology from generalizations based upon a static view of man. In so doing, we would also be in a position to begin to solve the generation-age controversy. In our present analysis, however, we have to rely upon one-shot evidence when making interpretations.

Generation, Residence, and Party

Within the limits described in the last section, we can try to gauge not only the significance of generational membership (or age) but also the pertinence of length of residence within the two major parties. You will recall how party preference failed to disturb the inverse relationship between length of residence and support for fair housing. Yet one wonders. Is length of residence

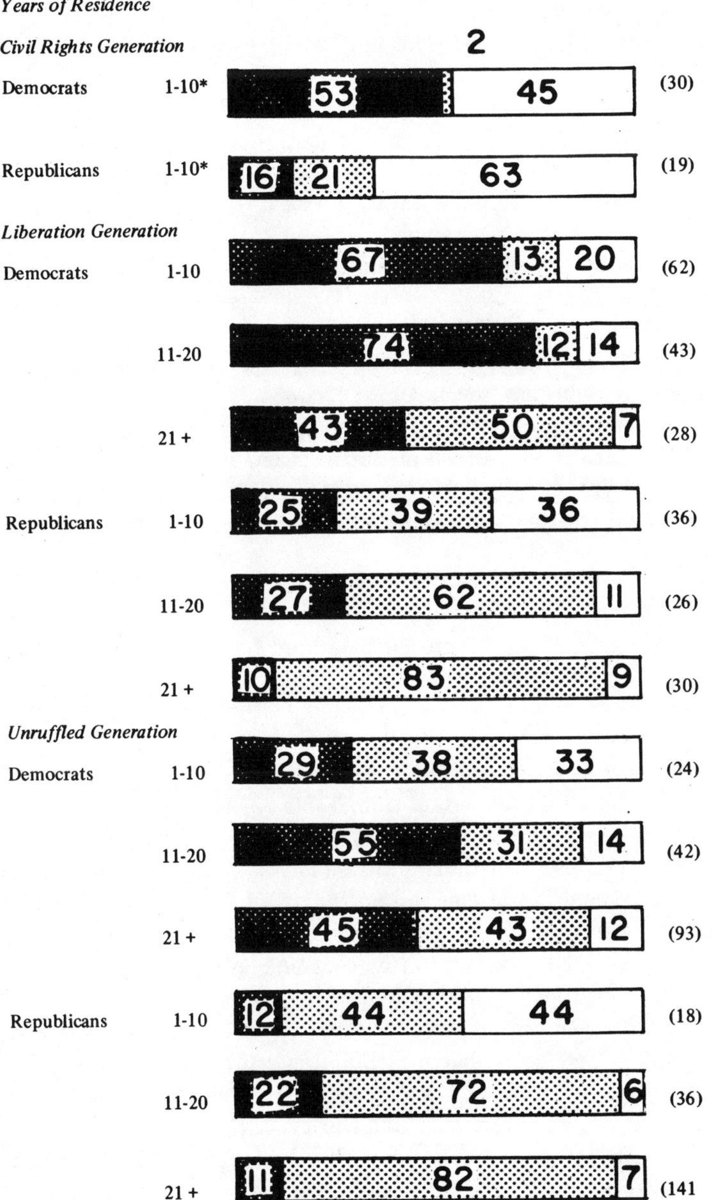

Table 32. Generation, Party, Length of Residence, and Fair Housing Vote

* There were too few applicable cases to extend analysis beyond 10 years of residence.

Key: See page 77.

that important? Perhaps what is actually significant is generational membership, not length of residence (see Table 32).

When we take into account the prior importance of generational membership and party preference and then relate length of residence to vote, we can observe the recurrent significance of residence longevity in those situations with enough cases to allow comparisons:

(1) Unfortunately, among the young Democrats and Republicans (ages 21-29), the limited information does not allow us to test our general notions on the significance of length of residence.

(2) However, within the liberation generation (ages 30-49), the residence factor holds up remarkably well among both Democrats and Republicans.

(3) Among the older Democratic residents within the liberation generation the predicted pattern stands, except among those living in Berkeley for six to ten years; among Republicans, the expected occurred.

(4) By contrast, among the unruffled, not much happens statistically.

On the whole, then, the information supports our hunches on length of residence but fails to diminish the importance of generation (age) which remains pertinent even when one takes into account residential longevity and party affiliation.

University, Party, and Residence

Perhaps residence and generation proved significant because of the relatively large number of University people in certain categories such as new residents and the civil rights generation. Let us first examine the residence possibility.

Presumably, the new residents might have been overwhelmingly in favor of fair housing because so many of them were attached to a university. At first glance we might draw this conclusion from Table 33. However, if length of residence were unimportant and University tie and party preference were the only vital considerations, then short-term, middle-term, and long-term residents should have voted in the same proportions for fair housing. This distribution occurred within the first cluster of interviewees. Among Democrats affiliated with the University, the differences among residence categories proved minimal. Surprisingly, among long-term residents we find that 20 voted for the ordinance, nobody went against it, and two failed to vote. However, among University-affiliated Republicans, there would appear to have been an inverse relationship between length of residence and vote for the proposal. Again, if one considers only non-University Republicans, the information followed almost the same pattern. Clearly, length of residence was pertinent. The exception was the University Democratic community. There, the norms and beliefs seemed sufficiently powerful to make residence irrelevant.

And generation? Almost the same pattern emerged within different genera-

Table 33. University Tie, Party, Length of Residence, and Fair Housing Vote

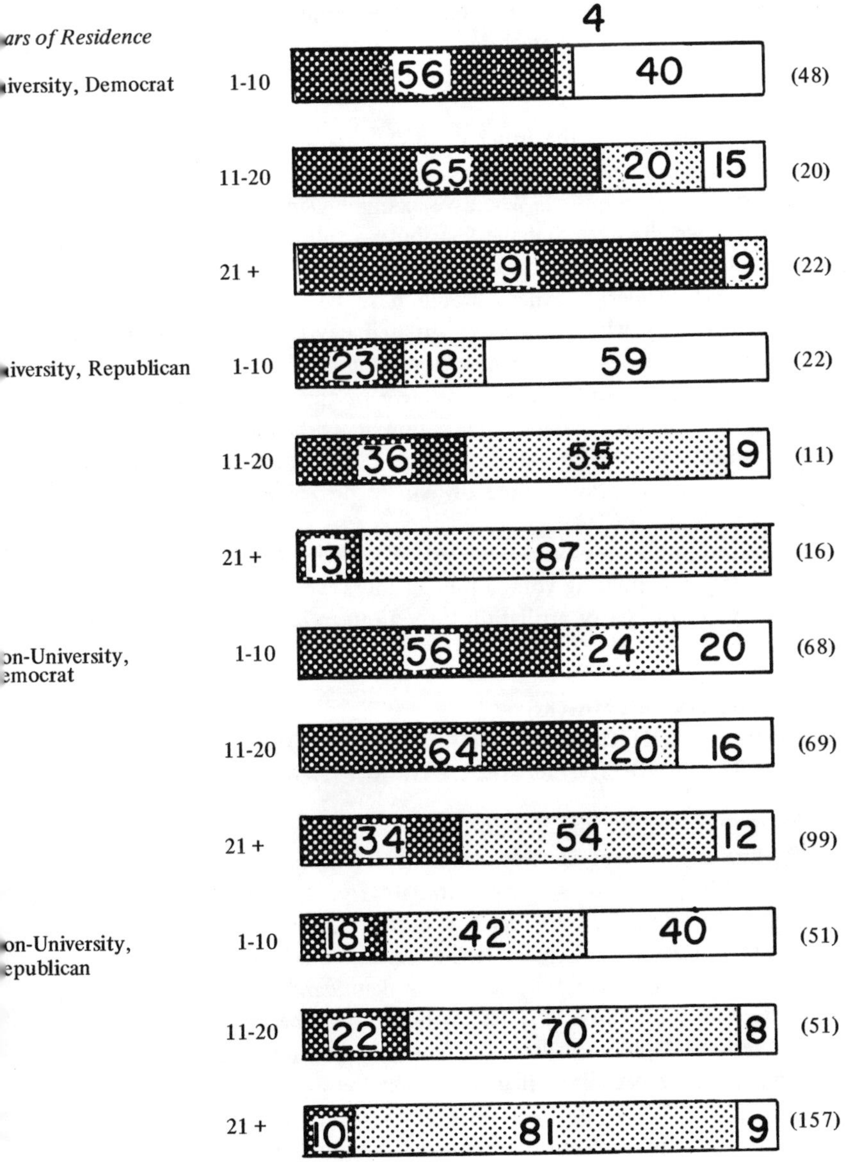

ars of Residence					
iversity, Democrat	1-10	56	4	40	(48)
	11-20	65	20	15	(20)
	21 +	91	9		(22)
iversity, Republican	1-10	23	18	59	(22)
	11-20	36	55	9	(11)
	21 +	13	87		(16)
on-University, emocrat	1-10	56	24	20	(68)
	11-20	64	20	16	(69)
	21 +	34	54	12	(99)
on-University, epublican	1-10	18	42	40	(51)
	11-20	22	70	8	(51)
	21 +	10	81	9	(157)

Key: See page 77.

tional categories when we took into account the simultaneous impact of University tie and party affiliation (see Table 34):

(1) Within the category of University Democrats, there were practically no differences among age categories. This pattern mirrored our findings on length of residence, when once again University Democrats proved to be a united lot.

(2) However, within the other three clusters, the relationship stood up as expected. Among the University Republicans, the younger generation split fifty-fifty on the proposal. When we examine Democrats unattached to the University, we discover that the distribution followed the expected pattern. The non-University Republicans acted in an identical way.

Republican property owners should have behaved the way we had expected, especially when they were situated beyond the University community. At the other extreme, University Democrats should have voted overwhelmingly for the ordinance irrespective of their ownership positions (see Table 35). Roughly speaking, that is how it worked out. In the case of the non-University population, home ownership was of slight significance among Republicans. By contrast, home ownership proved irrelevant among Democrats.

To sum up, liberating processes were of some importance in accounting for the Berkeley fair housing vote, although there were many instances in which University tie and party affiliation turned out to be the overriding considerations.

INTERPRETIVE REMARKS: CUSTOM, TRADITIONALISM, THE LAW OF EVOLUTIONARY POTENTIAL, AND THE PRIVILEGE OF BACKWARDNESS

If generation membership, length of residence, and to a lesser degree, home ownership are relevant considerations in determining choice on matters of accepting black minorities as semi-intimates, we must ask ourselves why. We have already referred to the cake of custom and the presence of liberation processes, but we failed to indicate the basis for their significance.

Perhaps we can explain why custom is significant by referring to the "law" of evolutionary potential.[10] This law holds that when a group becomes highly differentiated and specialized, the collectivity will be unable to adapt itself to novel ideas, especially if it believes that the implementation of these notions might disturb an agreeable adaptation. Hence, older professors might be hesitant to accept revolutionary concoctions in their own field, if only because (1) their adoption would disturb their professorial monopoly of commanding theories; (2) the older faculty would have to reevaluate the tried and tested formulas; and (3) the elderly scholars would find themselves in competition with young people unfettered by the reassessing process and hence

Table 34. University Tie, Party, Generation, and Fair Housing Vote

Generation				
University, Democrat				
Civil Rights (21-29)	52	5	43	(21)
Liberation (30-49)	67	5	28	(43)
Unruffled (50 +)	76	12	12	(26)
University, Republican				
Civil Rights	17	17	66	(12)
Liberation	35	35	30	(17)
Unruffled	15	80	5	(20)
Non-University, Democrat				
Civil Rights	44	56		(15)
Liberation	63	28	9	(90)
Unruffled	40	45	15	(131)
Non-University, Republican				
Civil Rights	(1)	(2)	(5)	(8)
Liberation	17	64	19	(76)
Unruffled	13	76	11	(175)

Key: See page 77.

Table 35. University Tie, Party, Home Ownership, and Fair Housing Vote

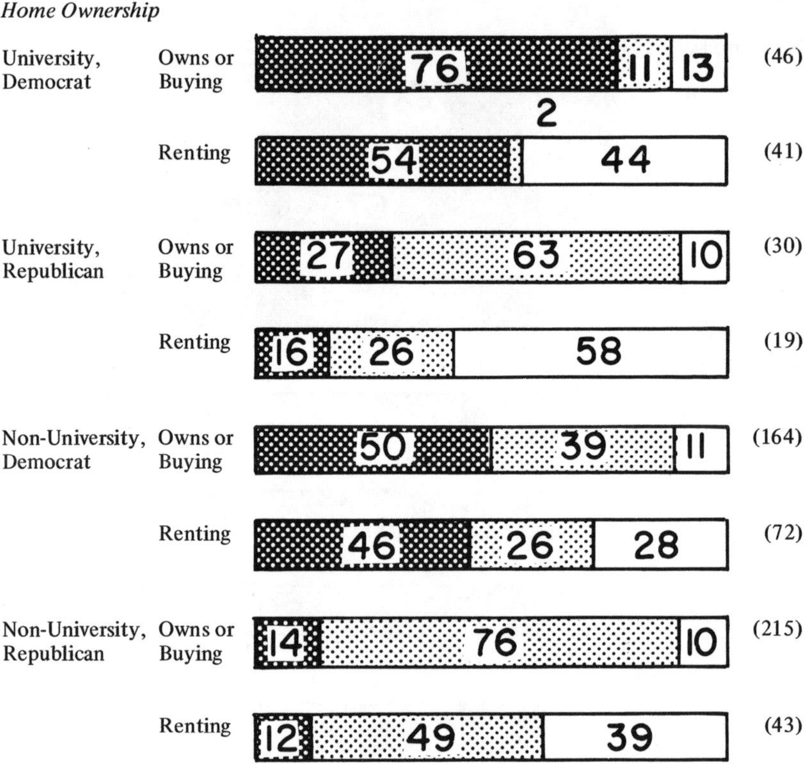

Key: See page 77.

groomed to grasp and to use the new approach. In another setting, an illustration would be the reaction of the personnel of a tired settlement house (run by professionals) to the newly created poverty groups (organized by young black militants). A mixture of conflict and co-optation would occur as the traditional agency (and the professional group) defended its monopoly of services and claim of skills.

These illustrations and this chapter's findings are in harmony with the law of evolutionary potential. Especially is this true of the older generation. After all, who are today's senior citizens if not the ones who had accepted a racist ethic, used it most of their lives, and now find themselves unable to relinquish it? By definition, the long-term residents are the ones, especially the elderly, who maintain they have a vested interest in retaining the present block and neighborhood arrangements. Their customary views and associated status provide them with justification to coerce others on neighborhood folkways concerned with a number of topics, including race.

The old-timers try to freeze reality to prevent change, if only because they can anticipate new structures they could not control. Let us develop this point. The elderly fear racial integration if only because the consequences would reveal their own inadequacies. Why? When senior citizens allow racial minorities to move into their neighborhoods, the white's decision and the black's in-migration indicate the nonutility of neighborhood folkways. When these rules become useless, they are suspect. At this point, many neighborhood residents seek other rules, perhaps arrangements more egalitarian. Should such actions take place and should they prove successful, there might well occur a dramatic rearrangement of power relations in the neighborhood, with the old-timers giving way to newcomers. New residents would be able to obtain and to retain these power positions partially because of their greater knowledge and obvious flexibility, both of which have a bearing on problems associated with the racial reorganization of the neighborhood and recurrent alterations of its services.

The knowledge factor would appear to be extremely important, and we can readily understand why old-timers might well lose their authority over what could and often does happen. Many of the older residents will have lost touch with problems of the neighborhood—such as keeping the elementary school up to date—if only because their children will have grown up and left the area. By contrast, many newcomers will have children who are involved in neighborhood interaction—such as elementary school activities. The short-term residents—both black and white—will be associated on a day-to-day basis with problems such as the integration of schools and reorganization of school curricula.

What is true of the aged and the long-term residents will also be true of many homeowners, especially when they belong to the party that has functioned as a repository of genteel as well as vicious racism. The property owners have exhausted considerable potential for change, for they have invested many economic resources and familial emotions in a particular home and neighborhood. After all, people—especially the elderly—have only a limited amount of both energy and affect to invest during their lives on these matters, and when there is some possibility of their efforts failing because of racial incursions, they move to restake their claims on habitat and to define them as inviolable.

By contrast, as we have already suggested, there are groups and categories that have a high degree of evolutionary potential. For example, if we observe the young with their relatively uncluttered and uncommitted heads, and the civil rights generation with its understandable concern over matters associated with racial injustice and elderly hypocrisy, we can see that the youth are in a fine position to support a proposal in favor of neighborhood integration. Their youth is adaptive and progressive, for it allows them to bypass unscientific notions on race. However, this potential may fail to be fulfilled unless the younger generation belongs to groups that push them in that direction. Consequently, we are not surprised when the current young include many who support an ordinance on fair housing, *especially when* they belong to both a progressive party and a university community.

The privilege of backwardness would also apply in this qualified sense to new residents and to home renters. On the whole, the new residents contain a relatively large number who favor fair housing, since few have high status and hence do not have powerful positions in their neighborhood. For them, there is an absence of vested interest in supporting the *status quo*, for on the whole their property is worth less, their power is generally minimal, and their prestige is accordingly low. Yet for many of the new arrivals there are multiple problems and novel ideas to be applied on how to tap and to reorder the neighborhood to make it more serviceable. When these fresh arrivals belong to both a progressive party and to a university community, they attach themselves to central sources of humanist impulse and scientific scrutiny concerned with promoting and maintaining both racial integration and pluralism.

CONCLUSIONS

We do not wish to give the impression that all levels of the University push equally for racial justice. Historically, it was not by chance that the white leaders in the race liberation struggles of the sixties turned out to be the students and the junior faculty, the renters and the short-term residents, as well as the key members of left-wing groups and progressive sections of the party of reform.

Roughly speaking, these were the young people, and they were involved in a dialectical relationship within the University as they encountered many senior faculty, school administrators, home owners, long-term residents, and party traditionalists. The elderly had remained dedicated to the ecological niche, vested interests, and traditional power positions.

Admittedly, there were exceptions to the law of evolutionary potential, the important one being members of the depression generation within the progressive section of this party of reform. In this case, youthful and harsh experiences guided many of the 1930 generation to vote in ways hardly consistent with what is now expected of the Establishment.

Even after we have completed our analysis of tradition and the law of evolutionary potential, we find it difficult to conclude that we have examined all relevant considerations. Perhaps there are other prime movers in this matter, specifically, authoritarian ideology, a topic explored in our next chapter.

NOTES

1. Ronald Freedman,Amos H. Hawley, Werner S. Landecker, Gerhard Lenski; and Horace M. Miner, in their *Principles of Sociology* (New York: Henry Holt, 1956), pp. 188-90 argue that:

> The normative integration of any group is the result of social mechanisms through which its norms acquire influence on its members, their attitudes, and conduct. In a small and relatively undifferentiated group, norms gain control over the individual through communication and mutual pressures among all of its members; that is, through means which involve the group as a whole. In more complex groups, however, particularly in societies and large communities, a number of component groups within the larger structure exert additional influence in support of social norms. In doing so, these subgroups act as instruments for the normative integration of the total group.
>
> In some instances, like that of the family, the subgroup plays this instrumental role because, as a primary group, it exerts a stronger impact upon the individual, especially in his formative years, than does society at large. Due to its intimacy it is in a position of strength and therefore of strategic importance for the normative integration of the total society. Some other supporting activities are performed by groups of a highly impersonal character, such as a court of law, which are formally established by a larger collectivity for the explicit purpose of promoting the effectiveness of its social norms. To the degree that a group facilitates the integration of the social system of which it is a component, it shall be designated as an *institution* of that system. Insofar as it aids in the normative integration of the system, it operates as a *normative institution* . . .
>
> As instruments of normative integration, institutions operate in various ways. While their understanding is furthered by distinguishing among several major categories of institutional activities, in practice they tend to be more or less interwoven with one another. The most essential service rendered by some groups as normative institutions is to act as agencies of *indoctrination.* In this role the group provides learning experiences in which the norms of society are internalized by the individual, especially in childhood. Families, churches, play groups and youth organizations, schools, and–in some limited respects–agencies of mass communication such as television and radio support normative integration in this manner, not without exerting simultaneous counterinfluences of varying magnitudes.
>
> Secondly, groups are normative institutions insofar as they strengthen their conformity to societal norms through *sanctions* . . .
>
> A third institutional activity is the *symbolization* of social norms . . .
>
> A fourth way in which an institution may contribute to normative integration is through the *implementation* of social norms . . .

Actually, I accept their definition, but for stylistic purposes I prefer to present a short-hand definition.

2. To my knowledge, there is little systematic treatment on the connection between property ownership and vote on matters of race. A possible exception might be Thomas W. Casstevens, *Politics, Housing and Race Relations: The Defeat of Berkeley's Fair Housing Ordinance* (Berkeley:

Institute of Governmental Studies, 1965), p. 94. However, even this study simply relates home ownership to vote and fails to simultaneously take into account other considerations that might be weighed when gauging the impact of home ownership. The author failed to use a multivariable analysis when treating vote.

3. *Lesser race* refers to a racial group with low prestige. This designation obviously does not have any genetic connotations.
4. However, not all speculators can control the processes they initiate. According to some, when businessmen attempt to control the processes of speculation they sometimes lose, as when a downtown business community supports urban renewal because it promises to review the deteriorating property at levels of profit well worth acceptance of urban renewal programs. However, many businessmen have failed in this regard, for the areas cease to attract businesses that are profitable. The net result is that large sections of the business community may lose in an effort that originally appeared to be anything but a gamble. For a discussion of this interesting thesis, see Martin Anderson, *The Federal Bulldozer* (Cambridge: M.I.T. Press, 1964), pp. 1-15, 73-91, and 216-30.
5. Home owners are not the only ones who should stand in the way of racial integration. Crucial also should be women, for they would appear to be among the vanguard of those committed to maintaining neighborhood honor and protecting neighborhood youth. The woman of the house shields the youngsters from threats that might arise within the neighborhood should black minorities move in as neighbors. She is the mother protector, and she assumes this role partially because the male breadwinner toils beyond the home and the neighborhood for much of the day and thereby declares himself less acquainted, less knowledgeable, and less sensitive, if not less sensible, on matters of preserving the status (honor) and the safety of the neighborhood. The wife is not the only female so concerned, for according to certain *mores,* all adult women should learn the proper racial and ethnic distinctions before they marry. Women are expected to be sensitive on this matter long before (and/or after) they marry. Prior to marriage, their ability to rank ethnics and to voice racist opinions fits into our pecking-order heritage, one deeply associated with courtship and marriage and undoubtedly related to male selection. Hence, adult women, not just the wives, should qualify as most traditional. We would expect fewer ladies—whether married or not—in favor of fair housing.

As you will recall, we interviewed females *only when* a male head of household failed to exist inside the dwelling unit. As a result, our sample included a large number of widows, divorcees, and single women who were secretaries, professionals and the like—not the typical housewife. As a result, or so it would seem, we obtained findings different from what we expected. Women did not differ from men when voting on the ordinance, even when we took into account the prior importance of occupation, education, and party affiliation.

6. Karl Mannheim formulated the theoretical basis for the impact of generations. See the relevant chapter, "The Sociological Problem of Generations," in *Sociology of Knowledge* (London: Routledge and Kegan Paul Ltd., 1964), pp. 276-322. More recently, Seymour Lipset, Paul Lazarsfeld, Allen Barton, and Juan Linz have observed:

> A number of sociologists in pre-Hitler Germany suggested that the concept of the "generation" had to be added to such structural categories as class or ethnic group to explain political behavior (Karl Mannheim, 1952; Behrendt, 1932; Neumann, 1939, 1942; Heberle, 1951b). They argued that just as men's attitudes differ as a consequence of their being in a different position in the stratification hierarchy, so men also differ as a result of belonging to different generations. Mannheim, a leading exponent of this concept, emphasized that common experiences at a given point—largely, in his opinion, late adolescence—create a common frame of reference within which people of the same age group tend to view their subsequent political experiences.
>
> In fact, those concerned with generations suggest that the political frame of reference in terms of which one first begins to think seriously about politics remains in force for the rest of one's life. Thus, they argue, to understand the basic values underlying the approach of the middle-aged groups who dominate the political life of any given society, one must go back and examine the political climate and problems which existed when they were young. Common experiences such as those deriving from depression, war, prosperity, or dictatorship act as socializing factors.
>
> This focus on the specific political environment of late adolescence is actually a sociological counterpart of the psychological concern with this life-cycle period discussed earlier. The German psychologist Spranger (1925) recognized this problem and began his discussion of adolescent politics by pointing out that "the political position of youth changes with specific historical circumstances" (p.212).
>
> Unfortunately, there has been no attempt to apply systematically the concept of generations to modern survey research techniques. A pre-Hitler student of German society, Arthur Dix (1930), did set up in tabular form the types of data that would be necessary for such research. He broke down the 1930 German electorate into age groupings and then presented data for each group on the political climate surrounding the first election in which they participated, as well as information about those times. From these data, he made assumptions concerning their role in the political events of the 1930's. With survey methods, one could easily test such hypotheses. The data describing the age composition and life experiences of members of the Nazi and Socialist parties tend to confirm some of the hypotheses about the role of different generations in German society (Gerth, 1940).
>
> Some American studies illustrate the usefulness of the generation concept. In a study of Negro voting in Harlem in 1944, Morsell (1951) found that 82 percent of the Negroes under forty-four voted for Roosevelt, as compared with 59 percent of those over that age. Many of the older Negroes were still responding to an image of the Republican Party as the party of Lincoln. The 1940 and 1944 panel studies reported that younger Catholics were more likely to vote Republican than their elders, while young Protestants were more prone to be Democratic than older ones (Lazarsfeld *et al.,* 1944; Korchin, 1946). This finding may be interpreted as an indication of youth's rebelling against parental patterns. An alterna-

tive hypothesis is that older Americans responded to the traditional religious basis of party cleavage, whereas younger ones reacted in terms of the class cleavages manifested in the politics of the 1930's. Thus young middle-class Catholics became Republicans, while young working-class Protestants became Democrats.

Studies of the 1948 and 1952 elections indicate that the new political generation, the first voters, are more Republican than those which immediately preceded them. Thus in Elmira in 1948 only 38 percent of the wage workers aged twenty-one to twenty-four voted for Truman, as compared with 54 percent among those aged twenty-five to thirty-four (Berelson *et al.,* 1954). Harris (1954), using national survey data, reports that 44 percent of the twenty-one to twenty-four age group were for Eisenhower in 1952, while only 38 percent of the twenty-five to thirty-four group preferred the Republican candidate.

These results, it is suggested, may be products of a situation in which persons who came of age during the depression or war have developed Democratic ties, whereas those who know these events only as history and whose first vote was cast in periods of prosperity are turning toward the Republican Party. If, in fact, it is the case that generations tend to vote left or right depending on which group was in the ascendancy during their coming of age, then it may be necessary to reconsider the popularly held idea that conservatism is associated with increasing age. The empirical evidence for this belief was gathered during periods of tremendous social instability, the 1930's and 1940's, when youth turned leftist while their elders tended to retain the more conservative beliefs of their youth. If a society should move from prolonged instability to stability, it may well be that older people would retain the leftist ideas of their youth, while the younger generations would adopt conservative philosophies.

See their "The Psychology of Voting: An Analysis of Political Behavior," in Gardner Lindzey, *Handbook of Social Psychology* (Cambridge: Addison-Wesley, 1954), pp. 1147-8.

7. The Negro liberation movement found expression not only inside the more advanced sections of the N.A.A.C.P. but the Old Left as well. Communists, Trotskyites, Socialists and others led in the fight against discriminatory employers, schools, churches, governments, and like institutions.

8. As note 5 indicated, our sample of females was anything but representative; hence we are not surprised to find another study of the same election coming up with quite different results. Thomas W. Casstevens' observations contained a more valid appraisal of the female vote. Basing his sample upon a cross-section of the Berkeley population, he found that 28 percent of the white females voted for the ordinance, while 68 percent went against it. There were no data on voting for 4 percent of the females. Among the women who voted, then, the vote was over 2 to 1 against the proposal. White males were more in favor of the proposal. Forty-one percent voted for while 56 percent voted against the ordinance; there was no information on the voting of 4 percent of the men.

Casstevens' information thereby supports the expectations presented in this chapter. See his *Politics, Housing, and Race Relations: The Defeat of Berkeley's Fair Housing Ordinance, op. cit.,* p. 94.

9. For our material on Ph.D. Republicans and the vote on fair housing, see *infra*, pp. 00-000.
10. For a discussion of the law of evolutionary potential, see Marshall Sahlins and Elman Service, *Evolution and Culture* (Ann Arbor: University of Michigan Press, 1960), pp. 93-122. For the crucial progenitor of this concept, see Leon Trotsky's discussion of the privilege of backwardness in his *The Russian Revolution* (Garden City: Doubleday Anchor Books, 1959), pp. 1-14.

EIGHT

The Impact of Authoritarian Ideology

Authoritarian ideology pervades America. Every class contains people who are ethnocentric, economically conservative, or culturally traditional, although authoritarianism is more heavily embedded in some groups than others. One part the product of the past, another the consequence of the economically insecure present, authoritarian ideology perhaps becomes most striking when it is absent, for so few people are free from its strictures. But when people are free in this respect, we wonder: Is there a connection between the *absence* of authoritarian ideology and *action* for minority rights? More precisely, the question is, how, if at all, do ideas and actions connect within the blue- as well as the white-collar worlds? Taking the problem one step farther, we might query: How does ideology help whites oppose *de facto* segregation? This is not to say that whites should attempt to impose desegregation on blacks—those days are gone forever—but that blacks should be legally free to move and to live where they see fit without running up against the stony "no" of grim realtors and individual householders. In this chapter we will focus on the traditional ideology of many such persons, be they realtors, bankers, or ordinary workingmen.

The vehicle for our study was a questionnaire designed to measure authoritarian personality, which for the purposes of our study has been redefined as *cultural traditionalism.* In this respect our efforts are innovational, for few if any studies have ever related the alleged attributes of the authoritarian personality to political behavior.

The questionnaire items used are shown in Figure 3. Each was to be answered on a five-point scale: *Strongly Agree–Mildly Agree–Mildly Disagree–Stongly Disagree–Don't Know.* Attitude areas covered by each group of questions are shown for reference, but did not, of course, appear on the questionnaire.

Figure 3. Questionnaire Items on Authoritarian Ideology (White Respondents Only)

Ethnocentrism

1. Most of our social problems would be solved if we could somehow get rid of the immoral, crooked, and feeble-minded people.
2. America may not be perfect, but the American way has brought us about as close as human beings can get to a perfect society.

Politico-Economic Conservatism

3. Labor unions should become stronger and have more influence generally.
4. Most government controls over business should be eliminated except during a war.
5. In general, full economic security is bad; most men wouldn't work if they didn't need the money for eating and living.
6. The businessman and the manufacturer are much more important to society than the artist and the professor.

Cultural Traditionalism

7. Obedience and respect for authority are the most important virtues children should learn.
8. If people would talk less and work more, everybody would be better off.
9. A person who has bad manners, habits, and breeding can hardly expect to get along with decent people.
10. Science has its place, but there are many important things that can never possibly be understood by the human mind.
11. Every person should have complete faith in some supernatural power whose decisions he obeys without question.
12. Young people sometimes get rebellious ideas, but as they grow up they ought to get over them and settle down.
13. What this country needs most, more than laws and political programs, is a few courageous, tireless, devoted leaders in whom the people can put their faith.

14. No sane, normal, decent person could ever think of hurting a close friend or relative.
15. Nobody ever learned anything really important except through suffering.
16. What youth needs most is strict discipline, rugged determination, and the will to work and fight for family and country.
17. An insult to honor should always be punished.
18. Sex crimes, such as rape and attacks on children, deserve more than mere imprisonment; such criminals ought to be publicly whipped or worse.
19. There is hardly anything lower than a person who does not feel a great love, gratitude, and respect for his parents.
20. When a person has a problem or worry, it is best for him not to think about it but to keep busy with more cheerful things.
21. Some people are born with an urge to jump from high places.
22. People can be divided into two distinct classes: the weak and the strong.
23. Some day it will probably be shown that astrology can explain a lot of things.
24. Wars and social troubles may someday be ended by an earthquake or famine that will destroy the whole world. (NOTE: Do not include H-bombs and their potential consequences.)
25. No weakness or difficulty can hold us back if we have enough will power.
26. Most people don't realize the high degree to which our lives are controlled by plots hatched in secret places.
27. Human nature being what it is, there will always be war and conflict.
28. Nowadays when so many different kinds of people move around and mix together so much, a person has to protect himself especially carefully against catching an infection or disease from them.
29. The wild sex life of the old Greeks and Romans was tame compared to some of the goings-on in this country.

The original study of the authoritarian personality, conducted over twenty years ago but still relevant, used these (and other) questions but failed to do so convincingly.[1] Since then, numerous studies have dwelt on various facets of the problem suggested by the questions posed in our introductory paragraph, but none has attempted to answer all of them, as we shall see at the end of this chapter.[2]

Much as other efforts have ignored the total problem, our analysis has so far failed to examine the impact of ideology on the political choices of working-

and middle-class people within the various political camps. However, we have assumed, and with good reason, that anti-minority group sentiments permeate sizeable chunks of the blue-collar and white-collar populations. Specifically, on the level of individual predisposition, we have assumed that a phenomenon such as authoritarian ideology—especially its traditional aspects—should be both widely accepted within the working class and generally expressed through partisan voting behavior against the acceptance of minorities.

As we have already observed in earlier chapters, some would argue that racial attitudes and correlated discriminatory actions arise from insecure group circumstances. Since working-class people as a whole are undoubtedly subject to economic and socializing conditions that foster the formation of anti-minority ideology, more blue- than white-collar people should be authoritarian and hence, by definition, reject minorities. However, there is an important qualification, one based upon our understanding of the coercive strength of group beliefs. When blue-collar workers evince authoritarian attitudes *but* belong to groups whose ideas demand fair play (behavior that runs counter to the person's traditional views), liberation norms and accompanying group commitments are often sufficiently powerful to push these persons into actions contrary both to their class norms and personal opinions, which are themselves to a large degree expressions of class ideology. Further, even when blue-collar workers are immersed in a subculture largely anti-minority in tone, a large number—especially when they belong to voluntary associations with liberation rules and commitments (for example, a progressive Democratic party organization)—will express nontraditionalist views.

Perhaps more important, groups that steer working-class members away from traditional ideology should also engender progressive economic views. When group members hold both liberation predispositions and progressive economic attitudes, a large number should favor minority rights. This should occur because the key sponsors of progressive ideas view both greater economic equity and minority group rights as inextricable; civil rights without economic rights are meaningless. The right of a black man to sleep under a white bridge is farce.

These propagandists of progressive views prod others to accept a consistent outlook and to link the overall view to fulfilling action. Similarly, when a political group fosters cultural traditionalism, it should also enhance economic conservatism—with predictable effects on voting behavior in race relations. Historically, groups that have sponsored the one have also promoted the other. Needless to say, we accept the idea that *traditionalism and conservatism* are mutually exclusive. However, we deny their alleged independence—one *does* have an accelerating influence on the other if only because the fulfillment of one depends upon the restatement and the realization of the other.

Thus, of those Berkeley blue-collar workers who belonged to the Democratic party in 1963, many should have rejected authoritarian ideology, and of those who did, a large percentage should have voted for fair housing–to a large degree because of the impact of the California Democratic Council on ordinary Democrats. For the same reason, of those blue-collar Republicans who stood to the right of center on ideology, very few if any should have voted for the ordinance, since the Grand Old Party linked ideology to a firm rejection of black rights.

This formulation on the impact of authoritarian ideology is consistent with our views on the significance of cultural traditionalism. As you will recall, we have defined authoritarian ideology as sufficiently inclusive to subsume cultural traditionalism (see Figure 3). Again, indicated in the book's earlier chapters, cultural traditionalism includes the working-class variety. To some degree this working-class subculture constitutes a refurbishing, a redefinition of beliefs, values, and norms associated with rural cultural traditionalism–an inheritance from a bygone pastoral way of life. Its verities have included anti-intellectualism, patriotism, and child-rearing authoritarianism.

One would have to be blind to ignore the popularity of these authoritarian attributes in a large section of the working class, although such beliefs are by no means beyond the middle class, as we shall see. Again, when we focus on traditional ties, we would have to be equally obtuse in judgment to overlook the popularity of rural-style recreation among many working-class people. Blue-collar workers in large numbers spend considerable time hunting and fishing; their favorite paintings frequently depict wooded lakes and streams or mountain splendor; Woolworth classics adorn many a working-class dwelling. (This is not to say that they are any better or worse than a Rembrandt or Picasso; it's all subculture.) Working-class calendars as often embrace the deer as the nude. Taken as a whole, working-class traditionalism thereby contains many rural as well as urban elements, but the blend creates an entirety both similar to, yet qualitatively distinct from, rural cultural traditionalism.

By contrast, liberation values consist of commitments antithetical to authoritarian ideology. Thus, liberation values would be anti-authoritarian, whatever their form.

THE AUTHORITARIAN PERSONALITY

Although the ideas are derived in part from Adorno, our formulation of authoritarianism is different, for our focus deliberately underplays the significance of personality. As Hyman and Sheatsley have indicated, personality loomed large in Adorno's pathfinding study:

> What guided The Authoritarian Personality was the general hypothesis that "the political, economic and social convictions of an individual often form a broad and coherent pattern. . . and that this pattern is an expres-

> sion of deep-lying trends in his personality." More specifically, anti-Semitism was seen as only a part of a larger constellation of anti-minority sentiments, which in turn were related to the politico-economic attitudes of a "potentially fascist" nature. It is also hypothesized that the personality structure within which these sentiments are imbedded [sic] is derived from actual early family experiences, and that these sentiments "could not be derived solely from external factors, such as economic status, group membership, or religion." A research design to test this theory was developed, and a massive array of data are presented in its support.[3]

Our approach to authoritarianism differs from Adorno *et al.*[4] not only on the question of personality but on other important aspects as well; perhaps we should summarize what's involved:

First, while Adorno *et al.* stressed the combined importance of three types of ideology plus a rigid personality to account for racist behavior, our approach has emphasized the significance of ideology and set aside matters of personality. For them, the important thing was the way in which deep-seated personality phenomena ordered the attitudes of anti-Semitism, ethnocentrism, and politico-economic conservatism, with both cause and consequence found within a syndrome itself largely derived from economic, social, and political conditions (the key determinants of personality). In our analysis, however, we ignore personality, focus on ideology (for example, ethnocentrism and politico-economic conservatism), and link it to class as well as other group attachments in order to predict acceptance of minorities as neighbors. Like Adorno *et al.* we stress the pertinence of group structure and rules in accounting for the emergence and perseverence of ideology. However, we do not consider personality, in part because of the immense obstacles to measuring it in a survey research setting. We do not consider white anti-Semitism (as they do) partially because of its subtle contemporary forms, expressions of which demand more than the insensitive door-step interview to calibrate.[5]

Second, we view the *measures of personality* formulated by Adorno *et al.* to be in fact *attributes of rural cultural traditionalism* in the United States. When one carefully inspects the statements they used to measure personality, one is struck by the way in which the queries tap multiple dimensions of rural American *geist,* perhaps more of the nineteenth- than the twentieth-century *genre.* It is as if the statements were designed to measure values seemingly popular among large sections of small-town Americana at the turn of the last century. Perhaps this is an intuitive hunch, but their statements and many of the answers move us to reconsider values perhaps more at home on the cover of the old *Saturday Evening Post* than in scaled dimensions of personality judged as authoritarian. The statements time and again touch on the rural verities and elicit replies that indicate adherence to an American cultural scene considerably more pervasive yesterday than today. The values of fundamentalism, patriotism, and propriety, among others, keep recurring with striking regularity.[6]

To be frank, we should confess that our reaction to the alleged personality measuring statements occurred only after we had used them in our interviews and only now are we trying to systematize which rural dimensions are involved. Consequently, we have tagged them in an *ad hoc* manner to suggest the rural qualities in question (see Table 36).

Third, while Adorno *et al.* do not link the authoritarian syndrome to action[7]—palpable, visible, anti-minority group behavior—our analysis does locate a connection between authoritarian ideology and voting. Thus, our approach hopes to determine not only some of the sources of relevant ideology, but to place these predispositions in their group settings before relating them to voting.

Fourth, we will not use measuring scales and then intercorrelate them as Adorno *et al.* did,[8] because the scale (or index) generally conceals more than it reveals about attitudinal and group importance. In using scales and scale types, one is never sure how groups differ on the multiple facets of each authoritarian attribute. By analyzing each particular opinion separately, we can observe the subtleties and differences too often lost in the labyrinth of scale types and correlation coefficients. Much of these materials will appear in Appendix B.

Fifth, in contrast to Adorno *et al.* we will use a cross-classificatory analysis in the last part of the chapter to demonstrate the separate as well as joint impact of ethnocentric ideology, politico-economic conservatism, and cultural traditionalism as all three *simultaneously* influence integration actions. In this sense, we will express a more positive orientation, being concerned with *both* the rejection and the acceptance of minorities as neighbors.[9]

Key Authoritarian Attributes

Ethnocentrism. One of the authors of *The Authoritarian Personality,* Daniel J. Levinson, defined ethnocentrism as a peculiar kind of ideological system, one that focuses on groups and group relations, distinguishing between ingroups (those with which the individual identified himself) and outgroups (those with which he does not have a sense of belonging and are regarded as antithetical to the ingroups). From Levinson's point of view, ethnocentrism exists when "outgroups are the objects of negative opinions and hostile attitudes; ingroups are the objects of positive opinions and uncritically supportive attitudes; and it is considered that outgroups should be socially subordinate to ingroups."[10]

To measure ethnocentrism, we used two of Levinson's statements from *The Authoritarian Personality*—1 and 2 on our questionnaire.

Table 36. Rural Cultural Traditionalism Subclasses

Questionnaire Statement No.	*Subclass*	*Definition*
7	Fundamentalism	Fundamentalism refers to an historically recent religious movement in American Protestantism, a religious revival that emphasizes the inerrancy of the Scriptures and Biblical miracles, especially the virgin birth and physical resurrection of Christ. It also makes a virtue of values stressed in the Old Testament, including submission to parental, male, and state authority.
8	Anti-intellectualism	Anti-intellectualism is the rejection of rational thought.
9	Rural propriety	Rural propriety refers to ruling class etiquette in nonurban areas. The chief carriers are found at all class levels, but the ethic finds decreasing support as one moves from the top to the bottom of the class structure.
10	Fundamentalism	
11	Fundamentalism	
12	Paternal familial affection	This kind of affection has its power center in the father, who sets the limits and regulates affectional display so as to exclude disruption of family ties so important in rural settings where uncles, aunts, cousins, and in-laws form webs of reciprocity. By contrast, companion familial affection is near-egalitarian and centered around the conjugal family, itself of lesser significance than the "web family" in rural settings.
13	Anti-intellectualism	
14	Paternal familial affection	
15	Fundamentalism	

Table 36 (continued)

Questionnaire Statement No.	*Subclass*	*Definition*
16	Rugged individualism	Individualism refers to a doctrine which assumes that the individual and not society is the paramount consideration or end. By extension, *rugged individualism* has reference to an ethic in which the individual allegedly has the potential of bending and shaping the world according to his desired ends, should he have the talent and energy to do so.
17	Fundamentalism	
18	Fundamentalism	
19	Paternal familial affection	
20	Anti-intellectualism	
21	Anti-intellectualism	
22	Fundamentalism	
23	Anti-intellectualism	
24	Fundamentalism	
25	Rugged individualism	
26	Suspicion of central government	Suspicion of central government refers to believing that the state will act in ways contrary to one's self-interest.
27	Fundamentalism	
28	Suspicion of outside groups	Suspicion of outside groups consists of believing that these groups will do harm to oneself and/or to highly regarded others.
29	Fundamentalism	

Politico-Economic Conservatism. Daniel Levinson has also defined politico-economic conservatism as support of the American *status quo,* resistance to social change, support of conservative values, and *laissez-faire* individualism. Conservatism emphasizes maintaining economic things the way they are. From this point of view, there is a predisposition to avoid alleged extremes when diagnosing problems and suggesting solutions, which are always framed to be consistent with personal ambition. In turn, social success is measured in financial terms, such as accomplishments in the business world. It is believed that gain in this area can be accomplished when there is minimal governmental intrusion in the economy. Economic conservatism, consequently, not only opposes the welfare state but looks askance at those groups such as labor unions, especially when they have the potential of becoming stronger.[12]

To gauge politico-economic conservatism, we once again selected statements from*The Authoritarian Personality*—3 through 6 for our questionnaire.

Rural Cultural Traditionalism. As we have already indicated, statements designed to measure the fascist personality did seemingly gauge aspects of rural cultural traditionalism. Although these values, beliefs, and norms have undoubtedly accompanied peoples' migration from the countryside to the city, they have by no means disappeared with the migrants, but remained in urban settings to become part of a cultural traditionalism so evident within a wide variety of political and other groups with considerable followings in both major classes. Not only political parties but church groups and recreational associations have fastened onto and sponsored these values to advance their own interests and provide cohesion for their members. Hence, these values are anything but cultural lag phenomena, as our earlier comments may have suggested; rather they are transplanted material with new missions and functions.

To suggest the form of rural American *geist* represented by each statement under this final category on our questionnaire, we have further broken down the 23 statements as shown in Table 36. Of course, these *ad hoc* classifications have only descriptive utility, although they might someday serve as the basis for a systematic specification of types of rural cultural traditionalism.

We do not want to give the impression that a pro or con reply to many of these statments is in any way indicative of personal access to ultimate truth. Indeed, the wild sex life of our Mediterranean ancestors *may* have been tame if one compares it to the United States scene of the 1960s. Likewise, our lives might very well be controlled to a high degree by plots hatched in secret places, if not in railroad directors' rooms (as was so often the case in the nineteenth century), then in paneled cloisters filled with politicians, militarists, and platonistic elitists; to argue that history is a gigantic plot is naive, but to believe that serious plots do not exist and are without consequence reveals a virginal naiveté. Our rural forbears created a multiplicity of beliefs—some authoritarian—not all of which deserve rejection.

WHAT HAPPENED: CORRELATION OF VIEWS AND VOTES

Let us first consider statistical descriptions of the results for each question. We can then observe the relationship between the various aspects of authoritarian ideology and the Berkeley 1963 fair housing vote.

Some might doubt the widespread acceptance of authoritarian values suggested by the statements posed. Especially might it seem unusual for large numbers of Berkeleyites to give authoritarian replies, since Berkeley, like many university towns, has the reputation of being pervasively, if not perversely, progressive on most matters. Table 37 should dispel any misconceptions on this matter of widespread acceptance of enlightened thought. Incredibly enough in this era of civilized reason, 25 percent of the whites agreed that "most of our social problems would be solved if we could somehow get rid of the immoral, crooked, and feeble-minded people." Again, in an epoch when we are supposedly moving into a stage of one-world humanism, we can observe that a full 69 percent (N=526) accepted this chauvinistic rhetoric: "America may not be perfect, but the American way has brought us about as close as human beings can get to a perfect society." At the same time, in a period when labor supposedly has been moving in the direction of playing a greater role in multiple community affairs, 73 percent of the study *disagreed* with the proposition that "Labor unions should become stronger and have more influence generally." Finally, at a time when Dr. Spock was extremely popular (1963), 62 percent of the study agreed that "obedience and respect for authority are the most important virtues children should learn."

Perhaps more of a shock is the close correlation between ideology and the fair housing vote. In almost every instance, as indicated in Table 38 (see Appendix B for additional relevant materials), those who strongly agreed with an authoritarian position (or strongly disagreed with a nonauthoritarian stance) voted disproportionately *against* fair housing. In every instance, the statistical differences were significant (at the .05 level), while the percentage gap between each of the categories assumed a staircase quality, with differences between the first and last of the four steps often 30 or 40 percent. For example, among those who strongly agreed that people should talk less and work more, 20 percent voted for fair housing. At the other attitudinal extreme, 52 percent voted for fair housing.

One might argue that the widespread popularity of authoritarian ideology and its link to the rejection of blacks as neighbors stemmed from the impact of working-class sentiment and working-class vote; workers being authoritarian in most cases, their numbers resulted in what appeared to be the widespread popularity of authoritarian views and voting choices. There is some

Table 37. Authoritarian Ideology: A Descriptive Presentation (Whites Only*)

	Strongly Agree	*Mildly Agree*	*Mildly Disagree*	*Strongly Disagree*	*Don't Know*	*Total*
Ethnocentrism						
1. Most of our social problems would be solved if we could somehow get rid of the immoral, crooked, and feeble-minded people.	(89) 12%	(102) 13%	(156) 21%	(402) 53%	(11) 1%	(760) 100%
2. America may not be perfect, but the American way has brought us about as close as human beings can get to a perfect society.	(287) 38%	(239) 31%	(138) 18%	(88) 12%	(11) 1%	(763) 100%
Politico-Economic Conservatism						
3. Labor unions should become stronger and have more influence generally.	(68) 9%	(119) 16%	(248) 33%	(309) 40%	(19) 2%	(763) 100%
4. Most government controls over business should be eliminated except during a war.	(155) 20%	(162) 21%	(207) 27%	(222) 29%	(17) 3%	(763) 100%
5. In general, full economic security is bad; most men wouldn't work if they didn't need the money for eating and living.	(141) 19%	(153) 20%	(185) 24%	(262) 34%	(22) 3%	(763) 100%
6. The businessman and the manufacturer are much more important to society than the artist and the professor.	(62) 8%	(84) 11%	(243) 32%	(344) 45%	(30) 4%	(763) 100%
Cultural Traditionalism						
7. Obedience and respect for authority are the most important virtues children should learn.	(329) 43%	(142) 19%	(130) 17%	(157) 20%	(4) 1%	(752) 100%
8. If people would talk less and work more, everybody would be better off.	(224) 29%	(212) 28%	(172) 23%	(129) 17%	(26) 3%	(763) 100%

*For all tables presented in this chapter.

Table 37 (continued)

9. A person who has bad manners, habits, and breeding can hardly expect to get along with decent people.	(345) 45%	(217) 29%	(94) 12%	(84) 11%	(23) 3%	(763) 100%
10. Science has its place, but there are many important things that can never possibly be understood by the human mind.	(280) 37%	(234) 31%	(127) 17%	(101) 13%	(21) 2%	(763) 100%
11. Every person should have complete faith in some supernatural power whose decisions he obeys without question.	(179) 24%	(108) 14%	(158) 21%	(304) 40%	(14) 1%	(763) 100%
12. Young people sometimes get rebellious ideas, but as they grow up they ought to get over them and settle down.	(287) 38%	(198) 26%	(161) 21%	(106) 14%	(11) 1%	(763) 100%
13. What this country needs most, more than laws and political programs, is a few courageous, tireless, devoted leaders in whom the people can put their faith.	(238) 31%	(123) 16%	(146) 19%	(236) 31%	(20) 3%	(763) 100%
14. No sane, normal, decent person could ever think of hurting a close friend or relative.	(263) 35%	(110) 14%	(183) 24%	(196) 26%	(11) 1%	(763) 100%
15. Nobody every learned anything really important except through suffering.	(69) 9%	(85) 11%	(169) 22%	(404) 53%	(36) 5%	(763) 100%
16. What youth needs most is strict discipline, rugged determination, and the will to work and fight for family and country.	(264) 35%	(203) 27%	(145) 19%	(136) 18%	(13) 1%	(761) 100%
17. An insult to honor should always be punished.	(99) 13%	(102) 14%	(237) 31%	(304) 40%	(14) 2%	(756) 100%
18. Sex crimes, such as rape and attacks on children, deserve more than mere imprisonment; such criminals ought to be publicly whipped or worse.	(150) 20%	(56) 7%	(146) 19%	(399) 53%	(10) 1%	(761) 100%

(Continued on p. 162)

Table 37 (continued)

19. There is hardly anything lower than a person who does not feel a great love, gratitude, and respect for his parents.	(173) 23%	(114) 15%	(209) 27%	(258) 34%	(8) 1%	(762) 100%
20. When a person has a problem or worry, it is best for him not to think about it but to keep busy with more cheerful things.	(145) 19%	(135) 18%	(216) 29%	(254) 33%	(9) 1%	(759) 100%
21. Some people are born with an urge to jump from high places.	(92) 12%	(170) 22%	(145) 19%	(304) 40%	(49) 7%	(760) 100%
22. People can be divided into two distinct classes: the weak and the strong.	(97) 13%	(93) 12%	(129) 17%	(436) 57%	(7) 1%	(762) 100%
23. Some day it will probably be shown that astrology can explain a lot of things.	(80) 11%	(96) 13%	(125) 16%	(434) 57%	(23) 3%	(758) 100%
24. Wars and social troubles may some day be ended by an earthquake or flood that will destroy the whole world. (NOTE: Do not include H-bombs and their potential consequences.)	(50) 7%	(112) 15%	(141) 18%	(433) 57%	(23) 3%	(759) 100%
25. No weakness or difficulty can hold us back if we have enough will power.	(214) 28%	(146) 19%	(163) 21%	(233) 31%	(6) 1%	(762) 100%
26. Most people don't realize the high degree to which our lives are controlled by plots hatched in secret places.	(91) 12%	(160) 21%	(128) 17%	(350) 46%	(27) 4%	(756) 100%
27. Human nature being what it is, there will always be war and conflict.	(298) 39%	(220) 29%	(127) 17%	(105) 14%	(11) 1%	(761) 100%
28. Nowadays when so many different kinds of people move around and mix together so much, a person has to protect himself especially carefully against catching an infection or disease from them.	(110) 15%	(116) 15%	(170) 22%	(356) 47%	(9) 1%	(761) 100%
29. The wild sex life of the old Greeks and Romans was tame compared to some of the goings-on in this country.	(82) 11%	(120) 16%	(257) 34%	(224) 30%	(71) 9%	(754) 100%

reason to doubt this thesis, however. Although workmen were disproportionately authoritarian, as indicated in Table 39, a sizeable chunk of the middle class also indicated a preference for authoritarian opinions. Because these views found considerable support within both strata, we could not ignore the impact of these ideas within the two classes, although our primary concern remained authoritarianism within the blue-collar world.

Some might hold that the important consideration is not information on what working-class people think and speculation on what they do, but rather statistical materials on the impact of thought on action. As the data in Table 40 indicate, when working-class people were non-authoritarian, they voted *overwhelmingly* against fair housing; the same pattern held true for middle-class people. Interestingly, we find certain unexpected results inside the blue- (and the white-) collar world. Of those who were working class *and authoritarian,* many voted for fair housing, thereby indicating the significance of phenomena other than attitude. Of those who were middle class and *non-authoritarian,* many voted against fair housing, once again suggesting the compelling influence of considerations other than personal opinion, perhaps the relevance of group rules and preferences.

Of those influences considered in our study, the most significant has proved to be political parties. When we take party influence into account and then consider the impact of ideology on blue- and white-collar people, we find at least four important patterns (see Table 41): (1) Among Democrats who were authoritarian, whether blue or white collar, more voted for fair housing than was the case among *comparable* nonauthoritarian Republicans. (2) If one were to compare *blue*-collar Democrats with *white*-collar Republicans who were ideologically the same, the blue-collar Democrats time and again were proportionately more for fair housing. Moreover, in those instances involving comparisons of *blue*-collar authoritarian Democrats with *white*-collar non-authoritarian Republicans, the majority of contrasts (specified in Appendix B) indicated that more blue-collar Democrats were for fair housing. (3) Among Democrats, more were for fair housing when they were nonauthoritarian. This was true in both the blue- and white-collar worlds. When *blue-collar* Democrats were nonauthoritarian on economic matters, they voted inordinately for the proposal. For example, when they favored unions becoming stronger, 39 percent voted for fair housing, 47 percent against, while 14 percent did not vote; on the other hand, when comparable workers rejected the idea of unions playing a stronger role in the community, 21 percent voted for and 71 percent against the ordinance. (4) If we consider Republicans only, especially the white-collar variety, we can observe that proportionately more voted for fair housing when they were nonauthoritarian. There were some exceptions to this pattern, but the unusual by no means obliterated the basic finding.

Table 38. Authoritarian Ideology and Fair Housing Vote

*Get rid of immoral people?(1)**				
Strongly Agree	17	64	19	(87)
Midly Agree	12	67	21	(102)
Mildly Disagree	28	51	21	(156)
Strongly Disagree	47	35	18	(397)
*Labor become stronger? (3)**				
Strongly Agree	51	31	18	(68)
Mildly Agree	53	28	19	(118)
Mildly Disagree	39	39	22	(244)
Strongly Disagree	19	62	19	(305)
*Obedience, respect best?(7)**				
Strongly Agree	16	67	17	(326)
Mildly Agree	28	51	21	(143)
Mildly Disagree	58	25	17	(128)
Strongly Disagree	62	14	24	(155)

*Numbers correspond to statements on questionnaire (Table 37, pp. 160-2); for full Table, see Appendix B.

Table 39. Class and Authoritarian Ideology

	Agree	Disagree	(N)
*Get rid of immoral people? (1)**			
White Collar	22	78	(637)
Blue Collar	46	54	(105)
*Labor becomes stronger?(7)**			
White Collar	23	77	(633)
Blue Collar	39	61	(104)
*Obedience, respect best?(3)**			
White Collar	59	41	(644)
Blue Collar	84	16	(107)

*Numbers correspond to statements on questionnaire (Table 37, pp. 160-2); for full Table, see Appendix B.

Key: Agree [diagonal hatching] Disagree [vertical lines]

On the whole, ideology proved to be an important determinant of vote; however, values did not eliminate the statistical significance of political party affiliation. If party affiliation and ideology have proved relevant when taken together, they may acquire even added importance when one links them to University tie, a consideration also found important in our previous analysis. In Table 42 we observe this to be the case, for when we examine only white-collar workers—there were so few blue-collar workers employed by the University—we note: (1) The triple impact of *University tie, Democratic party affiliation,* and *nonauthoritarian ideology* is by no means insignificant. For example, when we asked University Democrats the question dealing with "immoral people" (29) and scored only those who *disagreed* with this belief, we found that 57 persons voted for fair housing while six voted against it;

Table 40. Class, Ideology, and Fair Housing Vote

*Get rid of immoral people?(1)**				
White-collar, Agree	13	66	21	(141)
White-collar, Disagree	43	38	19	(496)
Blue-collar, Agree	19	65	16	(48)
Blue-collar, Disagree	25	50	25	(57)
*Labor become stronger?(3)**				
White-collar, Agree	60	22	18	(145)
White-collar, Disagree	29	51	20	(488)
Blue-collar, Agree	27	53	20	(41)
Blue-collar, Disagree	25	60	18	(63)
*Obedience, respect best?(7)**				
White-collar, Agree	20	62	18	(378)
White-collar, Disagree	61	18	21	(266)
Blue-collar, Agree	16	62	22	(90)
Blue-collar, Disagree	53	29	18	(17)

*Numbers correspond to statements on questionnaire (Table 37, pp. 160-2); for full Table, see Appendix B.

Table 41. Party Preference, Class, Authoritarian Ideology, and Vote

horitarian Ideology

Fair Housing Vote

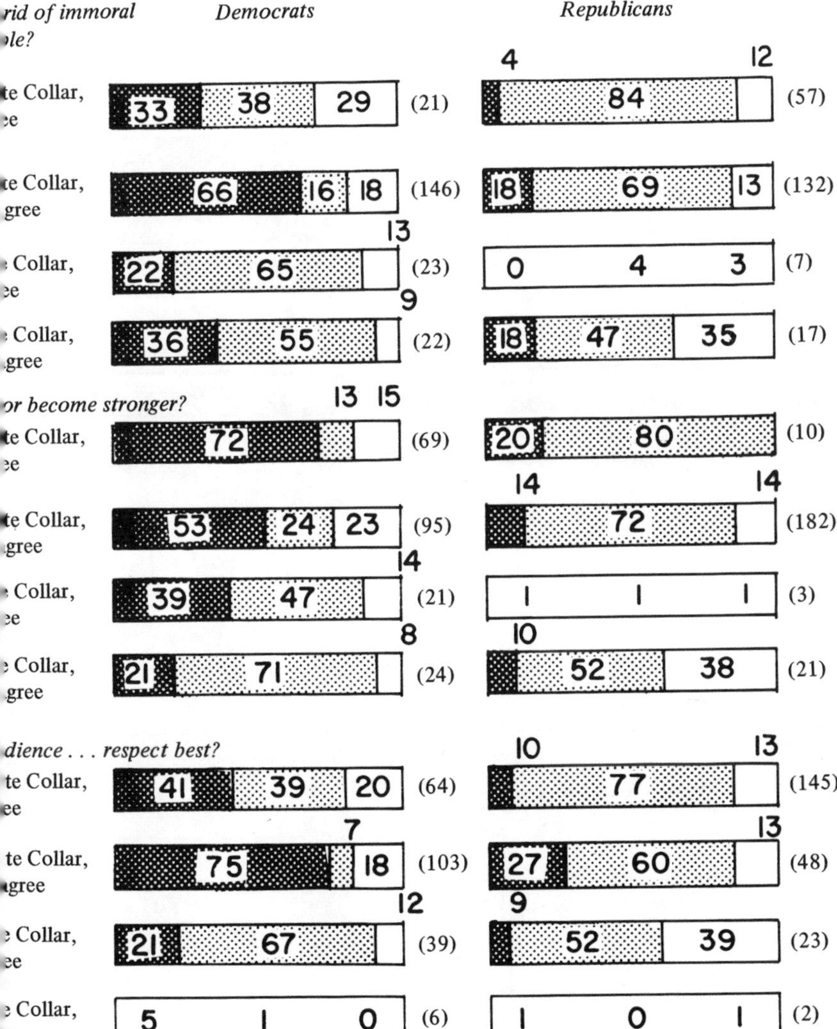

: See page 170.

Table 42. University Tie, Party, Ideology, and Fair Housing Vote (White-collar Only)

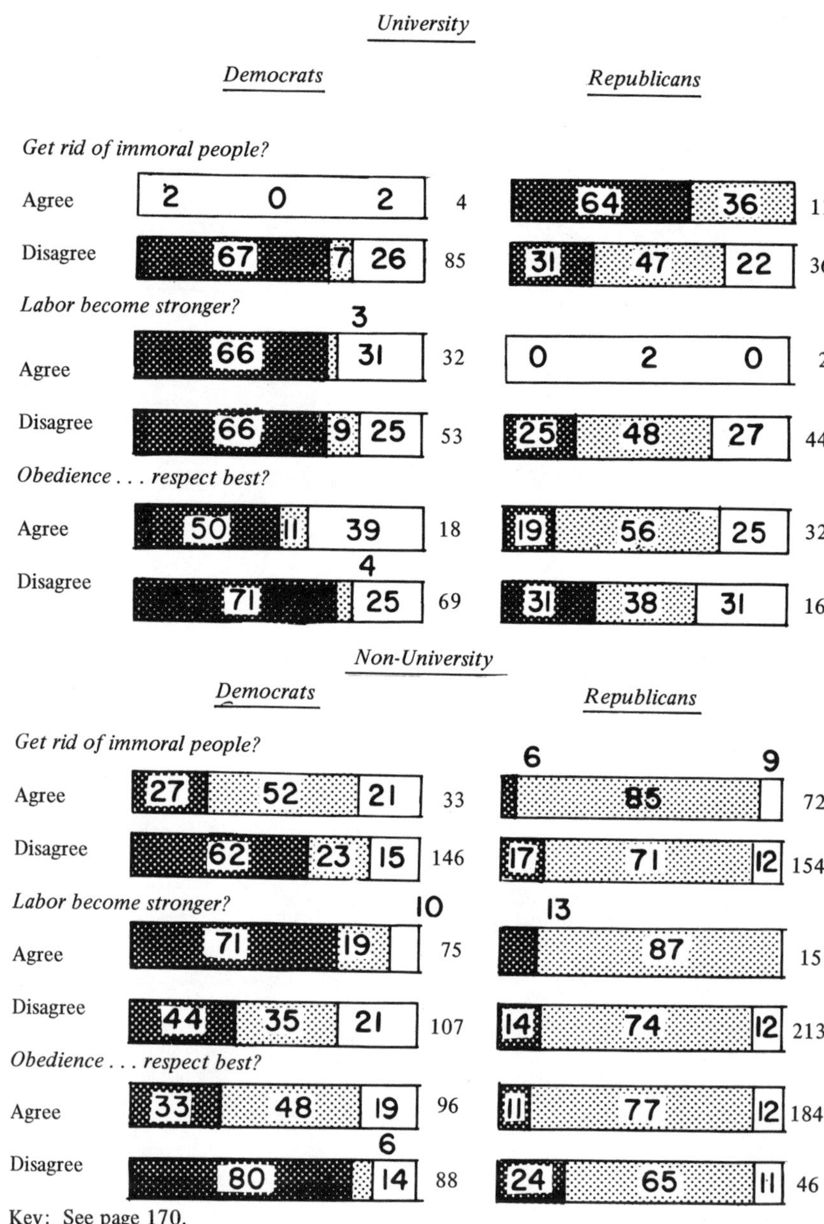

Key: See page 170.

there were so few people who *agreed* with the "morality" statement that we could not make a comparison. On the "America may not be perfect but it is the best" statement (2), the vote was 36 to 1 for fair housing among those University Democrats who *disagreed* with the superpatriotic formulation. The pattern was clear in almost every set of replies. (2) By contrast, the University, nonauthoritarian *Republicans* did not score as high on the vote, although they were well ahead of comparable authoritarians in the Republican ranks. (3) In the non-University world, the pattern of voting held up as expected. If we consider only non-University Democrats who were nonauthoritarian, they scored highest time and again in support of fair housing. For example, when we examine the distribution of people on the "immorality" statement (29), we note that of those who were nonethnocentric, the vote was 90 to 33 for the ordinance, while in the case of Democrats identical in every way except ideology, the vote was 9 in favor and 17 against. Among non-University Republicans, both ethnocentric and nonethnocentric, a comparable distribution occurred on almost every one of the statements.

If *University affiliation* and *ideology* should prove significant among white-collar people, *union tie* and *ideology* should be important in the blue-collar world, provided of course that one assumes unions have a positive influence on matters predisposing workers to favor fair housing. This last assumption is hard to accept, especially when one realizes that so many craft unions are decidedly racist, and many other unions only somewhat less so. At the same time, however, one should not overlook the ways in which certain West Coast industrial unions such as the longshoremen's and auto workers' unions have worked for civil rights over the decades.[23] Admittedly, their record is mixed (and to a large degree counter-balanced by most craft unions), but even if this is the case, one might still look for the positive impact of union affiliation on race vote. Unfortunately, there was a paucity of Caucasian blue-collar workers in the study, in large part because there were so few in Berkeley. Still, as Table 43 indicates, the combination of union tie, Democratic party registration, *and* nonauthoritarian ideology would appear to maximize the proportion of blue-collar workers voting for fair housing. For example, of those blue-collar workers who belonged to a union, registered as Democrats, and disagreed with statement 29, seven voted for the ordinance and ten cast their ballots against it. This combination of group pressures and personal attributes turned out a larger vote for fair housing than any other combination, either Democratic and Republican.

If it is true that the combination of *University (or labor union) tie, Democratic party affiliation,* and nonauthoritarian ideology has a predictable and positive impact on support for fair housing, what might we find should we *simultaneously* examine the two structural considerations plus three types of ideology? In attempting to answer this question, we will try to ferret out

Table 43. Union, Party, and Authoritarian Ideology (White, Blue-Collar Only)

	UNION											
	Democrats						*Republicans*					
Fair Housing Vote	*Get Rid of Immoral People . . . ?*		*Labor Become Stronger?*		*Obedience . . . Respect . . . Best?*		*Get Rid of Immoral People . . . ?*		*Labor Become Stronger?*		*Obedience . . . Respect . . . Best?*	
	Agree	Disagree	Agree	Disagree	Agree	Disagree	Agree	Disagree	Agree	Disagree	Agree	Disagree
For	5	7	8	4	7	5	0	1	1	0	0	1
Against	12	10	11	12	22	1	3	1	1	3	4	0
Did Not Vote	2	2	2	2	4	0	2	3	1	4	5	0
TOTAL (Frequencies Only)	19	19	21	18	33	6	5	5	3	7	9	1
	NON-UNION											
For	0	2	0	0	1	1	1	3	0	4	3	1
Against	8	2	4	6	10	0	3	7	2	10	10	0
Did Not Vote	1	0	1	3	1	0	2	2	0	3	4	1
TOTAL (Frequencies Only)	9	4	5	9	12	1	6	12	2	17	17	2

differences inside the *white-collar world only,* since there are insufficient blue-collar workers in the study to treat them simultaneously when examining so many dimensions.

In Table 44, in those instances where we focus exclusively on white-collar and University people, we singled out Democrats first and found that: (1) They voted overwhelmingly for fair housing when they were nonauthoritarian. (2) Slightly less voted for the ordinance when they were authoritarian on matters of economy but nonauthoritarian in terms of traditionalism. (3) Their opinions were remarkably homogeneous, as evidenced by the pile-up within the nonauthoritarian columns.

On the other hand, with non-University Democrats we observed a greater diversity in attitudes but similarity in results. For example, we found that the completely nonauthoritarian Democrats voted 37 to 2 for the ordinance, while those nonauthoritarian on all matters but economy voted for it 27 to 3. At the other extreme, when we focused only on non-University Democrats who were thoroughly authoritarian, we found that the vote was 4 in favor and 10 against. Appendix B materials point to the same pattern.

In the case of white-collar Republicans, the distribution occurred as expected, although there are so few cases among University Republicans that it is almost fruitless to comment on their distribution. Among non-University Republicans, however, Table 44 indicates that when they were nonauthoritarian in every way but economic, 8 voted for and 21 voted against the proposal. At the other extreme, when these people were so thoroughly authoritarian as to conform to the grimmest of academic stereotypes on town folk, two voted for and 51 against the proposal!

We can only conclude that authoritarian ideology does have an impact. Knowledge of people's values does add to our understanding of how they will vote on racial issues. This pattern holds true within the blue- and white-collar worlds, among Democrats and Republicans, University professors, and the town folk. However, ideological considerations do not supplant the importance of these structural considerations but supplement our understanding. Hence, where people stand *plus* what they think are of more importance than either of these considerations treated without reference to the other.[24]

Are These Findings Unique?

These results are consistent with what we already know about party and university as determinants and carriers of ideas. In an overlooked but significant study on opinion-formation in a crisis situation—the California loyalty oath fight of the early 1950s—Seymour M. Lipset interviewed 480 *students* at the University of California (Berkeley), a setting most appropriate for our study.[25] Selected randomly from the entire student body, the students chosen proved to be disproportionately against the loyalty oath and non-hir-

Table 44. University Affiliation, Ideology, and Fair Housing Vote (White-collar Only)

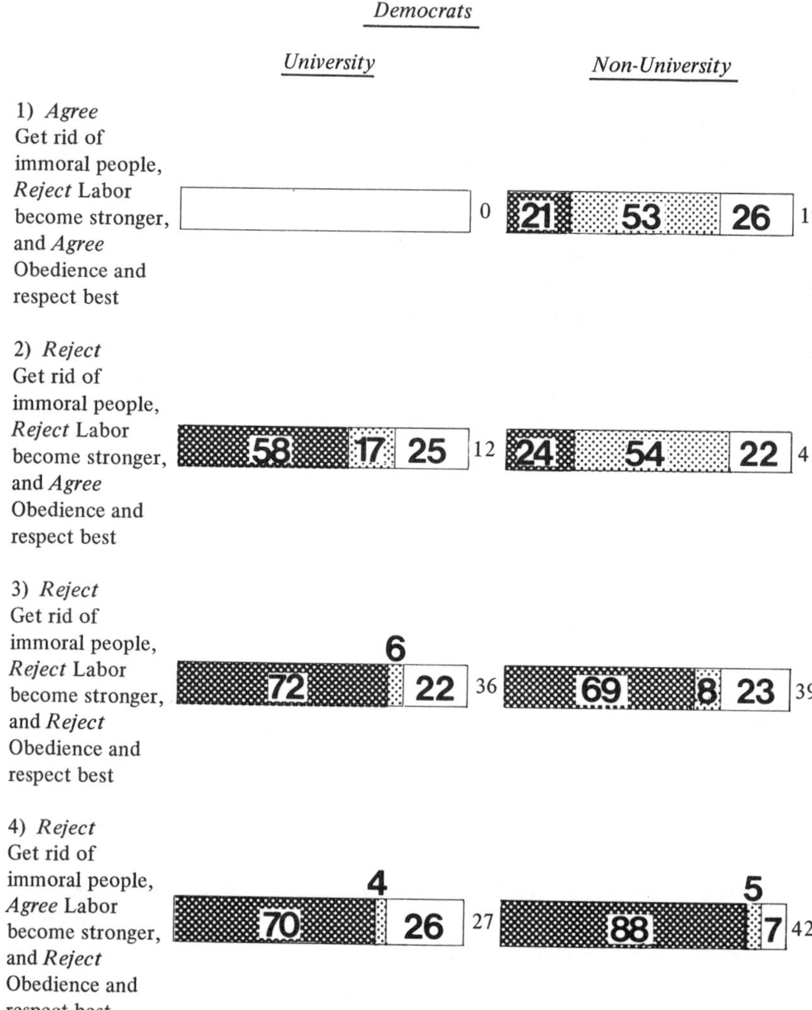

Table 44. Continued

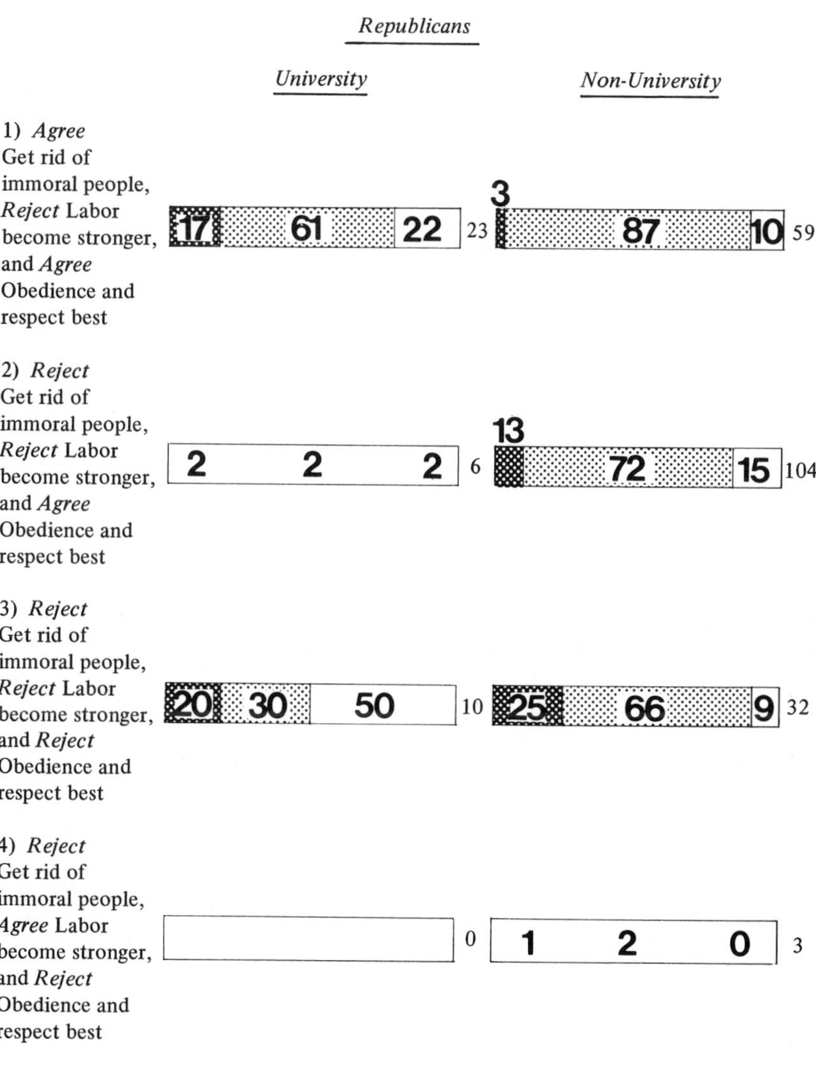

Key: See page 77.

ing of Communists by the University *when* they were Democrats with progressive opinions. (These political attitudes were gauged by focusing primarily on such economic matters as the Taft-Hartley Law, socialized medicine, government break-up of large corporations, government ownership of public utilities, and the British Labor Government.) Lipset found that the progressive Democrats, more than the Republicans, rejected the loyalty oath. These same progressive Democrats also rejected University policy on non-hiring of Communists to teach.

Perhaps most pertinent was Lipset's observation that when these students came from *working-class* families, they were disproportionately against the oath and the policy of not hiring Communists. Lipset made a distinction between students on the basis of their parental occupational backgrounds—fathers who were professionals, farmers, proprietors, business executives, or employed workers. The study found that when students came from the working class, they stood out in being opposed to the loyalty oath. Students of working-class background were only slightly behind the group having the largest proportion *against* the oath—students whose fathers were proprietors. (This last observation did not come as a surprise, because of those who were proprietors twenty years ago, a very large number were Jewish; and Jewish Berkeley students, as Lipset demonstrated statistically, scored well ahead of Protestants and Catholics, in that order, in opposition to the oath and the University policy on non-hiring of Communists.) When we consider these five occupational groups in terms of *support for* the oath and the non-hiring policy, students of working-class background contained the smallest proportion supporting these anti-civil libertarian views. In turn, these results are consistent with Lipset and Zetterberg's findings that middle-class people of working-class background are undoubtedly more leftist in sentiment and disproportionately concentrated in progressive and leftist political parties.[26]

This matter of party organization and attitude has come up in a host of other studies, including some of relevance to "the authoritarian personality." In California during the early 1960s, where issues of this kind kept cropping up, J.W. Ferguson and P.J. Hoffman dwelt on the Francis Amendment, a state constitutional proposal that provided strong measures for the control of "subversives."[27] Focused on the San Fernando Valley region of Los Angeles the study found that most Democrats but only a slight majority of Republicans were opposed to the measure. Whether these opponents were inordinately nonauthoritarian was not revealed. However, in another study—one consisting of an experiment investigating the relationship between F-scale (fascist) scores and preference for political candidates—Howard Leventhal, Robert L. Jacobs, and Nijole Z. Kurdirka observed a random selection of Yale students and found that when they scored high on F-scale (comparable to our measure of rural cultural traditionalism), they also preferred the Republican party and voted for Richard Nixon in the 1960 presidential election, while those who scored low preferred the Democratic party and voted for John F. Kennedy.[28] These authors believe the results reflect three significant situations: (1) both candidates clearly differed on matters of liberal and conservative ideologies; (2) the students in question possessed one of the two ideological outlooks; and (3) liberal or conservative values were more salient than other considerations in determining choice of candidates. It would seem that many conservative Republicans have a way of translating their ideas into political practice.

The Yale students' opinions are consistent with those of Berkeley students observed by Lipset (see note 25). However, Lipset's analyses are not all of one coin. Sidney Peck[29] as well as S. M. Miller and Frank Riessman[30] have commented on Lipset's less than skillful use of F-Scale and like materials to demonstrate the alleged authoritarian qualities of working-class life and practice. Pressed with criticism on this matter, Lipset has replied that under certain conditions, working-class people do support civil liberties, as was the case in Australia during the early 1950s when political rights were attacked by the middle-class conservatives out to ban the Australian Communist Party.[31] Although it would seem too much to expect Lipset or anybody else to specify the general conditions under which working-class people will vote heavily for the liberties and rights of beleaguered minorities, one can legitimately expect Lipset and others to take a more careful position on such matters as what the F-Scale measures.

William Peterson[32] and Arnold Rose[33] have indicated that the F-Scale taps a kind of cultural relativism disregarded by Adorno and the other authors of the original authoritarian personality study. In this sense, Peterson and Rose's views are not too different from our own, although they are less willing to speculate on what the F-Scale does in fact gauge. Elmer L. Struening and Arthur H. Richardson[34] have used the technique of factor analysis to discover what authoritarian items do calibrate. They found that authoritarianism is saturated with items that emphasize obedience to and respect for authority, improvement of one's social position, careful planning, family loyalty, and the value of attending religious services and working hard–what the authors perhaps inappropriately refer to as convential middle-class and especially lower middle-class ideology. Keeping in mind the classical distinction advanced by David Riesman,[35] Guy E. Swanson,[36] and William H. Whyte,[37] we would prefer to view authoritarian ideology as reaching its nadir during early American industrial capitalism, with its emphasis upon verities functionally linked to extraction of various resources from the soil, their processing, and saving. During this period, the key carriers might well have been the middle-class, both in rural and urban areas. Still, this class was by no means the only one to harbor such opinions.

If we assume that authoritarianism is largely a matter of values, we're still stuck with the problem of its origins. We cannot begin to solve this problem in this particular study, but we can suggest which considerations appear unrelated to the genesis of working-class authoritarianism. We have good reason to believe that prior and abrasive parental socialization in working-class settings fails to be entirely responsible for making people authoritarian. Miller and Riessman[38] have culled and analyzed the social psychological literature and made this point. So has William McCord[39] in one of those rare sociological studies on the familial basis of prejudice. Focusing on 45 lower-class males, he observed these youths (ages 9 to 12) between 1937 and 1940, and again in 1948. Both times, the boys' attitudes towards Jews and Negroes were obtained through interviews. The findings failed to confirm the generalizations proposed in the classical authoritarian personality study, namely, that bigots were more likely to come from families with harsh, severe discipline or with inconsistent discipline. In this developmental study—the Cambridge-Somerville project on juvenile delinquency—the bigoted and nonbigoted did not differ significantly on any family background dimension.

CONCLUSIONS

Much as Lipset has suggested, authoritarianism was widespread within the Berkeley working-class in 1963. As expected, this propensity was more true of cultural than economic beliefs. Elements of rural cultural traditionalism found large numbers of carriers inside the working class. Nonetheless, the popularity of the rural verities should not be confused with blanket working-class opposition to the acceptance of minorities as neighbors. Of those white workers who favored fair housing—and their numbers were by no means few—many could be found among those who rejected authoritarian views and who affiliated with groups containing liberation values. Hence, we find that blue-collar workers voted heavily for fair housing when they held progressive opinions *and* belonged to both labor unions and the Democratic party. Of all blue-collar groups, this particular category stood out in support of fair housing. Again, of those workers who were authoritarian but Democrats, a substantial minority voted for fair housing, thereby testifying to that party's influence on the working-class voter.

In the white-collar world where we had a sufficiently large number of respondents to permit a detailed, cross-classificatory analysis, we observed that when people held progressive economic views, there was a good chance of their rejecting cultural traditionalism as well, and when this was true, middle-class persons who belonged simultaneously to the Democratic party and University community voted overwhelmingly for fair housing.

Thus it would seem that although progressive economic views and liberation

Figure 4. Economic Ideology, Cultural Traditionalism, and Authoritarian Ideology

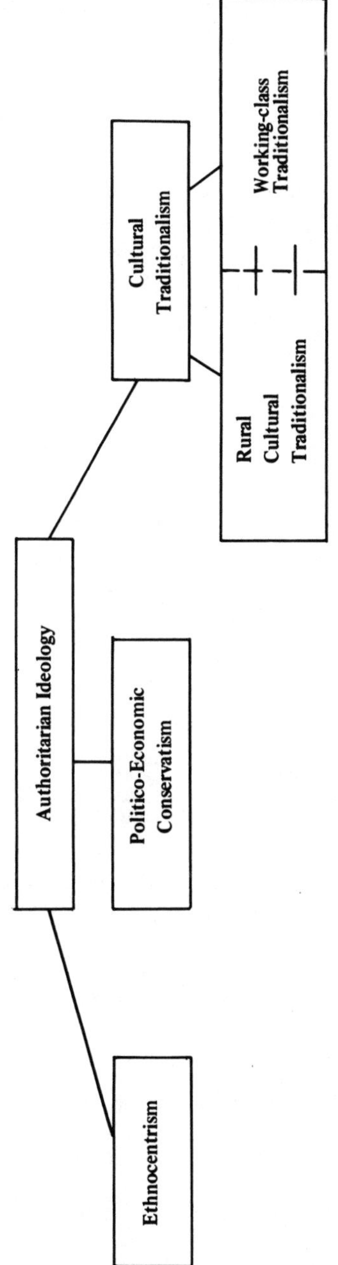

opinions are mutually exclusive, they are anything but unrelated to one another: knowledge of people's economic opinions allowed us to predict to their cultural views and vice versa, while information on people's economic opinions and cultural views allowed us to predict their vote on fair housing.

Perhaps we should make one more point to avoid misinterpretation of our findings. Our results by no means refute the authoritarian personality theory. Perhaps the authoritarian values discussed are harmonious with the needs of the authoritarian personality, with both ideology and personality having their genesis in economics, politics, and social institutions, much as the authoritarian personality study hypothesized.[40] Unlike Adorno and others, however, we do insist upon a distinction between people's values and their correlated personality characteristics. We should not confuse intercorrelation with equation.

NOTES

1. For the original publication of the study see T. W. Adorno, Else Frenkel-Brunswik, Daniel J. Levinson, and R. Nevitt Sanford, *The Authoritarian Personality* (New York: Harper and Row, 1950).
2. Perhaps the best effort to summarize these studies has been John P. Kirscht and Ronald C. Dillehay's *Dimensions of Authoritarianism* (Lexington: University of Kentucky Press, 1967).
3. See Herbert H. Hyman and Paul B. Sheatsley, "'The Authoritarian Personality' A Methodological Critique," in Richard Christie and Marie Jahoda, *Studies in the Scope and Method of 'The Authoritarian Personality'* (Glencoe: The Free Press, 1954), pp. 51-2.
4. See later edition of Adorno, *et al., The Authoritarian Personality, Part One* (New York: John Wiley and Sons, 1964), pp. 5-6, in which the authors make clear their position on the salience of social structure:

   > Since it will be granted that opinions, attitudes, and values depend upon human needs, and since personality is essentially an organization of needs, then personality may be regarded as a *determinant* of ideological preference. Personality is not, however, to be hypostatized as an ultimate determinant. Far from being something which is given in the beginning, which remains fixed and acts upon the surrounding world. personality evolves under the impact of social environment and can never be isolated from the social totality within which it occurs. . . . The major influences upon personality development arise in the course of child training as carried forward in a setting of family life. What happens here is profoundly influenced by economic and social factors. It is not only that each family in trying to rear its children proceeds according to the ways of the social, ethnic, and religious groups in which it has membership, but crude economic factors affect directly the parents' behavior toward the child. This means that broad changes in social conditions and institutions will have a direct bearing upon the kinds of personalities that develop within a society.

5. Bruno Bettleheim and Morris Janowitz have made this point in their *Social Change and Prejudice* (New York: Free Press of Glencoe, 1964), especially pp. 3-24. At the same time, antisemitic behavior remains commonplace in America, especially so in the East. See Edward D. Baltzell, *The Protestant Establishment* (New York: Random House, 1964). Much of the book deals with antisemitic practices among the upper-class bluebloods of Philadelphia.
6. After working in the clinical setting and observing the relationship between authoritarian personality traits and F-Scale type items, the authors (Adorno *et al., op cit.*) then extended their informal correlation technique to include *equivalence* of the two phenomena covarying, an analytical decision by no means acceptable since two things mutually exclusive cannot be the same no matter how intercorrelated they might be. Thus the classical correlation between sunspots and economic depressions does not allow us to use measures of economic depressions as indices of sunspots. Perhaps we can make this point clearer. R. Nevitt Sanford, T. W. Adorno, Else Frankel-Brunswik, and Daniel J. Levinson, in a chapter (of Adorno, *et al., op. cit.*, pp. 222-79) entitled "The Measurement of Implicit Anti-Democratic Trends," define the authoritarian personality as consisting of the following nine items: (1) conventionalism; (2) authoritarian submission; (3) authoritarian aggression; (4) anti-intraception; (5) superstition and stereotypy; (6) power and "toughness"; (7) destructiveness and cynicism; (8) projectivity; and (9) sex (exaggerated concern with sexual matters). In setting up their interview schedules, however, the authors did not measure these items but rather (what they had learned from clinical experiences to be) their correlates–beliefs, values, and norms apparently intertwined with authoritarian personality dimensions, thereby creating a doubtful index rather than a valid measure.
7. Of course the authors (Adorno *et al., op. cit.* viewed personality and ideology as having a direct bearing on political action. See, for example, Else Frenkel-Brunswik's brilliant essay on authoritarianism, "Interaction of Psychological and Sociological Factors in Political Behavior," in Daniel Katz *et al., Public Opinion and Propaganda* (New York: Dryden Press, 1954), pp. 363-80.
8. For a criticism of how Adorno *et al., op. cit.* intercorrelated various scales, see Hyman and Sheatsley, *op. cit.*, pp. 70-89.
9. If we were to examine the entire non-Jewish population, we would undoubtedly find considerable pro-semitism. Likewise, pro-black sentiments are widespread in the white population. Our understandable concern with prejudice and discrimination against various ethnic groups has unfortunately led us to overlook prejudice and discrimination *in favor* of minorities.
10. See Daniel J. Levinson, "The Study of Ethnocentric Ideology," in *The Authoritarian Personality, op. cit.* (1964 edition), pp. 103-4.

11. We used only a small number of questions since our primary concern consisted of F-Scale items.
12. See Daniel J. Levinson, "Politico-Economic Ideology and Group Memberships in Relation to Ethnocentrism," *ibid.*, pp. 151-207.
13. We used a large number of personality questions because we believed that personality would be strongly related to vote. However, only later, after careful scrutiny of the F (Fascist)-Scale personality items, did it occur to us that they failed to measure personality but rather gauged its presumed cultural correlates.
14. *Fundamentalism* refers to an historically recent religious movement in American Protestantism, a religious revival that emphasizes the inerrancy of the Scriptures and Biblical miracles, especially the virgin birth and physical resurrection of Christ. It also makes a virtue of values stressed in the Old Testament, including submission to parental, male, and state authority.
15. *Anti-intellectualism* is the rejection of rational thought.
16. *Rural propriety* refers to ruling class etiquette in nonurban areas. The chief carriers are found at all class levels, but the ethic finds decreasing support as one moves from the top to the bottom of the class structure.
17. *Paternalistic benevolence* refers to a fatherly desire to do good for others, including acts of kindness.
18. This kind of affection has its power center in the father, who sets the limits and regulates affectional display so as to exclude disruption of family ties so important in rural settings where uncles, aunts, cousins, and in-laws form webs of reciprocity. By contrast, companion familial affection is near-egalitarian and centered around the conjugal family, itself of lesser significance than the "web family" in rural settings.
19. *Individualism* refers to a doctrine which assumes that the individual and not society is the paramount consideration or end. By extension, *rugged individualism* has reference to an ethic in which the individual has the potential of bending and shaping the world according to his desired ends should he have the talent and the energy to do so.
20. By *patriotism* we mean love of one's country and a willingness to undergo hardship to defend its state.
21. *Suspicion of central government* refers to suspecting that the state will act in ways contrary to one's self-interest.
22. *Suspicion of outside groups* consists of believing that these groups will do harm to oneself and/or to highly regarded others.
23. Unfortunately, because of the *small number of unionists* as well as their wide *range of affiliations,* we were unable to analyze the impact of the various unions treated separately. However, we should mention that when we made the craft *vs.* industrial union distinction, we were unable to observe any differences on matters of vote for fair housing.
24. Still there is one more problem: Of what importance are the "cake of custom" commitments treated at length in Chapter 6? How about age,

length of residence, and home ownership, as all three relate to authoritarian ideology?

If it is true, for example, that age is an important source of support or opposition to fair housing, then the aged—everything else being equal—should be crusty, that is, contain more than their share of those who were ideologically authoritarian and against fair housing, even inside the Democratic party. If we examine only non-University white-collar *Democrats,* we can observe that the elders tend to include a disproportionately larger number of authoritarians, and of these, relatively more who voted against fair housing. For example, if we consider those who were Caucasian, white-collar, and non-University—a population sufficiently large to apply multiple statistical controls—we can note that within the fifty-years-and-older category, those who were thoroughly authoritarian included 3 for, 8 against, and 4 who did not vote. Younger Democrats were slightly more in favor of fair housing, although there were so few cases that a comparison was difficult. Among the older (50 plus) white-collar, non-University *Republicans* who were thoroughly authoritarian, 2 voted for and 45 against fair housing. The younger group voted none for and 6 against, while 2 didn't vote. Among those older Republicans who disagreed with the authoritarian position on immoral people but who were authoritarian on "unions" and "obedience," the vote was 11 in favor and 50 against the ordinance; their younger counterparts voted 3 for and 25 against. Thus, the age consideration did not prove significant among these Republicans. If anything, these younger ones were more *against* fair housing.

The same pattern held for length of residence and home ownership. Among non-University white-collar Democrats, the long-term residents (and to a lesser degree home owners) stood out in their support of authoritarian values and opposition to fair housing. If we examine non-University white-collar Republicans, like comparisons do not yield significant differences.

Thus, in this chapter, while the cake of custom considerations added somewhat to our understanding of who voted for fair housing, our knowledge of these phenomena by no means detracted from the overall impact of structural and ideological considerations already taken up.

25. Seymour M. Lipset, "Opinion Formation in a Crisis Situation," *Public Opinion Quarterly,* 17 (Spring 1953), pp. 20-46.
26. Seymour M. Lipset and Hans Zetterberg, "Social Mobility in Industrial Society," in Seymour Lipset and Reinhard Bendix, *Social Mobility in Industrial Society* (Berkeley: University of California Press. 1959), pp. 66-99.
27. See Jenniellen W. Fèrguson and Paul J. Hoffman "Voting Behavior: The Vote on the Francis Amendment in the 1962 California Election," *Western Political Quarterly,* 17 (December 1964), pp. 770-76.
28. Howard Leventhal, Robert L. Jacobs, and Nijole Z. Kudirka, "Authori-

tarianism, Ideology, and Political Candidate Choice," *Journal of Abnormal and Social Psychology,* 69 (November, 1964), pp. 539-49.

29. Sidney M. Peck, "Ideology and Political Sociology: The Conservative Bias of Lipset's Political Man," *American Catholic Sociological Review,* 23 (Summer, 1962), pp. 128-55.
30. S. M. Miller and Frank Riessman, "Working-Class Authoritarianism: A Critique of Lipset," *The British Journal of Sociology,* 12 (September, 1961), pp. 263-76.
31. Seymour M. Lipset, "Working-Class Authoritarianism: A Reply to Miller and Riessman," *The British Journal of Sociology,* 12 (September, 1961), pp. 277-81.
32. William Peterson, *The Politics of Population* (Garden City: Doubleday Anchor Books, 1965), pp. 244-5.
33. Arnold M. Rose, "Prejudice, Anomie, and the Authoritarian Personality," *Sociology and Social Research,* 50 (January, 1966), pp. 141-7.
34. Elmer L. Struening and Arthur H. Richardson, "A Factor Analysis Exploration of the Alienation, Anomie, and Authoritarian Domain," *American Sociological Review,* 30 (October, 1965), pp. 768-76.
35. David Riesman, *The Lonely Crowd* (New York: Free Press of Glencoe, 1961).
36. Daniel R. Miller and Guy E. Swanson, *The Changing American Parent* (New York: John Wiley, 1958).
37. William H. Whyte, Jr., *The Organization Man* (Garden City: Doubleday, 1957).
38. Miller and Riessman, *op. cit.*
39. William McCord, "Early Familial Experiences and Bigotry," *American Sociological Review,* 25 (October, 1960), 717-22.
40. See Adorno, *et al., op. cit.* (1964 edition), pp. 5-6.

NINE

The Minority Vote

If our earlier analysis on status crystallization has generality, then the overwhelming majority of white-collar blacks and "third world" peoples should have voted for fair housing.

BLACKS AND ASIANS

In the case of blacks, their middle-class population proved to be overwhelmingly in favor of the ordinance. But then working-class blacks also voted for the proposal. Table 45 demonstrates that racial solidarity overrode all other considerations, including those of status inconsistency. Only a very small fraction of the black population (2 percent) voted against fair housing, while approximately two-thirds favored it.

The black bloc vote should not come as a surprise, for there were a number of factors that compelled blacks to vote in solidary fashion. Of these considerations, three stand out: First, blacks were the central object of the ordinance conflict. The primary issue was black rights—black interests were obviously at stake. Second, many blacks were highly involved in the campaign. Third, the election had direct and visible consequences for black children.

Perhaps the presumed fate of black children was most relevant to their voting parents, since where they lived determined where they went to school. The neighborhood school was in operation at that time. Its operation meant that segregated black children went to all-black schools, while the white ghettoed generally attended all-white institutions. Since white schools had relatively high achievement levels, and since this success was common knowledge among black parents—whose children suffered from many inadequate school facilities, a dearth of adequately trained staff members, and low achievement levels–a sizeable proportion of the black community viewed a fair housing victory as a chance to move out of the ghetto and into neighborhoods where their children could grow up in a better school environment. So ran the argument. It seemed reasonable. People talked about it. Few doubted that the perceived interests of the kids pushed black parents to press simultaneously for neighborhood and school integration, with all that this meant for the occupational and pecuniary success of their children.

Yet despite what was at stake for blacks–and the child question was but one central motivating force–many blacks did not vote even when they were eligible. If we examine Table 46, we observe that nonvoters came from all categories of the population, although unusually large numbers were found among the young and the short-term residents; in these populations, whether black or white, everyday impediments associated with voting registration served to confuse those who might enter formal electoral politics should the state encourage them to do so. These observations and findings are consistent with those presented in summary form by Lipset and others, although we should observe that some of our results ran contrary to their findings.[1] Unlike Lipset, Lazarsfeld, and others, we found that education and religion were *unrelated* to voting turnout, at least among those eligible to participate in the election.[2] The Berkeley fair housing election, like all elections, had certain distinctive qualities, and perhaps these characteristics help to account for our unusual findings. The Berkeley black community, the lesser-educated, the blue-collar people, and the Catholics turned out in numbers relatively large in comparison to other elections. This may be partially explained by the occurrence of the fair housing fight within the context of a general social movement attempting to enlist the aid of all groups to fight for black liberation. This movement enlisted support from all sections of the population. By contrast, in most elections social movement politics are not involved, and the

Table 45. Race and Vote on Fair Housing

Vote	*% Black*	*% Asian*	*% White*
For	65 (131)	44 (17)	34 (258)
Against	2 (4)	23 (9)	45 (340)
Did Not Vote	33 (64)	33 (13)	21 (153)
Total	100 (199)	100 (39)	100 (751)

turnout more closely corresponds to the pattern depicted by Lipset and Lazarsfeld.

ASIANS

When we observe Asian peoples, we find that we must treat the two dominant groups (Chinese and Japanese) simultaneously because of the few cases in each category. Taken together, Japanese, Chinese, and other Asians voted approximately 2 to 1 for the ordinance.[3] A disproportionately large number of fair housing supporters were found among the lesser-incomed, the blue-collar workers, the Buddhists, the females, the young or middle-aged, the Republicans, and the University types as well as the home buyers. Thus, our previous remarks on the significance of liberation groups and processes (as well as status crystallization) would seem to have little if any application to the oriental population when taken as a whole. Why this should be so is difficult to ascertain. At this point, we would suggest that what is necessary is a careful study of each of the tightly-knit oriental communities to determine the variety of norms and values at work within each group. We stress "variety," because if our information is of any significance whatsoever, it suggests that there is no one set of integration values at work within each of the oriental groups.

Again we take the negative stance when we argue that our findings by no means demonstrate that the young minority group members—both black and Asian—today (1970) favor the breaking up of their respective ethnic ghettoes as the price paid for housing integration. Many of the young reject this alternative—the scattered and nominal integration of third world peoples and blacks into essentially all-white residential districts. For these young people, ethnic claims to neighborhoods and traditions would appear to be just as valid as an imposed blending of minorities into some bastardized form of Anglo substance and Saxon conformity. Many young blacks now reject integration when they call for the creation of revitalized neighborhoods and residential districts organized largely around the themes of black nationalism. (In the case of Asians, the norms would appear to dwell on the maintenance of ethnic primary ties and subcultural traditions.) In this sense, young blacks are attempting to refurbish and to extend a subculture within an organized subcommunity. In doing so, blacks (and Third Worlders) reinforce their own types of cultural traditionalism at the very time that a minority of whites calls for the elimination of all forms of traditional beliefs, values, and norms found within the minority subcommunity. For blacks and Asians, the answer to intended subcultural assimilation would appear to be subcommunity reassertion.

To eliminate anomie within the black community, many blacks are now staking out black territory whose boundaries coincide with those of their

Table 46. Blacks, Asians, Their Social Characteristics and Fair Housing Vote

(Figures in Absolute Numbers, Not Percentages)

	Negroes				*Asians*			
Social Characteristics	*For*	*Against*	*Did Not Vote*	*Total*	*For*	*Against*	*Did Not Vote*	*Total*
Blue Collar	113	2	53	188	10	7	7	24
White Collar	14	1	7	22	7	2	5	14
Education:								
0-8 grade	28	0	12	40	0	0	0	0
9-12 grade	68	1	36	105	3	3	6	12
12 and over	34	3	15	52	14	6	7	27
Income:								
Low (under $8,000)	87	3	54	144	12	5	8	25
High	40	1	9	50	5	4	5	14
Party:								
Republican	11	2	5	18	6	4	2	12
Democrat	107	2	46	155	10	4	9	23
University Affiliation:								
Non-University	120	4	47	171	13	6	11	30
University (includes students)	9	0	2	11	4	2	2	8

Social Characteristics	For	Against	Did Not Vote	Total	For	Against	Did Not Vote	Total
Religion:								
Protestants	103	3	53	159	6	- 5	6	17
Catholics	17	0	4	21	2	0	2	4
Buddhists	0	0	0	0	4	1	4	9
No Preference	11	1	5	17				
Age: (Year of Birth)								
1935-1942	14	1	18	33	2	2	3	7
1925-1934	24	0	21	45	6	1	2	9
1915-1924	46	0	12	58	6	2	4	12
1905-1914	32	1	9	42	1	4	2	7
1904 and before	14	2	3	19	2	0	2	4
Length of Residence in Berkeley:								
1½-5 years	22	0	29	51	4	1	3	8
6-10 years	33	0	14	47	5	3	3	11
11-20 years	54	2	14	70	4	2	5	11
21 plus	20	2	7	29	4	3	2	9
Lifetime	1	0	0	1	0	0	0	0
Home Ownership:								
Owns	20	3	5	28	5	1	4	10
Buying	49	0	11	60	8	5	5	18
Renting	59	0	44	103	3	3	4	10
Other	2	1	0	3	1	0	0	1
Sex:								
Male	97	2	48	147	14	8	12	34
Female	33	2	12	47	3	1	1	5

expanding ghettos. Following distinctions made by Sanford Lyman and Marvin B. Scott,[4] we would hold that ethnic minorities are laying out "home territories"–places where black participants can have relative freedom and a sense of intimacy and control over their residential areas. In this way, young blacks are reacting against the white propensity and define black housing integration efforts in hitherto all-white areas as "territorial encroachment" smacking of "contamination." The whites have united to engage in white "turf defense," but in so doing they have unknowingly helped to redefine for blacks what they have not until recently viewed as territory worth defending: black turf.

Many young blacks now jealously defend black residential areas that are so frequently sought for the purposes of "urban redevelopment," a euphemism for black removal and white real estate speculation, light industry installation, white freeway construction, white research and medical institute creation, and white downtown resurrection.[5] In every instance, whites take black turf for white benefit. Young blacks are becoming increasingly aware of the intent and consequences of these schemes. Accordingly, they oppose both the rationale and the activities associated with what they call–and with some accuracy–"Honky Redevelopment." After unloosing this counter-concept, they go on to argue that reforming whitey should begin with his soul, not the black man's territory and wallet. We are now learning that black opposition on the question of home territory finds ideological expression through black power formulations, matters we will discuss at length in the next chapter.

THE SPANISH AMERICAN VOTE

One more ethnic group demands our attention, even though our data on its voting behavior in the election is scant. Presented below is a table that describes how the various sample categories of Spanish-Americans voted in the Berkeley fair-housing election. As you can see, the miniscule frequencies at best dimly suggest the actual parameters. Still, some evidence is better than none. Not too surprisingly, the pattern appears to be very similar to the white population vote in general. This we expected to be the case in a Spanish-American community as heterogeneous as was Berkeley's, where Spanish-Americans differed not only on matters of background specified in Table B-1, but also in terms of nationality descent, with many coming from South as well as Central American countries.

Had our Spanish-American respondents been more homogeneous–had they been more like nearby Oakland's, that is, overwhelmingly Mexican by descent–we might well have found a "new breed" solidarity both *within* the Spanish-American community as well as *with* blacks on matters of fair housing. We emphasize "might," for even when Spanish-Americans were culturally homogeneous and hence politically unified, their traditional hostility towards

Table 47. Spanish-Americans and the Berkeley Fair Housing Vote

Social Characteristics	*For*	*Against*	*Did Not Vote*
Class			
Blue collar	1	3	1
White collar	2	1	2
Education			
0-8 years	1	1	1
9-12 years	0	1	1
12 plus	2	2	1
University Affiliation			
Non-University	3	3	3
*University**	0	1	0
Length of Residence			
1½-5 years	0	0	2
5-10 years	1	1	0
11-20 years	2	0	0
21 plus	0	2	1
Lifetime	0	1	0
Type of Residence			
Own home	1	0	0
Buying	1	1	0
Renting	1	3	2
Other	0	0	1
Religion			
Protestant	0	0	1
Catholic	2	3	2
No preference	1	1	0
Income			
Low ($8,000)	2	2	3
High	1	2	0
Party Preference			
Republican	0	1	1
Democrat	3	2	2
Independent	0	1	0
Sex			
Male	3	4	3
Female	0	0	0

Continued on p. 190

Table 47 (continued)

Social Characteristics	*For*	*Against*	*Did Not Vote*
Year of Birth			
1935-1942	0	1	2
1925-1934	1	1	0
1915-1924	2	0	0
1905-1914	0	0	1
1904 and earlier	0	2	0
Church Attendance			
Once a week	1	2	3
Few times a month	0	0	0
Once a month	1	0	0
Few times a year	0	1	0
Inappropriate	1	1	0

*Includes students

black Americans would have undoubtedly prevented (1963) bloc voting in favor of the ordinance.

Still, one should not rule out the possibility of interethnic solidarity among minorities reorganizing to assert their ethnic-class interests as beleaguered and exploited proletarianized ethnic communities. The objective similarities of their problems, interests, and enemies may someday move them to work together within the political framework of recurrent coalition.

CONCLUSIONS

In 1963, black Berkeleyans voted overwhelmingly for fair housing, while oriental members of the community went approximately 2 to 1 for the proposal. Although it is difficult to interpret the meaning of the oriental vote (in part because there were so few in the study), we have less such trouble understanding the bloc-vote effort of Berkeley's blacks. They were at the very center of the election issue. They also helped to mobilize themselves in what was an extremely close fight. But once they had lost, indeed, once the fight on fair housing was defeated in California (as well as elsewhere), many blacks turned toward black nationalism, toward the building of the black community, and away from blending residentially into a white dominated world. In changing their direction, some blacks, especially the young militant ones, have moved out with strident steps, a topic we will next discuss.

NOTES

1. See Seymour M. Lipset, *et al.*, "The Psychology of Voting: An Analysis of Political Behavior," *op. cit.*, p. 1127.
2. This population of *eligible* participants would probably be more limited than the one Lipset had in mind. His observations were undoubtedly based upon both those eligible and ineligible to participate in elections.
3. Approximately one-half of the Orientals were Japanese, while around one-fourth were Chinese. The remainder were Philippino, Asiatic Indian, and those few who were a mixture of Oriental groups.
4. Stanford M. Lyman and Marvin B. Scott, "Territoriality: A Neglected Sociological Dimension," in *Social Problems,* Fall, 1967, Volume 15, pp. 236-249.
5. For a general and critical analysis of urban renewal, see Martin Anderson's *The Federal Bulldozer* (Cambridge: M.I.T. Press, 1964). For material dealing specifically with urban renewal and America's blacks, see Paul A. Baran and Paul M. Sweezy's *Monopoly Capital* (New York: Monthly Review Press, 1966), pp. 289-300. Also see their earlier but still appropriate "Monopoly Capital," *Monthly Review,* Volume 14, July-August, 1962, pp. 178-189. Perhaps the best anthology on the subject is James Q. Wilson's *Urban Renewal: The Record and the Controversy,* (Cambridge: M.I.T. Press, 1967).

TEN

Epilogue:

Lessons Learned Since Berkeley

People sometimes describe the working class as if it were a homogeneous entity. Nowadays it is respectable to dismiss it as reformist on bread-and-butter issues but reactionary on race relations. In this closing chapter we consider a number of such popular assertions and comment on their relation to what we have found in our analysis of the 1963 fair housing vote. On this basis we turn to the question of why the struggle for racial reform in such areas as housing failed, yet at the same time paved the way for the creation of a rebellious and at times revolutionary mood within the black ghetto. Then, in the context of this kind of general unrest and government repression, we conclude with certain political recommendations.

MYTHS WE REJECT

Our study of the Berkeley vote on fair housing produced evidence at variance with some prevalent notions about class and politics. Here are six typical propositions and our reasons for disclaiming them.

1. *Authoritarianism is distinctly working class, hence we need only use the term "working-class authoritarianism" to depict this attitude and can, as a matter of course, dismiss any need to inspect the middle-class world for the presence of ethnocentrism, political-economic conservatism, or cultural traditionalism.* We have pointedly rejected this approach to ideology, arguing instead for the presence of authoritarianism in all classes, labeling it "working class" when it occurred among blue-collar persons and "middle class" when it

appeared in the white-collar population. This approach proved valid, for not only did we find authoritarianism in all groups but also discovered its predictable impact on race relations.

2. *The white working class is authoritarian, therefore it is antiblack.* This proposition assumes that white working-class people are all of one stamp. Yet we have learned from this and other studies that the proposition is demonstrably false. In Berkeley we observed a very sizeable minority of blue-collar workers who were anything but wholly authoritarian.

Further, we found that even when workers were markedly authoritarian, a small but significant minority voted for fair housing legislation. We suspect this paradox occurred in part because of the pressure exerted by a popular progressive political party, the California Democratic Council of the Democratic party organization.

We are not saying that authoritarian ideology was without importance. Indeed, it did affect working-class actions. Its strictures time and again exerted a predictable influence. But ideology was only one of many forces at work. It pushed in one direction, while other forces pressed workers to act contrary to their subcultural predispositions.

3. *Given the built-in bias of the working classes, only the white upper socio-economic status groups can take the lead on racial liberation, for only they have experienced the security of job, the predictability of income, and the enlightenment of formal education.* If our study has any generality whatsoever, we can lay this chestnut to rest. We found occupation largely irrelevant when we examined its importance, within both major parties. In fact, only among Democrats did white-collar people stand out in supporting the concept that blacks must have the legal right to live in some place other than the ghetto, should they opt for that alternative. Blue-collar Democrats and Republicans led white-collar Republicans in support of fair housing. The same pattern occurred on matters of family income and formal education. As you will recall, only a very tiny minority of highly educated Republicans voted for fair housing. Again, and by contrast, the Democrats followed the expected pattern. Within this population, as education (and income) increased, so did the proportion of people who voted for the proposal.

What these findings strongly suggest is that increased education by itself will not do the trick. More important, where one stands politically—and this is to a large degree based upon a person's prior class and status experiences—sets the context within which one's present educational achievement has impact. When persons are politically conservative and culturally traditional, there is a very good chance that higher education will make only more facile their creation of rationalizations designed to foster ongoing racist practices. (Do not forget our Ph.D. Republicans!)

4. *The Democratic party has the answer.* Not in the year 1970. The old

Democratic party coalition of minorities, professionals, a section of the upper class, and the progressive working class—the 35-year alliance established by Roosevelt and seemingly ended with Sirhan's bullet—has disintegrated. In its place, certainly in California, one finds a fragment of a Democratic party organization unified only by a desire to win elections and suppress black militants. The desire to win among many leading Democrats has taken such forms as the recent California spectacle of many politicians seriously entertaining the proposal that S. I. Hayakawa of San Francisco State fame—and repression—run for a leading office in order to outdo G.O.P. reaction. As of 1970, the California Democratic party organization is in shambles, divided on matters of ideology and organization.

Perhaps a third party alternative would make sense. In the present context, a Peace and Freedom party or its equivalent might be able to bring together a confederation of the various protesting tribes not only in California but elsewhere. But there are numerous obstacles to the success of such a party, not the least of which is the nature of state and federal electoral laws. They penalize a third party. These structural obstacles—such as the absence of proportional representation and the massive signature campaigns needed to obtain a ballot position and keep it—make difficult the completion of a takeoff phase for any third party. And political progressives are aware of these roadblocks.

Consequently, we suspect that most dissidents in the United States will remain inside the Democratic party, even though it is a wreck. In California and in similar situations across the country, such persons will use up a good deal of their energy to fight those who wish only to win—with reaction if need be. Under these conditions, efforts toward racial liberation, both white and black, will be few and attenuated. Organizational fights, alliances, and compromises will consume most of their energies. This kind of activity will simply turn off those who want change now—or even in the long run.

In short, the possibilities of working successfully within either the Democratic party or a third party movement appear gloomy.

5. *All whites are racists, and therefore black people should forget about creating political coalitions to deal with black problems.* If we define racism in both idea and action terms, we must reject this narrow, black nationalist formula. Clearly, a minority of whites were (and are) not in a racist bag, either in terms of votes or attitudes. In fact, it is precisely because of this minority in the white population that the militant Black Panthers can call for a united front against the growth of fascism in the United States. And the Panthers have sought those groups we have found to be in support of black interests, to wit: the university population in general; the younger university crowd in particular; and the progressive professionals. From another perspective, perhaps the Panthers and similar groups gather support from white mid-

dle-class people who are continuously on the move—younger university instructors, graduate students, writers, and professional students. These persons are not resident in an area long enough to become wedded to a traditional and conservative way of organizing people's lives; hence they are in a position to endorse novel and radical proposals on property and race enunciated by black writers such as Eldridge Cleaver.

6. *All blacks want to integrate and assimilate.* Hardly. What many blacks—certainly a sizeable segment of the urban young—want is the legal right to live where they choose, either beyond or inside the ghetto. However, even should they live outside the ghetto, this does not mean that they prefer to assimilate to a white, middle-class life style. Often the desire to leave the ghetto is motivated by a belief that they can pay lower rents for better housing and give their children better schooling. Living beyond the ghetto nonetheless may lead to assimilation. Environment may well structure black lives to make them more like those of white, traditional, middle-class America. Blacks, too, may inadvertently become part of a middle class without distinctiveness, commitment, or soul.

Yet years of urban rebellion have served to reinforce black detachment from the ethos of the white mainstream. These struggles are not rooted in free choice but rather in material conditions for which political progressives as well as reactionaries are at least partially responsible. We must take these circumstances, many of them stark everyday tragedies, into account before we can make political recommendations.

FAILURE AND REBELLION: THE CONTEXT OF OUR RECOMMENDATIONS

Any political suggestions must be based on an examination of the mood of the black community, especially its younger members. Their anger springs directly from the failures of the 1960s. One of them is the continuation of exploitative ghettoization that has contributed to the organization of militant working-class blacks. The Malcom Xs, Stokeley Carmichaels, Rap Browns, Eldridge Cleavers, Huey Newtons, and Bobby Seales have moved a small minority of whites to call for either drastically changing or immediately breaking up the American system. Of course, the overwhelming majority of white responses to black demands has been negative. The reaction has at times been furious, as in Chicago, where publicly condoned beatings as well as police raids on Panther headquarters have clearly indicated high levels of collective hate associated with white rejection of black demands.

But white backlash ain't the only one. When we study the failure of integration efforts during the 1950s and 1960s, we must examine its successors and offspring—black backlash. Black backlash constitutes a new ideological form. As yet inchoate, its ideas nonetheless clearly reject the goals of both assimilation on matters of culture and integration in the realm of work as well as intimacy. Black backlash asserts the right of black people to control all aspects of the black community. Whitey can leave. But black backlash becomes more than rational anger when it takes insurrectionary form. Whatever black power becomes–and its present dizzy pace makes yesterday's manuscript cold and archaic only several months later–black power goals would appear to have been quite frequently revolutionary.

These black power objectives–those most clearly articulated by writers such as Malcolm X and Eldridge Cleaver–contrast vividly with what the civil rights movement originally wanted. What happened to create this change? It would appear that the failure of Martin Luther King and others to abolish discrimination and to integrate blacks–indeed, the dismal record of the civil rights movement in general, especially in the realm of housing–has paved the way for the black call to reorganize black people for a fight quite different from the one waged a short time ago. Even though black power goals smack of the vagueness of newness, even though its militant forms have attracted the active, committed support of only a minority of the young–black power's strongest base–the black power effort would appear to be crystallizing around the following principle: black people must extend and refurbish the subculture and substructure of a black population to be rejuvenated through nationalism–one ringing with anticolonial declarations.

These nationalist efforts had their origins largely in the inability of American institutions to budge significantly. That period of door pounding is behind us. Black people are now building their fortress.

WHY INTEGRATION FAILED

Why wasn't racial integration achieved during the crucial period, the one that began with the United States Supreme Court decision on schools in 1954 and clearly ended with King's assassination in 1968? There are at least three alternative explanations advanced on this matter of civil rights defeat: (1) the failure of the American Ethos; (2) the efforts of white working-class authoritarians; (3) the impact of white cultural traditionalism and the weakness of white liberation forces. Let us examine each of these separately.

The Failure of the American Ethos

In the case of the American Ethos argument, the American people *as a whole* are judged as having racist values not in keeping with democratic practices; yet these people are assessed as being capable of relinquishing their racist attitudes to resolve the contradiction between vulgar predispositions and a sense of fair play, a value more pronounced, more abiding, than the transitory commitment to racism. Nonetheless, in the short run these racist values have moved Americans in general–so goes the argument–to reject racial integration and, hence, to facilitate the introduction of black nationalism.

The trouble with this argument is its disregard of statistical reality. Objectively, we can count people who have articulated libertarian racial commitments *and* struggled time and again to create both an integrated division of labor and a brightened world of interracial intimacy. In some cases, their liberated bodies lie at the bottom of swamps as well as in more traditional final resting places. Less dramatically, tens of thousands of whites have laid their jobs on the line to abolish racism. Clearly, their ethos was nontraditional but democratic in the best French Revolutionary sense. By contrast, the values and behavior of most white Americans have been traditional, and we have little reason to believe that they will fail to continue to be what they have always been. However, and this point is the important one, their present thoughts and actions fail to represent the entire population. To generalize from the discrimination and prejudice of an aggregate—admittedly a majority—to *all* white Americans, is to confuse the sizeable part with the heterogenous whole, an illogical exercise not worthy of further attention.

Blue-Collar Authoritarianism

The second position holds the blue-collar world responsible for continued racism in America. Presumably within the working-class lies a cauldron of racist sentiment, the crucial source of racist behavior in America. From this point of view, authoritarianism pervades the entire working class and creates racist behavior in the entire white section of the working class. This behavior has been largely responsible for any black backlash against enlightened white efforts to integrate America. By contrast, so goes the argument, the white-collar world has taken the lead on matters of integration.

For better or for worse, as we have already indicated, the facts fail to match the outline. Admittedly, a majority of workers are undoubtedly racist. But their equivalents can also be found inside the middle-class world. Undoubtedly a majority of white-collar persons—including most American business leaders—have continued to discriminate not only at work but in residence. Clearly, our study found that a majority of white-collar Berkeleyans refused to help outlaw the discriminatory housing practices of slumlords, real estate associations, banks, and others connected with continued racial segregation. Moreover, this choice was strongest within the political party representing the business community. Nor was our study unique. Other white-collar populations have done so as well. In the western residential districts middle-class Republicanism constitutes a substantial minority middle-class enclave—the only one in this overwhelmingly working-class, largely Democratic community—the residents (Census Tracts 37 and 38) participated in a fair housing referendum in 1968 and voted approximately 2 to 1 *against* a fair housing ordinance. This kind of behavior runs counter to the working-class, bogeyman theory. From our point of view, Jim Crow collective sentiment covers the entire community and helps make the majority of blue- and white-collar persons reject blacks as semi-intimates.

Cultural Traditionalism and Racial Liberation

This theory acknowledges the widespread cultural character of the racist ethos, observes its attitudinal counterparts within both classes, notes liberation values at work within voluntary associations, and argues that the rules, values, and beliefs of progressive groups can both liberate people from racist practices and traditions and reinforce enlightened practices and commitments. However, this analysis admits the overall weaknesses of these progressive groups, as indicated earlier. Hence, progressive groups neutralize few traditional predispositions. Looking at the United States as a whole, we can safely say progressive collectivities have made only a slight dent in racist traditions. These weaknesses have been pronounced even in university towns such as Berkeley, a community where the Enlightenment should have affected the largest number of people. Elsewhere, beyond university- and college-influenced communities, cultural traditionalism and corresponding attitudes remain more or less untouched, although "all brothers under the skin" rhetoric generally keeps the most vicious pronouncements below the surface. Nonetheless, cultural traditionalism affects black brothers above the skin. Apparently what has actually happened is that most voluntary associations have remained racist in practice. But in order to appear fair, and hence supportable, many groups have quietly taken advantage of public but polite racist sentiment to articulate a carefully-reasoned racist ideology to justify discrimination on matters of housing and related items. Real estate associations, for example, do not have to sound off like Senator Eastland. They can rely upon a highly educated public to support a racial ideology cast to include the general pronouncements of both real estate boards guarding racist practices and gentlemen bigots running for public office. In effect, smooth running, well financed, voluntary associations can help bring together ideology, attitude, money, and politicians to maintain a pattern of discrimination initially put together by the less subtle and the more undignified.

Let it be said that historically the United States did not contain sufficiently powerful forces during the 1950s and 1960s to overcome these traditional barriers and to reconstruct itself along nonracial lines. Let it also be hypothesized that most Americans, including many of its intellectuals, remain unaware of the consequences of this failure. Finally, we should note the double-edged character of racial concessions now being made to blacks. These compromises may well in fact foster black nationalism and not interracial tenderness. New black jobs generally contribute to black dignity, not the happy interracial life envisioned earlier by many whites. Negro scholarships help young blacks with natural hair cuts go to the university and join the black student union. And so on. We have crossed the Rubicon.

THE CONSEQUENCES OF INTEGRATION FAILURE

Of those observers who have turned towards the consequences of integration failure—an analysis quite different from one focusing on those responsible for the civil rights flop—many subscribe to one of the following three hypotheses: the Failure of the American Dream; a Statistical View; or Black Colony and Black Power.

The Failure of the American Dream

We cannot overlook those earnest liberals who lament the failure of the American Dream—the white acceptance of blacks as equals and hence as intimates. But we might ask: Whose dream? Perhaps liberals may be projecting their own sentiments onto others. Perhaps it is fair to say that some liberal analysts have ignored the real content of many real nonmythological dreams. For large numbers of white American people, the American Dream has undoubtedly contained many elements of nightmare. When these ordinary folk ponder the liberal conception of the American Dream, their associations undoubtedly give them the creeps, the sweats, and fleeting moments of panic. These widespread thoughts and feelings—should they occur, and I believe they do—would make false the rhetoric that assumed all Americans deeply favored integration, the realization of the American Dream. We suspect that the American Dream, however well intentioned, was never more than surface veneer, a self-enhancing ideology propounded through the mass media by and for people who preferred to define themselves as enlightened and to live in lily-white suburbs. *That* was not enough.

A Statistical View

A more hard-headed appraisal of what's happening would analyze the consequences of failure in purely statistical terms. From this point of view, when housing integration fails, measurable millions of Americans continue to live within enumerated, segregated residential districts inside mapped central cities populated by quantifiable people and an estimated number of rats. Here the analyst emphasizes the aggregate of blacks and their fellow ghetto occupants charted in reports, numbers of blacks wrecked by low quality education before they reach twelve years of age, police brutality observed by social scientists from inside police cars, employment opportunity denied by so many thousand employers, and other additive phenomena structured largely by housing segregation in fifty years.

There's nothing terribly wrong with this kind of analysis. Indeed, as sociologists, we like this routine, for it's our bread and butter. It's what graduate schools wisely taught us to do best.

But once again, unfortunately, the statistical view fails to contain propositional materials on the unanticipated and collective reactions of black Americans against a largely unyielding Jim Crow system. But, then, we shouldn't be too critical of this theoretical omission. Perhaps this oversight stems in large measure from the methodological difficulties involved in quantifying the collective behavior of insurrectionaries. However, we should not forget Karl Mannheim's observation that the hesitance to grapple with methodological problems may well derive from a social structural incapacity to face an unsavory political possibility, in this case–revolution-torn America.

Black Colony and Black Power: the Ecological Base

The third interpretation develops a global view pointing towards the importance of collective behavior, although this direction frequently lacks methodological sophistication. This position uses statistical materials, neglects careful methodological considerations, but tries to link what we know to a theoretical frame bent on understanding racial bipolarization and class-racial struggle. This Black Colony and Black Power perspective holds that continued segregation contributes to the creation of a rebellious, if not revolutionary, black population caught within a system in many ways analagous to classical colonialism. In this situation, real estate–and the related questions of labor and commodities–are both the center of controversy and a principal cause of discontent.

Land is a chief bone of contention and a source of insurrection *precisely* because it is an exploitative resource in a society that turns most human relations into assets and liabilities. These resources include the very ground occupied by most blacks. Hence, land has become central in the black revolution. *Land misuse* prepared many blacks to sharply criticize the system. *Land-people segregation* angers them yet fosters subcultural *similarities* which in turn help communication on common problems–including land use–that cannot be solved by working through the ongoing political party system. *Turf invasion* and *outsider pollution* of black land, especially in the case of the police, precipitates the initial phases of insurrection. *Land-people density* allows for ready agitation and other translating exercises increasingly sponsored by paramilitary organizations.

Preparatory Conditions

But land is not the only important consideration in a colonial-like situation. Perhaps as important would be the way in which significant sections of the white community define blacks as sources of labor and consumers of commodities. White businessmen have traditionally treated blacks as a source of cheap labor, much of which can be found in the pool of unemployed, especially during economic recessions. Generally unskilled, blacks have found this occupational status further and negatively compounded by the stigma of racial discrimination, another colonial-like phenomenon. High unemployment, low skill level, plus discriminatory practices combine with exploitative land use, as well as shark-like merchant behavior, to create the material base for discontent. As in the colony, the white merchant class unloads the shoddiest goods at the highest prices through generally discredited retail practices. But this is not enough to set many black people in motion.

When white realtors and others reject fair housing referenda (and their equivalents in other areas), they help prepare disillusioned blacks for militant action. Not only do these white groups deny blacks decent housing, they view black ghetto property as sources of profitable rent to be derived from unmaintained housing ultimately destined to be razed profitably through federally sponsored programs which (1) pay exorbitant prices for ramshackle slum housing, and (2) subsidize the subsequent construction of housing for high-income renters. More precisely, many white businessmen view black tenants as quantifiable units whose thin pay envelopes and welfare checks nonetheless guarantee exorbitant rents for rat-infested housing whose eventual removal allows for lucrative sales of land to private developers (often themselves), and whose structural high-rent successors earn top dollar for the owners.

Land is bought and sold, rents are raised and seldom lowered, rats are fostered and obliged, children are shunted and stunted, people's neighborhoods are demolished and "reconstructed," people are uprooted and forgotten—all to maximize an urban redevelopment organized to heighten private profit for whites who winter vacation in the Bahamas and Hawaii. On this matter, there can be little doubt. The analyzed data are plentiful, and although there may be exceptions—the soulful landlords—they serve only to make more stark the common pattern of urban renewal, black removal, and indiscriminate dump. The steam shovel digs, lifts, and drops poor blacks in nearby areas being readied for another urban renewal. Where will it all end? What are the blacks to make of this recurrent process? How, if at all, can blacks stop whites from treating them like objects in the land-profit maximization game?

FACILITATION: THE OTHER SIDE OF DISCRIMINATION

Whatever black power formulations become—and they are now only partially articulated and crystallized—they will derive in part from the fact that segregation promotes discussion within the black community at the very time that the quantity of black burdens has become objectively unbearable. Segregation has meant for blacks the packing of large numbers into relatively small areas where the congested population density and exacerbated housing problems oppress them but yet, ironically, allow them to talk about slumlords, urban renewal, police, unemployment, and schools. It's as if segregation can and does work to black advantage. Blacks are spatially contiguous, population dense, and racially pocketed. Hence, relational contacts become easy, especially in a context where their common place of origin—almost all blacks are first and second generation Southern born—and their common subculture facilitates discussion of the land question and agreement on problems of exploitation. Our analysis should not be misconstrued to mean that blacks, especially the urban working class, are without cultural anomie and personal alienation, both of which work against collective problem solving. There is plenty of both. We are saying, however, that a common origin, fate, and subculture facilitates black interaction with a multiplicity of informal and formal groups. Neighborhood conversation and block club groups, residential gangs and religious associations, ghetto-wide liberation groups and black trade union associations—among others—are the artifacts of unsolved problems and packed proximity.

Supporting Conditions

However, even when militant black churches, block clubs, race protection, and militant associations—both moderate and radical—arrive at nonviolent solutions to their problems, even when they make proposals to either integrate or black nationalize—they find that they cannot use the going political system to solve their problems. If we have learned anything from the 1960s, it is that the blacks cannot rely upon the Democratic party (and certainly not the Republican) to achieve racial justice; both major parties have proven themselves less concerned with justice than with the maintenance of "law and order." In almost all communities, blacks cannot work through the Democratic party, mainly because its key components are traditional. In the South, the situation is obvious; the data are overwhelming. In the North as well as in the West, Democratic party organizations are time and again ethnic dominated and craft union oriented, when they are not splintered. These general observations should not come as a shock. They should simply remind us of realities. When we observe the ghettoed colony, we should keep in mind how the city and state political machines rule the parties, pack the courts, run the conventions, administrate the laws, and damn the blacks generally to continued white colonialism. There are occasional exceptions, such as the Berkeley Democratic Party in 1963. But once again, they illuminate the rule. And the rule contributes to black restlessness.

Precipitating Events: Normal Phenomena

Under these circumstances of black inability to solve basic problems such as real estate fleecing of black neighborhoods and police muggings of those under suspicion, there has emerged a normal statistical rate of white atrocities against blacks, including both the murdering of black youth suspected of committing lesser felonies (such as car stealing) and the slapping and beating of blacks who object to the officious attitude and behavior of the police. Any one of these "normal" police efforts can set in motion an angry crowd leading to a riot committed to extracting on-the-spot redistributive justice within areas as tightly packed and exercised as our black ghettos.

Translating Groups and Processes

These "precipitating" events, however, do not become the basis for an insurrectionary struggle unless certain translating mechanisms are present. Here a distinction between the short-term and long-term insurrection would seem to be in order relative to black uprisings within colonial-like communities. In the case of the *short-term* insurrection, the collective upheaval lasts for several days. It is of short duration precisely because it depends almost exclusively upon the efforts of informally organized opinion leaders without paramilitary organizations. The informal coordination is *ad hoc,* as was the case in Detroit in 1967. By contrast and in general terms, when the long-term insurrection takes place, the uprising lasts longer and depends upon local opinion leaders who connect to a paramilitary group established along the lines of democratic centralism. The fighting group is led by charismatic leaders with a rational program for the blacks. The paramilitary organization is committed to the dissemination of charismatic pronouncements through the articulation of concrete and abstract ideologies made available for the insurgent masses and intellectuals. (Briefly, the fusion of democratic centralism and paramilitary organization takes the following form: (1) the revolutionary counterelite specifies issues to be discussed; (2) all levels of the organization debate the merits of the arguments advanced by the contending subgroups; (3) the central committee at the top of the organization takes a variety of views into account as it makes policy decisions, maps strategies, and specifies tactics; (4) the remainder of the organization accepts the formulations, commands its members to work for the realization of the policies accepted, and disciplines those who deviate on principles, strategy, and tactics.) Whether on the level of concrete referrents or abstract formulas, translating ideas find expression through charismatic leaders. In the United States, these leaders time and again define the black housing problem as one of classical colonial use of land within a colony to be liberated by black insurgency when blacks are ready to move.

WHAT NOW FOR THE WHITE LIBERAL?

By the standards of the civil rights movement of the early 1960s, black power ideology and action must seem wild, crazy in the extreme. The classical liberal slumlord must find these reformulations hard to believe, let alone accept. Not housing integration in the near future nor the elimination of the ghetto within the confines of capitalism, but ghetto redefinement and ghetto rejuvenation through paramilitary organizations having international commitments are the demands of the day. For the black nationalists—and they are today becoming increasingly popular—liberation from cultural traditionalism means both the total rejection of intimate integration and the wholehearted creation of a black community welded together through the myth and the reality of black power.

And where does this leave white liberals, the various piqued ones, as they gaze at the growth of black nationalism within the most segregated landscapes? Clearly white liberals are without their former influence inside the Negro community. Even their language has become archaic, quaint. For those of us previously involved in domineering, self-celebrating, self-indulging, and self-congratulatory efforts to integrate housing and to relieve our guilt-ridden souls, what can we do? As one "Afro" told a friend of mine, "Stay away." But that's not all.

Perhaps we should reassess our own failures during the 1960s and realize that widespread Negro integration—and hence assimilation—into white, middle-class residential areas might well have been grotesque. Had housing integration succeeded, it would have, by definition, scattered blacks residentially. Had the scattering included the movement of many blacks into white-collar areas and the creation of intimate ties with whites, many blacks would have accepted many white, suburban practices. Integration and assimilation would have meant the casting of many new black suburbanites replete with bricked patio, charcoal broiler, Bermuda shorts, polished golf clubs, serial promiscuity, *Time* magazine subscriptions, and political gutlessness—the whole panoply shared by so many American suburbanites. However, housing discrimination worked. As events have turned out, a lot of young blacks are now among the more articulate, militant Americans. They do not have a stake in suburban living nor American empire building. Hence, they need not accept domestic formulas and overseas atrocities. They can take the lead, take advantage of the privilege of white discrimination. Rap Brown, Eldridge Cleaver, Dick Gregory, Malcolm X, and even Martin Luther King in his later years—not all youngsters by any means—have helped us keep our chubby, opulent consciences aware of how the other three-quarters of the world gets by on greens, grits, and pig tails. The black spokesmen have done so by pointing to the overseas wretched and publicizing the domestic exploited. These spokesmen have insisted that we see the intercontinental parallels, the cross-cultural circumstances, the ways in which international capitalism has created both black and brown misery by stealing land, exploiting labor, ignoring grievances, and selling junk.

In the short run, alienated blacks will undoubtedly fail to create the basis for a triumphant anticolonial coalition against the American Empire. In the

United States, the blacks, browns, and whites eligible for the revolutionary adventure are today too few in number, even if they could coalesce on issues of joint material interest. Yet blacks have rebelled, if only to discover positive identity. But their doing so has not revolutionized America. Blacks have failed to fashion a humanist utopia—at least in our time—for the police and military have all but obliterated "translating mechanisms" such as the Black Panther organization. Their doing so has been generally popular. On the whole, this country is near frozen to international racist traditions and practices, integrated television commercials notwithstanding. If anything, black uprisings have helped create a larger political base for sophisticated racists now more vulgar, more bold, more violent than ever before.

Given the insurmountable military odds, black insurrections may nonetheless, in the short run, help foster what most white Americans deserve: a police state not too different from those partially created and heavily supported by United States military and civilian authorities working abroad in such countries as Guatemala, the Dominican Republic, Greece, and Vietnam—to name but a few. King may have been right: the consequence of recurrent black insurrections in America may well be fascism. The jailing of insurgent blacks, their incarceration in the twelve prison camps vacated by the Japanese Americans twenty-five years ago and until recently furbished for political undesirables, the white establishment's inadequate but explainable responses of more effective military arms, police tactics, and summer circuses rather than the elimination of class-racial injustices—all of these trends make clear what might well be in store for blacks in general and black militants in particular. But fight blacks must, for their struggle is determined, just, and necessary. The black revolutionaries are right: without revolution we would still be serfs. Without revolution, blacks, browns, yellows, and whites will never be free from an international capitalism no longer able to cope simultaneously with insurrections at home and revolutions abroad. In part, because of heavy and expensive overseas commitments, there is little domestic federal money available for structural changes—only small amounts for token projects and military controls. Patch-work reforms have failed to move many blacks to do anything other than become more angry as they react to heightened but unmet expectations, while recurrent police brutality only further angers them. Riots and insurrections continue to occur. In trying to cope militarily with these domestic and overseas rebellions and revolutions, the United States tightens its archaic laws, threatens its judiciary, represses its proletarian minorities, wiretaps its suspected subversives, regulates its tamed labor leadership, justifies massive annihilation of its overseas obstinates, grapples with its recalcitrant universities, drafts its student troublemakers, indicts its foremost critics, and promises its middle classes greater affluence if they will accept the new adjustment. For many of those who stand to lose during the movement toward, and the realization of, middle fascism, revolution would appear to be the only alternative. For others, a united front perhaps would be the order of the day.

But in the long run, can we not count on the positive impact of formal education, as many of the moderate antimilitants have hoped? Perhaps, but I doubt it. Apparently when traditional people are located in traditional groups, education makes them more clever in their construction of racial rationalizations on the sacredness of property and the rejection of interracial intimacy. Most white politicians sensitively understand those who concoct self-righteous ideologies. That's why antidiscriminatory laws go unenforced. Politicians know when to break the law by not enforcing it, and why their doing so goes unchallenged. Many young blacks also understand this reciprocal affair between educated white people and practical politicians, and some of them work to dynamite this tidy relationship. In short, the near future promises interesting confrontations.

POLITICAL RECOMMENDATIONS

But dynamite and Molotov cocktails have not removed colonial-like conditions common to the ghetto. Nor does massive material deprivation appear to be on the wane. A trip through any ghetto will convince anyone of that. Nor can we say that ghetto realities will improve sharply if at all during the next decade. Powerful politicians and big businessmen have decided to slightly modify and repress rather than eliminate or seriously upgrade the ghetto. In this context, what can we do politically? "We" refers to those academic people who have lodged themselves on the American left—often in tenuous coalition with the young against the academic mandarins—those academics who service big corporations, government, and industry. Perhaps we antimandarins can begin by indicating areas where we can expect to have little political impact in the next five years, for if nothing else, the 1960s have been instructive. They have taught us our limitations, especially when working through government programs. First we must admit what we can *not* do. Then we can move to the question of what we *must* do to get ourselves organized to help ourselves as well as blacks. For some academic people have also come under attack because of their participation in anticolonial struggles.

In the short run, we cannot end the exploitation of black people. We cannot eliminate even a small amount of those conditions that drive blacks to rebel. Whether in the areas of housing, jobs, or commodities, we fail to control the distribution of apartments, homes, jobs, or goods, since we do not own the private property associated with their creation and political control. We do not own the housing corporations, construction companies, the factories, the mines, the shopping centers, or the lumber companies. We do not highly influence or control the senators, the congressmen, the governors, or the assemblymen through corporate-based contributions. Although not too different in this respect from our mandarin colleagues, we are powerless in almost every area where we could hope to alleviate the conditions of black, brown, yellow, and other subjugated populations. Of course, we can and must complain. But let's not confuse our insignificant influence with the ability to get things done.

We cannot remove the walls of the ghetto, or the ghetto itself—should we even want to do so. Most whites actively or tacitly insist upon their retention. Most blacks are refusing the struggle to leave the ghetto. Meanwhile the leading white politicians flit from formula to formula in order to guarantee this walled retention. "Keep the niggers out of the suburbs"—that's still the standing order of the day. Failures in housing integration have accompanied unmet goals in social welfare. Generally, most federal programs for blacks can be reduced to government subsidy of welfare organizations. These groups compete to malservice the poor blacks and perpetuate the very conditions they are presumed to alleviate. Indeed, these agencies know that if they could remove the deplorable conditions of the ghetto—or the ghetto itself—they would have little reason to exist. Like national safety councils, they don't help much and they won't go away. Like Topsy, they just grow. In fact many of these public service organizations, as they are inappropriately called, can report success, no matter what happens. If ghetto conditions improve minimally, perhaps even momentarily, on matters of welfare or safety, they can interpret the gains as the basis for continued community tax support of their organizations; if ghetto material conditions deteriorate further, they can argue for more money to alleviate a worsening situation. This insight—one stated most precisely eight years ago by Charles Silberman,[1] clearly indicates that more than inertia and obvious discrimination serve to maintain much of the black population as separate and poor. So let's stop talking about welfare services as part of a "solution." The federal government will not even be able to unload them in efforts to directly subsidize and train the poor, for welfare organizations know how to lobby successfully for their continued participation

Police malpractices parallel "benign neglect" in housing and social welfare. And we will not be able to eliminate the normal rate of police brutality in our black communities—although the black brothers may make a dent in this area—for we do not have the coercive strength to do so even publicly, but we should not mistake the symbolic denunciation of the act with the structural eradication of the practice; intellectuals are most prone to accept this symbolic fantasy. Worse, many antimandarins are likely to try to convince the dispossessed others, especially those who suffer police abuses, that government reports, professional meetings, panel discussions, and university conferences on police misuse of force somehow constitute improvements in black lives. In this sense and insofar as these intellectuals are successful in symbol sales, they help create a false sense of consciousness among that dwindling minority of blacks who still take white critics seriously. What white intellectuals should do is publicly admit the ineffectiveness of spoken and written protest–in a word, dissent–in minimizing the brutality of those civil servants employed to hold the lid on a system no longer capable of fully subordinating populations through the dissemination of myths. The biggest lie is the power of the freely spoken word. Let's point that out. For example, during the 1968-9 Black Panther repression, one involving the deaths of dozens of Panthers as well as the illegal and extra-legal harassment of hundreds of others, white journalists and academics either ignored the false arrests, the incredible beatings, and the street corner slayings, the gunning down of the Chicago Panther leadership, or exonerated their humanist souls by writing the occasional article about what was happening. Their writing did not abate the pace of violent illegality mounted by our blue-uniformed civil servants. Let's admit publicly that we have done little to stop the killings, the beatings, the office-smashing, the gassing, and the open harassment largely because we have no way to affect public officials and bigoted police who forge false interpretations of the law.

What can we antimandarins do? Our first task is to get our own house in order. Of those professors interested in effecting an elimination of domestic racism, many are in deep trouble because of establishment represssion of their protest activities during the 1960s, whether as supporters of the black liberation movement or anti-Vietnam war mobilizations. Professors have been fired, and little has been done to help them. We must end this acquiescence. We must take care of our casualties, as does any army, or fold up our tents. Our own careerism leads us to duck controversies like taking on the entrenched faculty on matters of employing those fired elsewhere. Worse, our careerism leads us not to support students when they put themselves on the line. A minority of our students have energetically and morally organized a Children's Crusade against the upper classes, their institutions, their mandarins, and their corrupt ways. Yet we give little support to the young unless and until these students are injured in clashes with mobilized police. Then we back the students only so long as they adamantly protest, for somehow we wish a return to order. When those students who have not been suspended or turned off by our hypocrisy return to our classrooms, as we urge them to do, we slump back in our casual ruts and forget about the campus institute for defense analysis, the campus corporate recruitment office, and the napalm canisters.

And these are not the only problems facing the antimandarin faculty. We know we must communicate with people beyond the campus in order to stop the move towards fascism in America. But we don't make sacrifices, like giving up two weeks of our summer vacations to organize to reach potential allies whose present conceptions of world events outrage what we know of evidence and logic. As a beginning, we already should have organized an underground tabloid for workers and others who have genuine material grievances. But we haven't. As generally satisfied Platonists covered by the state payroll, flattered by the federal hog trough, and/or honored by the benevolent endowment, we have acquired a perspective as false as the ones common to most workers. We have tried to account for the civil rights failure by blaming the lesser educated whose authoritarian views do in fact derive from mystifications imposed upon them through the very institutions we understand but refuse to expose. We use the tax money of white, black, and brown working people to create our own intellectual good fortune of near no-work. We neglect the dissemination of knowledge to working people through already existing organizations, groups to which we have potential access. Our community organizational efforts are almost nil.

But to reach those around us–should we opt to do something–we must shelve temporarily our general strategy of direct action, for this approach has been misinterpreted successfully by the propertied media to create massive opposition to it. This opposition is most noticeable among the very ones we wish to change and might hope to bring over to our side. Let us be blunt. We will not stem the tide towards fascism, let alone move forward, unless we create some kind of mass base for our movement. We don't have money, so we're going to need numbers. For this kind of mass base we will have to recruit blue-collar workers, both white and black. But we won't get the numbers if we continue direct action, at least at present. It's that simple. The next time we move into a period of direct action, and its present use appears to be on the wane, we must do so with masses of people lining up on our side, not with the Ronnie Reagans.

To obtain working-class support, we must go through a period of creating a united front. What we need presently is a coalition of those very groups that Robert Kennedy attempted to weld together. But such a unity seems unlikely unless we have a political party and an agreement to work for diverse as well as common interests. The party will have to be a third party-despite all the limitations inherently involved-for the Democratic party is hopeless. The issues will have to be of the gut variety–work pace and working conditions, unemployment and job creation, housing conditions and slumlord violations, police practices and repressions, food prices and their continued inflation, corporations and their connection to food-price inflation, selective service and selected deaths–for chosen wars which benefit only the few at the top and their servants. These are the kinds of interracial issues to be publicized through the unpropertied media, the workers' own underground newspapers, and wherever possible, their radio stations. We can distribute these papers and raise these questions within labor unions as well as neighborhood groups, tenants-rights organizations, welfare-rights groups, union-organizing campaigns, and the like. But we must do so in an egalitarian spirit, with an absence of counter-elite self-righteousness. Let there be two, three, many Berkeley *Barbs* geared to working class taste in every state in the Union. It will be our task to help erase the false conceptions held by so many of our potential allies. It will be our job to create a more sociological view of how institutions operate to shortchange those within our coalition. Let's struggle for ourselves, as mixed as we are in background. Let's forget about working as false prophets of benevolent change through the federal bureaucracy.

Admittedly this is a reformist program. But then our potential allies are not ready for a more trenchant strategy. Perhaps later, *if* we have been able to demonstrate the futility of social reform and *if* we can create a fully conscious coalition, we can then opt for a militant course of action. Unless we do our homework, nothing will work out.

NOTES

1. Charles Silberman, *Crisis in Black and White* (New York: Random House, 1964).

Appendix A

A Statistical Addendum

Included in Appendix A are materials referred to in the second major section of Chapter 7. Entitled "White Tradition and the Law of Evolutionary Potential," the section analyzes the striking impact of political party affiliation on fair housing choice among union members and various categories of mobile and non-mobile persons. This appendix, then, adds the supportive documentation to this analysis.

Table A-1. Union Membership and Fair Housing Vote (Whites Only)

Blue- and White-collar Workers				
Nonunion	36	45	19	(620)
Union	28	47	25	(135)
Blue-collar Only				
Nonunion	18	57	25	(44)
Union	22	55	23	(65)

Key: See page 77.

Table A-2. Party, Union Membership, and Fair Housing Vote (Blue-collar Whites Only)

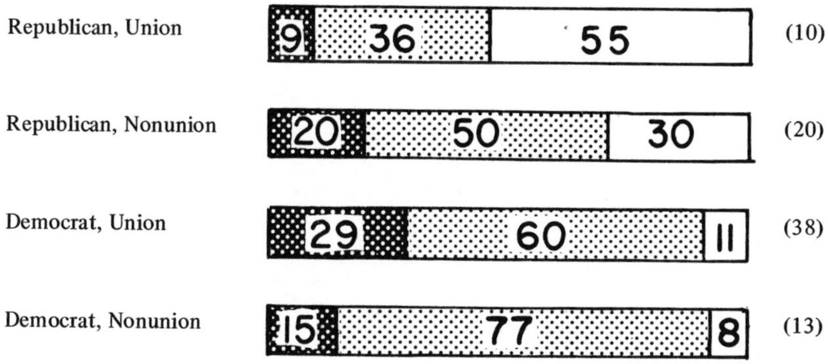

Republican, Union	9	36	55	(10)
Republican, Nonunion	20	50	30	(20)
Democrat, Union	29	60	11	(38)
Democrat, Nonunion	15	77	8	(13)

Key: See page 66.

Table A-3. Union Membership and Class Identification (Only Blue-Collar Democrats) as They Relate to the Fair Housing Vote (Whites Only)

Union Membership	*Class Identification*	*Vote on Fair Housing*			
		For	*Against*	*Did Not Vote*	*Total*
Union Member	Middle Class	7	18	2	27
	Working Class	3	4	1	8
	Lower Class	0	1	1	2
	Refused to Identify	1	0	0	1
Nonunion Member	Middle Class	2	5	0	7
	Working Class	0	4	1	5
	Lower Class	1	0	0	1
	Refused to Identify	0	1	0	1

Table A-4. Intergenerational Mobility and Vote on Fair Housing (Whites Only)

Mobility Level	*Father's Occupation*	*Respondent's Occupation*		*Vote on Fair Housing*			
				For	*Against*	*Did Not Vote*	*Total*
Middle-Class Stationary	White Collar	White Collar	Middle Class	(149) 40%	(159) 43%	(65) 17%	(373) 100%
Upwardly Mobile	Blue Collar	White Collar	Middle Class	(39) 30%	(59) 46%	(31) 24%	(129) 100%
Working-Class Stationary	Blue Collar	Blue Collar	Working Class	(5) 10%	(30) 57%	(17) 33%	(52) 100%
Skidder	White Collar	Blue Collar	Working Class	(13) 28%	(25) 54%	(8) 18%	(46) 100%

Table A-5. Party Preference, Intergenerational Mobility vs. Vote on Fair Housing (Whites Only)

Father's Occupation	*Respondent's Occupation*	*Vote on Fair Housing*			
		For	*Against*	*Did Not Vote*	*Total*
Middle-Class Democrats					
White Collar	White Collar	(103) 70%	(27) 18%	(22) 12%	(152) 100%
Blue Collar	White Collar	(24) 44%	(14) 26%	(16) 30%	(54) 100%
Working-Class Democrats					
Blue Collar	Blue Collar	(4) 21%	(15) 58%	(5) 21%	(24) 100%
White Collar	Blue Collar	(6) 30%	(14) 70%	(0) 0%	(20) 100%
Middle-Class Republicans					
White Collar	White Collar	(22) 13%	(116) 71%	(26) 16%	(164) 100%
Blue Collar	White Collar	(12) 20%	(38) 66%	(8) 14%	(58) 100%
Working-Class Republicans					
Blue Collar	Blue Collar	(1) 8%	(5) 38%	(7) 54%	(13) 100%
White Collar	Blue Collar	(4) 27%	(7) 36%	(4) 27%	(15) 100%

Table A-6. Union Membership, Party Preference, Father's Class and Respondent's Class vs. Fair Housing Vote

Union Membership	*Party Preference*	*Father's Occupation*	*Respondent's Occupation*		*Vote on Fair Housing* For	Against	Did Not Vote	Total
Union	Democrat	White Collar	White Collar	Middle Class	(12) 57%	(4) 19%	(5) 24%	(21) 100%
		Blue Collar	White Collar		(6) 40%	(6) 40%	(3) 20%	(15) 100%
		Blue Collar	Blue Collar	Working Class	(4) 21%	(11) 48%	(4) 21%	(19) 100%
		White Collar	Blue Collar		(6) 43%	(8) 57%	(0) 0%	(14) 100%
	Republican	White Collar	White Collar	Middle Class	(0) –	(8) –	(1) –	(9) –
		Blue Collar	White Collar		(1) –	(6) –	(1) –	(8) –
		Blue Collar	Blue Collar	Working Class	(0) –	(1) –	(3) –	(4) –
		White Collar	Blue Collar		(1) [illegible]	(2) [illegible]	(2) [illegible]	(5) [illegible]

Non-Union	Democrat	White Collar	White Collar	Middle Class	(91) 68%	(23) 19%	(17) 13%	(131) 100%
		Blue Collar	White Collar	Middle Class	(18) 47%	(8) 20%	(13) 33%	(39) 100%
		Blue Collar	Blue Collar	Working Class	(0) –	(4) –	(1) –	(5) –
		White Collar	Blue Collar	Working Class	(0) –	(6) –	(0) –	(6) –
	Republican	White Collar	White Collar	Middle Class	(22) 14%	(106) 70%	(25) 16%	(152) 100%
		Blue Collar	White Collar	Middle Class	(11) 22%	(34) 65%	(7) 13%	(52) 100%
		Blue Collar	Blue Collar	Working Class	(1) –	(4) –	(4) –	(9) –
		White Collar	Blue Collar	Working Class	(3) 30%	(5) 50%	(2) 20%	(10) 100%

Table A-7. Selected Vertical Mobility Considerations Among Union Democrats (Blue-Collar), Amount of Formal Education and Vote on Fair Housing (Whites Only)

Selected Vertical Mobility	*Education Level*		*Vote on Fair Housing*			
			For	*Against*	*Did Not Vote*	*Total*
Skidders	Grade School 1-8	(1)	(1)	(3)	(0)	(4)
	Some High School 9-11	(2)	(1)	(1)	(0)	(2)
	High School 12	(3)	(1)	(2)	(0)	(3)
	College up to M.A.	(4)	(3)	(2)	(0)	(5)
	M.A.	(5)	(0)	(0)	(0)	(0)
Blue-Collar Stationary	Grade School 1-8	(1)	(0)	(6)	(1)	(8)
	Some High School 9-11	(2)	(1)	(0)	(0)	(1)
	High School 12	(3)	(1)	(3)	(2)	(6)
	College up to M.A.	(4)	(1)	(2)	(0)	(3)
	M.A.	(5)	(0)	(0)	(1)	(1)

Appendix B

APPENDIX B

Fair Housing and Authoritarian Ideology

This appendix presents material in support of the assumptions and hypotheses advanced in Chapter 8. Table B-1 relates class to vote on fair housing while taking into account ideology and party affiliation. You will note how we treat, first, ethnocentrism, then politico-economic conservatism, followed by cultural traditionalism. For brevity, only the first part of each relevant question is given in the table; the exact wording can be found on pages 000-000.

When we consider Question 1 on ethnocentrism—"Most of our social problems would be solved if we could somehow get rid of immoral, crooked, and feeble-minded people"—together with class and party positions, we can observe the combined impact of idea and structure on action. In this case, the behavior is voting. At one extreme is the 22 percent that voted for fair housing, 65 percent against (and 13 percent who did not vote) who were simultaneously traditional, blue collar, and Democratic. By contrast, 66 percent of the Berkeley people who were anti-traditional (on this item), white collar, and Democrat, voted for the ordinance, 16 percent against, with 18 percent not voting.

More importantly, whatever the spread in votes, Democrats were always more progressive than comparable Republicans. Compare, for example, non-traditional, white-collar Democrats with the equivalent category of Republicans, and you will find almost 50 percent differences on voting. Both patterns—a wide span of differences within the Democratic camp *and* consistent differences among comparable Republicans and Democrats—occur throughout the remainder of the table.

Clearly, then, we are not arguing for the exclusive relevance of either ideas or structural position. It is the interaction of people's minds and *their* positions that jointly determines what they do.

All the remaining data–too much to be presented in this book–clearly support this basic, social psychological principle.

Table B-1. Party Preference, Ideology, Class, and Vote on Fair Housing (Ethnocentrism and Politico-Economic Conservatism Only)

	Democrats				*Republicans*			
	% Agree		*% Disagree*		*% Agree*		*% Disagree*	
Vote on Housing	*Blue Collar*	*White Collar*	*Blue Collar*	*White Collar*	*Blue Collar*	*White Collar*	*Blue Collar*	*White Collar*
Question No. 1: Problem solving and immoral people . . . (Ethnocentrism)								
For	22 (5)	33 (7)	36 (8)	66 (96)	– (0)	4 (2)	18 (3)	18 (24)
Against	65 (15)	38 (8)	55 (12)	16 (24)	57 (4)	84 (48)	47 (8)	69 (91)
Did Not Vote	13 (3)	29 (6)	9 (2)	18 (26)	43 (3)	12 (7)	35 (6)	13 (17)
Total	100 (23)	100 (21)	100 (22)	100 (146)	100 (7)	100 (57)	100 (17)	100 (132)
Question No. 2: America may not be perfect . . . (Ethnocentrism)								
For	27 (10)	56 (50)	– (2)	68 (50)	14 (3)	13 (21)	– (0)	17 (6)
Against	65 (24)	27 (24)	– (3)	11 (8)	50 (11)	74 (116)	– (1)	69 (24)
Did Not Vote	8 (3)	17 (16)	– (2)	21 (16)	36 (8)	13 (20)	– (2)	14 (5)
Total	100 (37)	100 (90)	– (7)	100 (74)	100 (22)	100 (157)	– (3)	100 (35)
Question No. 1: Labor unions become stronger . . . (Politico-Economic Conservatism)								
For	39 (8)	72 (50)	21 (5)	53 (50)	– (1)	20 (2)	10 (2)	14 (25)
Against	47 (10)	13 (9)	71 (17)	24 (23)	– (1)	80 (8)	52 (11)	72 (132)
Did Not Vote	14 (3)	15 (10)	8 (2)	23 (22)	– (1)	0 (0)	38 (8)	14 (25)
Total	100 (21)	100 (69)	100 (24)	100 (95)	– (3)	100 (10)	100 (21)	100 (182)

Question No. 2: Eliminate most government controls . . . (Politico-Economic Conservatism)

For	27	(7)	31	(9)	32	(6)	68	(93)	7	(1)	8	(8)	–	(2)	22	(19)
Against	65	(17)	35	(10)	53	(10)	15	(21)	50	(9)	81	(85)	–	(5)	64	(54)
Did Not Vote	8	(2)	34	(10)	15	(3)	17	(22)	43	(6)	11	(12)	–	(2)	14	(12)
Total	100	(26)	100	(29)	100	(19)	100	(136)	100	(14)	100	(105)	–	(9)	100	(85)

Question No. 3: Full economic security is bad . . . (Politico-Economic Conservatism)

For	19	(3)	51	(28)	34	(10)	67	(74)	14	(2)	8	(8)	10	(1)	22	(19)
Against	63	(10)	24	(13)	59	(17)	19	(19)	50	(7)	79	(82)	50	(5)	65	(56)
Did Not Vote	18	(3)	25	(14)	7	(2)	16	(17)	36	(5)	23	(14)	40	(4)	13	(11)
Total	100	(16)	100	(55)	100	(29)	100	(110)	100	(14)	100	(104)	100	(10)	100	(86)

Question No. 4: Businessman more important than professor . . . (Politico-Economic Conservatism)

For	33	(7)	48	(10)	25	(6)	64	(92)	–	(1)	2	(10)	12	(2)	18	(24)
Against	57	(12)	29	(6)	63	(15)	18	(26)	–	(3)	89	(40)	53	(9)	68	(93)
Did Not Vote	10	(2)	23	(5)	12	(3)	18	(26)	–	(3)	9	(4)	35	(6)	14	(19)
Total	100	(21)	100	(21)	100	(24)	100	(144)	–	(7)	100	(45)	100	(17)	100	(136)

(Cultural Traditionalism Only)

Question No. 1: Obedience and respect for authority best for kids . . . (Cultural Traditionalism)

For	21	(8)	41	(26)	–	(5)	75	(77)	9	(2)	10	(14)	–	(1)	27	(13)
Against	67	(26)	39	(25)	–	(1)	7	(7)	52	(12)	77	(111)	–	(0)	60	(29)
Did Not Vote	12	(5)	20	(13)	–	(0)	18	(19)	39	(9)	13	(20)	–	(1)	13	(6)
Total	100	(39)	100	(64)	–	(6)	100	(103)	100	(23)	100	(145)	–	(2)	100	(48)

(Continued on p. 226)

	Democrats								*Republicans*							
	% Agree				*% Disagree*				*% Agree*				*% Disagree*			
Vote on Fair Housing	*Blue Collar*		*White Collar*		*Blue Collar*		*White Collar*		*Blue Collar*		*White Collar*		*Blue Collar*		*White Collar*	
Question No. 2: Talk less, work more . . . (Cultural Traditionalism)																
For	27	(8)	45	(34)	29	(4)	74	(63)	6	(1)	10	(13)	–	(2)	25	(14)
Against	63	(19)	29	(22)	57	(8)	12	(10)	59	(10)	78	(100)	–	(2)	61	(35)
Did Not Vote	10	(3)	26	(20)	14	(2)	14	(12)	35	(6)	12	(16)	–	(4)	14	(8)
Total	100	(30)	100	(76)	100	(14)	100	(85)	100	(17)	100	(129)	–	(8)	100	(57)
Question No. 3: Bad manners and getting along with decent people . . . (Cultural Traditionalism)																
For	23	(9)	52	(56)	–	(3)	82	(40)	13	(3)	10	(15)	–	(0)	33	(12)
Against	64	(25)	24	(26)	–	(2)	8	(4)	50	(12)	78	(121)	–	(0)	53	(19)
Did Not Vote	13	(5)	24	(26)	–	(0)	10	(5)	37	(9)	12	(20)	–	(1)	14	(5)
Total	100	(39)	100	(108)	–	(5)	100	(49)	100	(24)	100	(156)	–	(1)	100	(36)
Question No. 4: Science has its place . . . (Cultural Traditionalism)																
For	26	(9)	57	(52)	36	(4)	67	(47)	10	(2)	13	(18)	–	(1)	17	(9)
Against	59	(20)	22	(19)	64	(7)	19	(13)	50	(10)	78	(106)	–	(2)	60	(32)
Did Not Vote	15	(5)	21	(20)	0	(0)	14	(10)	40	(8)	9	(12)	–	(1)	23	(12)
Total	100	(34)	100	(91)	100	(11)	100	(70)	100	(20)	100	(136)	–	(4)	100	(53)
Question No. 5: Faith in supernatural and obedience . . . (Cultural Traditionalism)																
For	24	(7)	34	(11)	40	(6)	69	(93)	17	(3)	7	(5)	–	(0)	19	(22)
Against	63	(19)	41	(13)	53	(8)	14	(19)	44	(8)	79	(57)	–	(4)	70	(79)
Did Not Vote	13	(4)	25	(8)	7	(1)	17	(23)	39	(7)	16	(12)	–	(2)	11	(13)
Total	100	(30)	100	(32)	100	(15)	100	(135)	100	(18)	100	(74)	–	(6)	100	(114)

Question No. 6: Young people as rebellious . . . (Cultural Traditionalism)																
For	23	(8)	39	(26)	50	(5)	76	(75)	17	(3)	12	(18)	–	(0)	22	(9)
Against	69	(23)	35	(23)	40	(4)	9	(9)	50	(9)	75	(114)	–	(3)	63	(25)
Did Not Vote	11	(4)	26	(17)	10	(1)	15	(15)	33	(6)	13	(19)	–	(4)	15	(6)
Total	100	(35)	100	(66)	100	(10)	100	(99)	100	(18)	100	(151)	–	(7)	100	(40)
Question No. 7: Country needs fewer laws, programs, more leaders . . . (Cultural Traditionalism)																
For	30	(9)	44	(22)	21	(3)	71	(79)	0	(0)	8	(8)	27	(3)	21	(19)
Against	53	(16)	34	(17)	79	(11)	11	(12)	57	(8)	83	(80)	37	(4)	62	(56)
Did Not Vote	17	(5)	22	(11)	0	(0)	18	(21)	43	(6)	9	(9)	36	(4)	17	(16)
Total	100	(30)	100	(50)	100	(14)	100	(112)	100	(14)	100	(97)	100	(11)	100	(91)
Question No. 8: Decent person wouldn't hurt close friend . . . (Cultural Traditionalism)																
For	23	(7)	52	(30)	39	(5)	68	(74)	14	(2)	14	(16)	–	(1)	15	(11)
Against	68	(21)	26	(15)	46	(6)	16	(17)	50	(7)	74	(86)	–	(5)	69	(52)
Did Not Vote	9	(3)	22	(13)	15	(2)	16	(18)	36	(5)	12	(14)	–	(3)	16	(12)
Total	100	(31)	100	(58)	100	(13)	100	(109)	100	(14)	100	(116)	–	(9)	100	(75)
Question No. 9: Learning through suffering . . . (Cultural Traditionalism)																
For	35	(6)	48	(12)	26	(7)	66	(90)	–	(0)	7	(2)	13	(2)	16	(25)
Against	47	(8)	24	(6)	70	(19)	17	(23)	–	(6)	83	(25)	40	(6)	70	(110)
Did Not Vote	18	(3)	28	(7)	4	(1)	17	(24)	–	(2)	10	(3)	47	(7)	14	(23)
Total	100	(17)	100	(25)	100	(27)	100	(137)	–	(8)	100	(30)	100	(15)	100	(158)

(Continued on p. 228)

	Democrats								Republicans							
	% Agree				% Disagree				% Agree				% Disagree			
Vote on Fair Housing	*Blue Collar*		*White Collar*		*Blue Collar*		*White Collar*		*Blue Collar*		*White Collar*		*Blue Collar*		*White Collar*	
Question No. 10: Youth needs discipline, fight for country . . . (Cultural Traditionalism)																
For	24	(9)	48	(27)	–	(4)	70	(75)	10	(2)	13	(20)	–	(1)	19	(7)
Against	65	(24)	33	(19)	–	(3)	11	(12)	57	(12)	75	(116)	–	(0)	62	(23)
Did Not Vote	11	(4)	19	(11)	–	(1)	19	(20)	33	(17)	12	(18)	–	(3)	19	(7)
Total	100	(37)	100	(57)	–	(8)	100	(107)	100	(21)	100	(154)	–	(4)	100	(37)
Question No. 11: Insult to honor and punishment . . . (Cultural Traditionalism)																
For	22	(6)	36	(8)	40	(6)	66	(91)	8	(1)	11	(6)	16	(2)	16	(21)
Against	63	(17)	41	(9)	53	(8)	16	(22)	50	(6)	79	(45)	46	(6)	70	(92)
Did Not Vote	15	(4)	23	(5)	7	(1)	18	(25)	42	(5)	10	(6)	38	(5)	14	(18)
Total	100	(27)	100	(22)	100	(15)	100	(138)	100	(12)	100	(57)	100	(13)	100	(131)
Question No. 12: Sex crimes and punishment . . . (Cultural Traditionalism)																
For	28	(5)	27	(7)	30	(8)	68	(95)	–	(0)	7	(5)	20	(3)	18	(22)
Against	56	(10)	46	(12)	63	(17)	14	(20)	–	(5)	80	(54)	47	(7)	69	(83)
Did Not Vote	16	(3)	27	(7)	7	(2)	18	(25)	–	(4)	13	(9)	33	(5)	13	(15)
Total	100	(18)	100	(26)	100	(27)	100	(140)	–	(9)	100	(68)	100	(15)	100	(120)
Question No. 13: Bad not to love parents . . . (Cultural Traditionalism)																
For	24	(8)	33	(11)	42	(5)	68	(91)	7	(1)	7	(6)	20	(2)	19	(21)
Against	64	(21)	43	(14)	50	(6)	14	(18)	47	(7)	80	(68)	50	(5)	67	(72)
Did Not Vote	12	(4)	24	(8)	8	(1)	18	(24)	46	(7)	13	(11)	30	(3)	14	(15)
Total	100	(33)	100	(33)	100	(12)	100	(133)	100	(15)	100	(85)	100	(10)	100	(108)

	Question No. 14: Forget about worries and keep busy . . . (Cultural Traditionalism)															
For	27	(7)	47	(19)	28	(5)	67	(84)	–	(3)	14	(10)	0	(0)	14	(17)
Against	65	(17)	29	(12)	56	(10)	15	(19)	–	(4)	76	(53)	53	(8)	72	(84)
Did Not Vote	8	(2)	24	(10)	16	(3)	18	(22)	–	(2)	10	(7)	47	(7)	14	(17)
Total	100	(26)	100	(41)	100	(18)	100	(125)	–	(9)	100	(70)	100	(15)	100	(118)
	Question No. 15: Born to jump from high places . . . (Cultural Traditionalism)															
For	39	(7)	58	(27)	23	(6)	66	(68)	–	(2)	20	(15)	7	(1)	9	(10)
Against	56	(10)	23	(11)	62	(16)	17	(17)	–	(3)	71	(55)	64	(9)	74	(81)
Did Not Vote	5	(1)	19	(9)	15	(4)	17	(18)	–	(4)	9	(7)	29	(4)	17	(18)
Total	100	(18)	100	(47)	100	(26)	100	(103)	–	(9)	100	(77)	100	(14)	100	(109)
	Question No. 16: People divided: weak and strong . . . (Cultural Traditionalism)															
For	32	(7)	35	(9)	26	(6)	67	(93)	0	(0)	8	(4)	20	(3)	16	(23)
Against	59	(13)	38	(10)	61	(14)	15	(21)	50	(5)	84	(40)	47	(7)	69	(99)
Did Not Vote	9	(2)	27	(7)	13	(3)	18	(25)	50	(5)	8	(4)	33	(5)	15	(21)
Total	100	(22)	100	(26)	100	(23)	100	(139)	100	(10)	100	(48)	100	(15)	100	(143)
	Question No. 17: Astrology will someday explain . . . (Cultural Traditionalism)															
For	25	(6)	40	(8)	33	(6)	65	(94)	0	(0)	15	(5)	25	(3)	14	(22)
Against	63	(15)	25	(5)	56	(10)	19	(27)	40	(4)	76	(25)	58	(7)	72	(114)
Did Not Vote	12	(3)	35	(7)	11	(2)	16	(24)	60	(6)	9	(3)	17	(2)	14	(23)
Total	100	(24)	100	(20)	100	(18)	100	(145)	100	(10)	100	(33)	100	(12)	100	(159)

(Continued on p. 230)

Vote on Fair Housing	*Democrats*				*Republicans*			
	% Agree		*% Disagree*		*% Agree*		*% Disagree*	
	Blue Collar	*White Collar*	*Blue Collar*	*White Collar*	*Blue Collar*	*White Collar*	*Blue Collar*	*White Collar*
Question No. 18: Troubles ended by earthquake or flood . . . (Cultural Traditionalism)								
For	25 (5)	52 (16)	32 (8)	65 (84)	– (0)	11 (4)	18 (3)	15 (23)
Against	65 (13)	26 (8)	56 (14)	18 (24)	– (4)	76 (28)	47 (8)	72 (107)
Did Not Vote	10 (2)	22 (7)	12 (3)	17 (22)	– (3)	13 (5)	35 (6)	13 (20)
Total	100 (20)	100 (31)	100 (25)	100 (130)	– (7)	100 (37)	100 (17)	100 (150)
Question No. 19: The power of will power . . . (Cultural Traditionalism)								
For	17 (5)	31 (15)	50 (7)	74 (86)	11 (2)	11 (12)	– (1)	17 (15)
Against	67 (20)	42 (20)	50 (7)	10 (12)	50 (9)	75 (78)	– (3)	70 (61)
Did Not Vote	16 (5)	27 (13)	0 (0)	16 (19)	39 (7)	14 (15)	– (3)	13 (11)
Total	100 (30)	100 (48)	100 (14)	100 (117)	100 (18)	100 (105)	– (7)	100 (87)
Question No. 20: Lives controlled by plots . . . (Cultural Traditionalism)								
For	28 (7)	45 (18)	26 (5)	69 (80)	– (1)	10 (7)	13 (2)	16 (20)
Against	64 (16)	30 (12)	58 (11)	15 (18)	– (4)	80 (54)	50 (8)	69 (84)
Did Not Vote	8 (2)	25 (10)	16 (3)	16 (19)	– (2)	10 (7)	37 (6)	15 (19)
Total	100 (25)	100 (40)	100 (19)	100 (117)	– (7)	100 (68)	100 (16)	100 (123)
Question No. 21: Human nature and war . . . (Cultural Traditonalism)								
For	24 (9)	49 (41)	– (4)	75 (59)	5 (1)	12 (19)	– (2)	22 (8)
Against	62 (23)	25 (21)	– (4)	13 (10)	48 (10)	76 (119)	– (2)	59 (21)
Did Not Vote	14 (5)	26 (22)	– (0)	12 (10)	47 (10)	12 (18)	– (0)	19 (7)
Total	100 (37)	100 (84)	– (8)	100 (79)	100 (21)	100 (156)	– (4)	100 (36)

Question No. 22: Mobility and infectious disease . . . (Cultural Traditionalism)

For	24	(6)	32	(10)	32	(6)	69	(92)	18	(2)	5	(3)	7	(1)	19	(24)
Against	64	(16)	42	(13)	58	(11)	13	(18)	46	(5)	83	(52)	50	(7)	67	(87)
Did Not Vote	12	(3)	26	(8)	10	(2)	18	(24)	36	(4)	12	(8)	43	(6)	14	(18)
Total	100	(25)	100	(31)	100	(19)	100	(134)	100	(11)	100	(63)	100	(14)	100	(129)

Question No. 23: Wild sex life: U.S. . . . (Cultural Traditionalism)

For	36	(8)	41	(12)	21	(4)	67	(83)	20	(2)	5	(2)	–	(1)	17	(24)
Against	55	(12)	31	(9)	63	(12)	16	(20)	40	(4)	81	(34)	–	(7)	69	(95)
Did Not Vote	9	(2)	28	(8)	16	(3)	17	(21)	40	(4)	14	(6)	–	(1)	14	(19)
Total	100	(22)	100	(29)	100	(19)	100	(124)	100	(10)	100	(42)	–	(9)	100	(135)

Name Index

Subject Index

1 2 3 4 5 6 7 8 9 10 11 12 13 14 15 – H – 77 76 75 74 73 72